The Shorter Catechism Illustrated

The
Shorter Catechism Illustrated

John Whitecross

Solid Ground Christian Books
PO Box 660132 ~Vestavia Hills AL 35266

SOLID GROUND CHRISTIAN BOOKS
PO Box 660132, Vestavia Hills, AL 35266
205-443-0311
sgcb@charter.net
http://www.solid-ground-books.com

The Shorter Catechism Illustrated:
from Christian Biography and History

by John Whitecross

Taken from the 1968 edition by *Banner of Truth Trust*

Special thanks to the Banner of Truth Trust for their faithfulness to the cause of
God and truth for more than 45 years, and especially for their willingness to
permit Solid Ground Christian Books to do this limited edition of this precious
book from the past.

Published by Solid Ground Christian Books

Classic Reprints Series

First printing of hardcover edition June 2003
First printing of paperback edition July 2004

ISBN: 1-932474-08-0 (hardcover)
ISBN: 1-932474-47-1 (paperback)

Manufactured in the United States of America

PREFACE

The Westminster Assembly's Shorter Catechism has been long and justly esteemed an excellent compendium of religious knowledge. To illustrate it, Explanatory Catechisms, and even Bodies of Divinity, have been composed. Parents and teachers have used it for the purpose of initiating the young in the principles of religion. To contribute to their assistance in a labour so important, is the design of the following compilation.

Having been in the habit of selecting an anecdote or two, suited to the subject of instruction in the Sabbath School formerly under his charge, the compiler was led to conceive the plan of this little work. It will be generally allowed, that anecdotes and stories are calculated to engage the attention of children, which, gained by this means, may be happily kept, while directed to other parts of instruction.

While, from the similarity of several of the questions, it was found difficult to prefix to each its appropriate anecdotes, it is hoped there will be few, if any, altogether misplaced. Care has been taken to admit, as far as possible, only those of a religious nature, which may, with propriety, be related by a Christian parent or teacher, when instructing his children or scholars on a Sabbath evening.

Though this little volume is to be used as chiefly adapted to the use of parents and Sabbath School teachers, it may not be uninteresting to the general reader. The questions under which they are arranged will serve as a guide in selecting anecdotes suited to particular circumstances; and something may be found fitted to please and to instruct.

If, through the Divine blessing, this work in any measure serve the purpose designed, the compiler will rejoice that his humble labours have not been in vain.

THE SHORTER CATECHISM
ILLUSTRATED

Q. 1. *What is the chief end of man?*

A. Man's chief end is to glorify God, and to enjoy Him for ever.

1. Lady Glenorchy, in her diary, relates how she was seized with a fever which threatened her life, 'during the course of which,' she says, 'the first question of the Assembly's Catechism was brought to my mind—"What is the chief end of man?" as if some one had asked it. When I considered the answer to it—"To glorify God, and to enjoy Him for ever"—I was struck with shame and confusion. I found I had never sought to glorify God in my life, nor had I any idea of what was meant by enjoying Him for ever. Death and judgment were set before me; my past sins came to my remembrance; I saw no way to escape the punishment due unto them, nor had I the least glimmering hope of obtaining the pardon of them through the righteousness of another.' From this unhappy state she was shortly after delivered, by believing on the Lord Jesus as the only Saviour of the guilty.

2. Such was James Hervey's strict piety, that he suffered no moment to go unimproved. When he was called down to tea, he used to bring his Hebrew Bible or Greek Testament with him; and would either speak upon one verse or upon several verses, as occasion offered. 'This,' says William Romaine, 'was generally an improving season. The glory of God is very seldom promoted at the tea-table; but it was at Mr Hervey's. Drinking tea with him, was like being at an ordinance; for it was sanctified by the Word of God, and prayer.'

3. An eminent minister, after having been silent in company for a considerable time, on being asked the reason, signified that the powers of his mind had been solemnly absorbed with the thought of eternal happiness. 'Oh, my friends,' said he, with an energy that surprised all present, 'consider what it is to be for ever with the Lord—for ever, for ever, for ever.'

4. A French officer, who was a prisoner upon his parole at Reading, met with a Bible, read it, and was so struck with its contents, that he was convinced of the folly of sceptical principles, and of the truth of Christianity, and so resolved to become a Protestant. When his gay associates rallied him for taking so serious a turn, he said in his vindication, 'I have done no more than my old school-fellow Bernadotte, who has become a Lutheran.' 'Yes, but he became so,' said his associates, 'to obtain a crown.' 'My motive,'

said the Christian officer, 'is the same; we only differ as to the place. The object of Bernadotte is to obtain a crown in Sweden, mine is to obtain a crown in heaven.'

5. Mr Robinson, a member of the presbytery of New Brunswick, was the son of a wealthy Quaker in England. Being permitted to pay a visit to an aunt in London, from whom he had considerable expectations, and becoming very fond of the dissipations of the town, he incurred debt, which so involved him, that he determined to quit his native country, and seek his fortune in America. Soon after his arrival, he had recourse, for subsistence, to teaching in a school in New Jersey. After he had been for some time engaged in this business, without any practical sense of religion, he was riding at a late hour one evening, when the moon and stars shone with unusual brightness. While he was meditating on the beauty and grandeur of the scene, and was saying to himself, 'how transcendently glorious must be the Author of all this beauty and grandeur!' the thought struck him with the suddenness and force of lightning—'But what do I know of this God? Have I ever sought His favour, or made Him my friend?' This happy impression, which proved, by its permanency and effects, to have come from the best of all sources, never left him until he took refuge in Christ, as the hope and life of his soul.

Q. 2. *What rule hath God given to direct us how we may glorify and enjoy Him?*

A. The Word of God, which is contained in the Scriptures of the Old and New Testaments, is the only rule to direct us how we may glorify and enjoy Him.

1. A gentleman, travelling in a stage coach, attempted to divert the company by ridiculing the Scriptures. 'As to the prophecies,' said he, 'in particular, they were all written after the events took place.' A minister in the coach, who had hitherto been silent, replied, 'Sir, I beg leave to mention one particular prophecy as an exception, 2 Pet. 3. 3, "Knowing this first, that there shall come in the last days *scoffers*." Now, sir, whether the event be not long after the prediction, I leave the company to judge.' The mouth of the scorner was stopped.

2. When the famous Duke of Wellington was, in the early part of his career—he was then Sir Arthur Wellesley—stationed in India, an officer, dining at the mess where he presided, was sporting his infidel sentiments. Sir Arthur wishing to put down such conversation, said, S——, did you ever read Paley's Evidences? The reply was in the negative. 'Well then,' said Sir Arthur, 'you had better read that book before you talk in the way you are doing.' The occurrence passed away, and the conversation was soon forgotten; but the reference to Paley's work led Colonel S. to inquire after it, and having obtained a copy, he read it with the most serious attention. He rose from the perusal of it with the fullest conviction of the falsehood of the

system he had formerly adopted, and of the divine origin of Christianity. But he did not stop here, he was determined to examine the Book itself, which he was thus satisfied was a revelation from God. The result was, that he cordially received this revelation of mercy, saw and felt his need of a Saviour, and believing in Jesus, became a Christian, not in name only, but in deed and in truth. Colonel S. feeling his obligation to Sir Arthur, afterwards wrote to him, thanking him for his kindness, in recommending to him Dr Paley's valuable work; and earnestly advising him not to be satisfied with merely knowing the external evidence of Christianity, but to inquire what this divine communication really contains. It is not known whether any reply was made to this communication.

3. Naimbanna, a black prince from the neighbourhood of Sierra Leone, arrived in England in 1791. The gentleman to whose care he was entrusted, took great pains to convince him that the Bible was the Word of God, and he received it as such, with great reverence and simplicity. Do we ask what it was that satisfied him on this subject? Let us listen to his artless words. 'When I found,' said he, 'all good men minding the Bible, and calling it the Word of God, and all bad men disregarding it, I then was sure that the Bible must be what good men called it, the Word of God.'

4. 'A few Sabbaths ago,' says one, 'a little boy, about six years of age, just after entering the school, came and asked me for the charity-box. I inquired what he wanted with it. "I want to put a halfpenny into it," said he. To examine his motives, and his knowledge of divine things more particularly, I asked him what good he supposed it would do to put his money into the charity-box. "I want to send it to the heathen," he replied. "Do you know," said I, "who the heathen are?" "They are folks who have not got any Bible, and live a great way off." "What is the Bible?" "The Word of God." "Of what use would it be to the heathen, if they had it?" "It would tell them to love God, and be good." "Where did the Bible come from?" "From heaven." "Was it written in heaven?" "No, the prophets and good men wrote it." "If good men wrote it, how then is it the Word of God, and came from heaven?" "Why, the Holy Ghost told them how to write it." "Did they see the Holy Ghost, and did He speak to them?" "No, but He made them *think* it." This was enough. I presented to him the charity-box; he dropped in his money; a smile of joy glowed upon his countenance; and he returned to his seat filled with the luxury of doing good.'

5. The learned Salmasius of Burgundy said on his death-bed, 'O! I have lost a world of time! If one year more were added to my life, it should be spent in reading David's Psalms, and Paul's Epistles.'

6. John Locke, a little before his death, being asked what was the shortest and surest way for a young gentleman to attain a true knowledge of the Christian religion, made this reply; 'Let him study the Holy Scriptures, especially the New Testament; therein are contained the words of eternal life. It has God for its author, salvation for its end, and truth, without any mixture of error, for its matter.'

7. It was customary, in Cromwell's time, for his soldiers to carry each a Bible in his pocket; among others, a profligate young man, who was ordered out to attack some fortress. During the engagement, a bullet had perforated

his Bible, and gone so far as to rest opposite these words in Ecclesiastes; 'Rejoice, O young man, in thy youth, and let thy heart cheer thee in the days of thy youth; and walk in the ways of thy heart, and in the sight of thine eyes: but know thou, that for all these things God will bring thee into judgment.' These words so appropriate to his case, powerfully affected his mind, and proved, by the blessing of God, the means of his conversion. He used to observe that the Bible had been the happy means of saving both his soul and his body.

8. During days of war a godly man visited a camp of French soldiers at Toulon, taking with him a number of French New Testaments which he distributed to the men, many of whom seemed pleased with the gift. He had at length exhausted all his store, with the exception of one copy; this he offered to a man standing near him. The man took it, opened it, and turning to a companion said sneeringly, 'Oh, this will do to light my pipe with.' A discouraging enough reception; but the book, having been once given, was beyond recovery.

About a year and half after this occurrence, the distributor of the Testaments was on a short journey through the South of France, and stopped on his way at a roadside inn for refreshment and a night's lodging. On entering the house, he soon perceived that something of a sad nature had happened to the landlady. On inquiring what it was, she informed him that her eldest son had been buried that very week. She went on very naturally to dilate on his many excellencies, and spoke of his happy deathbed. 'And sir,' said she, 'all his happiness was got from a little book that was given him sometime ago.' The traveller inquired further concerning the little book. 'You shall see it,' said the mother, 'it is upstairs.' She soon returned with the book. On opening it, he found it to be French New Testament, and identified it as the very one he had himself given, so many months before, to that seemingly unpromising soldier at Toulon. He discovered that five or six of the early pages had been torn out, thus indicating that the man had actually commenced the fulfilment of his threat to use the book to light his pipe with. This was not all. On the inside cover were written the words: 'Given to me at Toulon on —day; first despised, then read, and finally blessed to the saving of my soul.'

9. Two men came one night to a missionary in Madagascar. They had walked a hundred miles out of their way to visit him. 'Have you the Bible?' asked the missionary. 'We have seen it and heard it read,' one man said, 'but we have only some of the words of David, and they do not belong to us; they belong to the whole family.' 'Have you the words of David with you now?' asked the missionary. They looked at each other but would not answer. Perhaps they were afraid, but the kindness of the speaker moved one of the men to put his hand into his bosom and to take out what seemed to be a roll of cloth. He unrolled it and, after the removal of a few wrappers, there appeared a few old, torn, dingy leaves of the Psalms which had been read, passed round, lent and re-read, until they were almost worn out. Tears came into the missionary's eyes when he saw them. 'Have you ever seen the words of the Lord Jesus, or John or Paul or Peter?' he asked. 'Yes,' they said, 'we have seen and heard them, but we never owned them.' The mis-

sionary then brought out a Testament with the Book of Psalms bound up with it, and showed it to them. 'Now,' said he, 'if you will give me your few words of David, I will give you all his words, and all the words of the Lord Jesus, and John and Paul and Peter besides.' The men were amazed and delighted. But they wanted to see if the words of David were the same in the missionary's book, and when they found that they were, and thousands more of the same sort, their joy knew no bounds. They willingly gave up their poor, tattered leaves, seized the volume, thanked the missionary, bade him good-bye, and started off upon their long journey home, rejoicing like those who had found a great spoil.

10. A peasant in the county of Cork, understanding that a gentleman had a copy of the Scriptures in the Irish language, begged permission to see it. He asked whether he might borrow the New Testament in his own tongue that he might make a copy of it. The gentleman said that he could not obtain another copy, and that he was afraid to trust it with him so that he might take a copy in writing. 'Where will you get the paper?' he asked. 'I will buy it.' 'And the pens and ink?' 'I will buy them.' 'Where will you find a place to do the work?' 'If your honour will allow me your hall, I will come after I have done my work in the day, and take a copy by portions of time in the evening.' The owner of the book was so struck with his zeal that he gave him the use of the hall and a light, in order to make the copy. The man was firm to his purpose, in course of time finished the work, and produced a copy of the New Testament in writing by his own hand. A printed copy was later given him in exchange for it, and the written one was placed in the hands of the President of a Bible Society as a monument of the desire of the Irish to know the Scriptures.

Q. 3. *What do the Scriptures principally teach?*

A. The Scriptures principally teach what man is to believe concerning God, and what duty God requires of man.

1. David Hume was dining at the house of an intimate friend. After dinner, the ladies withdrew; and in the course of conversation, Mr Hume made some assertion, which caused a gentleman present to observe to him, 'If you can advance such sentiments as these, you certainly are what the world gives you credit for being, an infidel.' A little girl whom the philosopher had often noticed, and with whom he had become a favourite by bringing her little presents of toys and sweets, happened to be playing about the room unnoticed. She, however, listened to the conversation, and on hearing the above expression, left the room, went to her mother, and asked her, 'Mother, what is an infidel?' 'An infidel! my dear,' replied her mother, 'why should you ask such a question? an infidel is so awful a character, that I scarcely know how to answer you.' 'Oh! tell me,' said the child, 'I must know what an infidel is.' Struck with her eagerness, her mother at length replied, 'An infidel is one who believes that there is no God, no heaven, no

hell, no hereafter.' Some days afterwards, Hume again visited the house of his friend. On being introduced into the parlour, he found no one there but his favourite little girl; he went to her, and attempted to take her up in his arms, and kiss her, as he had been used to do; but the child shrunk with horror from his touch. 'My dear,' said he, 'what is the matter? do I hurt you?' 'No,' she replied, 'you do not hurt me, but I cannot play with you.' 'Why not, my dear?' 'Because you are an infidel.' 'An infidel, what is that?' 'One who believes there is no God, no heaven, no hell, no hereafter.' 'And are you not very sorry for me, my dear?' asked the philosopher. 'Yes, indeed, I am sorry!' replied the child, with solemnity; 'and I pray to God for you.' 'Do you, indeed! and what do you say?' 'I say, O God, teach this man that Thou art!'—A striking illustration of the words of sacred Scripture, 'Out of the mouth of babes and sucklings Thou hast ordained strength, because of thine enemies, that Thou mightest still the enemy and the avenger' (Ps. 8. 2).

2. Dr Elliot, who was well acquainted with Colonel Allen, an infidel in America, visited him at a time when his daughter was seriously ill. He was taken to the library, where the Colonel read to him some of his writings with much self-complacency, and asked, 'Is not that well done?' While they were thus employed, a messenger entered, and informed Colonel Allen that his daughter was dying, and desired to speak with him. He immediately went to her chamber, accompanied by Dr Elliot, who was desirous of witnessing the interview. The wife of Colonel Allen was a pious woman, who had instructed her daughter in the principles of Christianity. As soon as her father appeared at her bedside she said to him, 'I am about to die; shall I believe in the principles you have taught me, or shall I believe in what my mother has taught me?' He became extremely agitated; his chin quivered, his whole frame shook; and after waiting a few moments, he replied, 'Believe what your mother has taught you.'

3. An English officer, who was lately in Valenciennes, states the following fact, which came under his own observation. A number of Bibles, in French, had been sent from England to that city, for sale or distribution. Many of the people received them with gratitude, and read them with avidity; but the priest, getting information of the matter, ordered all the Bibles to be returned. The English officer, who was acquainted with him, asked the reason of this; to which he gave the truly Popish reply, 'I teach the people every thing that is necessary for them to know!'

4. A poor boy, going to a Sabbath School, was met by a companion, who invited him to play truant; but he absolutely refused, and went to school. When this came to be known, the boy was asked what it was that kept him from complying with the temptation? He answered, 'Because I read in my Bible, "My son, if sinners entice thee, consent thou not" ' (Proverbs 1. 10).

5. It was remarked by one, 'If I have been honoured to do any good in my day; if I have been of any use to the church of Christ, to my family, and to my fellow-creatures; if I have enjoyed any happiness in life (and I am happy to say I have had a large share); if I have any hope beyond the grave, and that hope I would not exchange for a thousand worlds—I owe all to the Bible.'

6. A considerable time ago, a motion was made in Parliament for raising and embodying the Militia; and, for the purpose of saving time, to exercise them on the Sabbath. When the motion was likely to pass, an old gentleman stood up and said, 'Mr Speaker, I have one objection to this, I believe in an old book, called the Bible.' The members looked at one another, and the motion was dropped.

7. 'I once attended, on his dying bed,' says a writer, 'a man whose early history had given promise of better things, but whose goodness was as the morning cloud and the early dew. As I entered the room, he fixed his eyes upon me, with a fearful expression of countenance, and in the spirit and almost in the very language of the Gadarene demoniac, exclaimed,— "Why are you come to torment me?" I replied, "I am not come to torment you; I am come to tell you that there is mercy, mercy yet, and mercy even for you." He raised his arm with vehemence, and said, "No mercy for me; no mercy for me; no mercy for me. I have sinned through all; I have despised all; I am dying, and I am damned!" His arm fell, and he apparently ceased to breathe. I thought him dead, but was mistaken; there was life still, there was even consciousness. Fetching a long-drawn breath, as if for some desperate effort, and covering his face, with the evident intention of concealing the agony which was written there, he uttered the most awful groan I ever heard, and then expired. If any thing could increase the horror of that scene, it was the following circumstance. That man ascribed the ruin of his soul to a popular preacher, whom, on some public occasion, he heard deliver a sermon which deeply affected him, and whom, at the close of the service, he was delighted to meet at the house of a mutual friend. But great was his disappointment. The individual who, in the pulpit, was a Boanerges, in the parlour played the mountebank, and in either character he seemed perfectly "at home." His adventures, jokes, and anecdotes, kept the company, till past midnight, in a roar of laughter. The consequence may be easily imagined. The unhappy man, who was doomed to witness that incongruous scene, persuaded himself that Christianity was disbelieved by its professional advocates, and thenceforth he treated it as unworthy of his notice.'

8. In the spring of the year 372, a young man in the thirty-first year of his age, in evident distress of mind, entered a garden near Milan. This was no other than the afterwards eminent Augustine. The sins of his youth—a youth spent in following after the sins of the flesh and in impiety—weighed heavily on his soul. Lying under a fig-tree, moaning and pouring out abundant tears, he heard from a neighbouring house a young voice saying and repeating in rapid succession, 'Tolle, lege! Tolle, lege' (Take and read! Take and read!). Receiving this as a word of counsel from God to read the Holy Scriptures, he returned to the place where he had left his friend Alypius, to procure the roll of the Epistles of Paul, the apostle of the Lord, which he had a short time before left with him. 'I seized the roll,' says he, in describing this occurrence: 'I opened it and read in silence the chapter on which my eyes first alighted.' It was the thirteenth chapter of the Epistle to the Romans: 'Let us walk honestly as in the day; not in rioting and drunkenness, not in chambering and wantonness, not in strife and envying.

But put ye on the Lord Jesus Christ, and make not provision for the flesh, to fulfil the lusts thereof' (Rom. 13. 13-14). All was decided by that word. 'I did not want to read any more,' says Augustine, 'nor was there any need; every doubt was banished.' The morning star had risen in his heart. Old things had passed suddenly away and all things had as suddenly become new. His saved soul entered a new world of grace and mercy and peace, and to God he gave all the glory.

9. William Hone, writer and bookseller, having been taught to read from the Bible only, turned against the Word of God in the days of his youth and earned for himself the reputation of a leader of the freethinkers and un-believers of his day. In 1817 he was prosecuted for parodying one of the great creeds of the Christian Church and for doing his utmost to bring the Christian religion into public contempt. Remarkably, in later life he was con-victed of his sins, humbled before God, and turned into a firm advocate of the faith which formerly he had hated so bitterly. The Lord used several circumstances to bring about this happy result, and among them was the following.

One day, riding through a part of Wales, he arrived at a cottage and saw a little girl sitting at the door reading a book. He stopped and spoke to the girl. 'Oh, you are reading the Bible.' 'Yes, sir, it is the Bible.' 'I suppose you are performing your task,' he said. 'Task? Task?' she replied. 'Yes, I suppose your mother has set you so much to read.' 'Mother set me so much to read?' said the little girl. 'Yes, I suppose you would not read the Bible unless she had done so; it is a task, is it not?' 'Oh no, sir,' was the reply, 'I only wish I could read it all the day long. It is my joy and delight when my work is done to get a few minutes to read this lovely book.'

The simple testimony touched the heart of the hard unbeliever as nothing else had done. It was with William Hone as it had once been with Job when he said, 'God maketh my heart soft,' and ere long he was brought out of darkness into God's marvellous light. Later he wrote a tribute of praise to God of which the following is the opening verse:

'The proudest heart that ever beat
   Has been subdued in me:
The wildest will that ever rose
   To scorn Thy cause or aid Thy foes
Is quelled, my God, by Thee.'

10. In the *Memoirs of Thomas Boston* of Ettrick appears the following: 'Singing at family worship Psalm 121, this view of the Bible was given me, namely, that whatever were the particular occasions of the writing of it or any part thereof, I am to look upon it as written for me as much as if there were not another person in the world, and so is everybody else to whose hand it comes.'

11. When Thomas Charles of Bala, North Wales, met a man or woman on the road, he used to stop his horse and make the inquiry, 'Can you read the Bible?' He was so much in the habit of doing this, that he became known everywhere from this practice. 'The gentleman who kindly asked the poor

people about the Bible and their souls' was a description of Thomas Charles. Meeting one day with an old man on one of the mountains, he said to him, 'You are an old man and very near another world.' 'Yes,' said he, 'and I hope I am going to heaven when I die.' 'Do you know the road there? Do you know the Word of God?' 'Pray, are you Mr Charles,' said the man. He suspected who he was from his question. He was often thus questioned when asking the poor people he met with about their eternal concerns. When he had time, he scarcely ever passed a man on the road without talking to him about his soul and his knowledge of the Bible. When he found any ignorant of the Word and unable to read it, he put to them, in a kind and simple way, the duty and necessity of becoming acquainted with it, and with pity and much feeling he set before them the awful state of those who leave the world without any knowledge of the Word of God and faith in the glorious Redeemer that it presents to view. He sometimes persuaded them to learn to read, and the good he did in this way was undoubtedly very great.

Q. 4. *What is God?*

A. God is a Spirit, infinite, eternal, and unchangeable in His being, wisdom, power, holiness, justice, goodness, and truth.

1. Thomas Raffles, in his interesting Alpine Tour, relates a circumstance worthy of notice. 'Yet,' says he, 'amid these scenes, surrounded by the sublimest demonstrations of the eternal power and Godhead of the Almighty, a wretch has had the hardihood to avow and record his atheism, having written over against his name in the Album, at Montanvert, "An atheist". It seems as if some emotions of shame touched him at the time, for he has written it in Greek. It caught the eye of a divine who succeeded him, and he very properly wrote underneath, in the same language, "If an atheist, a fool,—if not, a liar." '

2. Simonides, a heathen poet, being asked by Hiero, king of Syracuse, What is God? desired a day to think upon it; and when that was ended, he desired two; and when these were past, he desired four days; thus he continued to double the number of days in which he desired to think of God, before he could give an answer. Upon which the king expressed his surprise and asked him what he meant by this strange behaviour? To which the poet answered, 'The more I think of God, He is still the more unknown to me.'

3. A certain man went to a Mohammedan friar, and proposed three questions: 1, 'Why do they say that God is omni-present? I do not see Him in any place; show me where He is. 2, Why is man punished for his crimes, since whatever he does proceeds from God? Man has no free will, for he cannot do any thing contrary to the will of God, and if he had power, he would do everything for his own good. 3, How can God punish Satan in hellfire, since he is formed of that element? and what impression can fire make on itself?' The friar took up a large clod of earth, and struck him on

the head with it. The man went to a judge and said, 'I proposed three questions to such a friar, who flung such a clod of earth at me, as has made my head ache.' The judge, having sent for the friar, asked, 'Why did you throw a clod of earth at his head, instead of answering his questions?' The friar replied, 'The clod of earth was an answer to his speech. He says he has a pain in his head; let him show me the pain, and I will make God visible to him. And why does he make a complaint to you against me? Whatever I did was the act of God; I did not strike him without the will of God; and what power do I possess? And, as he is compounded of earth, how can he suffer pain from that element?' The man was confounded, and the judge highly pleased with the friar's answer.

4. 'The Jews would not willingly tread upon the smallest piece of paper in their way, but picked it up; for possibly, said they, the Name of God may be on it. There was some superstition in this . . .. But trample not on the soul of any. There may be some work of grace that thou knowest not of. The Name of God may be written on that soul thou treadest on. It may be a soul that Christ thought so much of as to give His precious blood for it. Therefore despise it not.'

5. The teacher of a Sabbath School in Bristol, discoursing with the children, asked among other things, 'Where is God?' One of the elder boys immediately answered, 'In heaven.' The teacher not appearing satisfied with this reply, repeated the inquiry, when a lad, younger than the other, answered, 'Everywhere.' Requiring still further explanation, the question was again put, 'Where is God?' when a third boy called out, 'God is here.' The views of the teacher were now met; and he endeavoured to impress upon the minds of the children the important truth, that God is in heaven—God is every where—God is here.

6. It was a fine reply that a pupil of the Deaf and Dumb Institution of Paris made to the following question, put by a gentleman visiting it, 'What is eternity?' 'It is the life-time of the Almighty!'

Q. 5. *Are there more Gods than one?*

A. There is but One only, the living and true God.

1. A little boy being asked, 'How many Gods are there?' replied, 'One.' 'How do you know that?' 'Because,' said the boy, 'there is only room for one, for He fills heaven and earth.'

2. An Indian chief, having sent for Hiacoomes, a converted native, with the view of receiving religious instruction from him, asked him, 'How many Gods do the English worship?' Hiacoomes answered, 'One and no more.' On which the chief reckoned up about thirty-seven principal gods which he had. 'And shall I,' said he, 'throw away all these thirty-seven for the sake of one only?' 'What do you yourself think?' said Hiacoomes; 'for my part, I have thrown away all these, and many more, some years ago, and yet I am preserved, as you see to this day.' 'You speak true,' said the

chief, 'and therefore I will throw away all my gods too, and serve that one God with you.' Hiacoomes proceeded more fully to instruct him, and the rest of the company with him; and the chief having promised to worship the true God, and serve Him only, was as good as his word, for he carried himself as a true servant of God, all the days of his life after.

3. 'I never had a sight of my soul,' says the Emperor Aurelius, 'and yet I have a great value for it, because it is discoverable by its operations; and by my constant experience of the power of God, I have a proof of His being, and a reason for my veneration.'

4. A child about eight years old who lived in that part of India known as the Northern Circars, and who had been educated in Christianity, was ridiculed on that account, by some heathens older than himself. In reply, he repeated what he had been taught respecting God. 'Show us your God!' said the heathens. 'I cannot do that,' answered the child; 'but I can soon show you yours.' Taking up a stone, and daubing it with some resemblance of a human face, he placed it very gravely upon the ground, and pushing it towards them with his foot, said, 'There is such a god as you worship.'

5. 'When I lately arrived,' says a missionary, 'at a large village north-west of Amboyna (East Indies), upwards of eight hundred persons, in order to convince me of the reality of their faith in the only true and living God, brought all their idols before me, and acknowledged their foolishness. I advised them to pack them up in a large box, to put a heavy load of stones upon them, and to drown them all in the depths of the sea in my presence. They all agreed to follow my advice: a boat was made ready for the purpose, and, with a great shout, they were carried out of the village, and launched into the bottom of the deep. After this business was over, we sang the first four verses of the 136th Psalm.'

Q. 6. *How many persons are there in the Godhead?*

A. There are three persons in the Godhead, the Father, the Son, and the Holy Ghost; and these three are one God, the same in substance, equal in power and glory.

1. 'Sitting lately,' says one, 'in a public room at Brighton, where an infidel was haranguing the company upon the absurdities of the Christian religion, I could not but be pleased to see how easily his reasoning pride was put to shame. He quoted such passages as, "I and my Father are one;" and "I in them, and Thou in me". Finding his hearers not disposed to applaud his blasphemy, he turned to one gentleman, and said with an oath, "Do you believe such nonsense?" The gentleman replied, 'Tell me how that candle burns?" "Why," answered he, "the tallow, the cotton, and the atmospheric air, produce the light." "Then they make one light, do they not?" "Yes." "Will you tell me *how* they are one in the other, and yet but one light?" "No, I cannot." "But you believe it?" He could not say he did

B

not. The company, smiling at his folly, instantly made the application; upon which the conversation was changed. This may remind the young and in-experienced, that if they believe only what they can explain, they may as well part with their senses, being surrounded by the wonderful works of God, "whose ways are past finding out." '

2. Two gentlemen were once disputing on the divinity of Christ. One of them who argued against it, said, 'If it were true, it certainly would have been expressed in more clear and unequivocal terms.' 'Well', said the other, 'admitting that you believed it, were authorized to teach it, and allowed to use your own language, how would you express the doctrine to make it indubitable?' 'I would say,' replied he, 'that Jesus Christ is *the true God*.' 'You are very happy,' replied the other, 'in your choice of words; for you have happened to hit upon the very words of inspiration. John, speaking of the Son, says, "This is the *true God*, and eternal life" ' (1 John 5.20).

3. Dr Sewall, in a tour in Europe, in company with a Unitarian clergyman from New England, paid a visit to the justly-celebrated writer of the *History of the Reformation*, Merle d'Aubigné. Soon after their introduction, d'Aubigné inquired of the clergyman to what denomination of Christians he belonged. With some little hesitancy he replied that he was a Unitarian. A cloud of grief passed over the face of the pious historian, but again all was as before. The hour passed pleasantly, and the moment of parting came. D'Aubigné took the hand of the Unitarian, and fixing a look of great earnestness upon him, said: 'I am sorry for your error. Go to your Bible, study it, pray over it, and light will be given you. "God WAS manifest in the flesh." '

4. Robert Hall, of Bristol, in the early part of his ministry, doubted the distinct personality of the Holy Spirit; but, increasing in the spirituality of his mind, and becoming more ardently attached to secret devotion, he found that, whenever in private prayer he was in the most deeply devotional frame, most overwhelmed with the sense that he was nothing, and God was all in all, he always felt himself inclined to adopt a Trinitarian doxology. This circumstance occurring frequently, and being more frequently meditated upon in a tone of honest and anxious inquiry, issued at length in a persuasion that the Holy Spirit is really and truly God, and not an emanation.

Q. 7. *What are the decrees of God?*

A. The decrees of God are His eternal purpose, according to the counsel of His will, whereby, for His own glory, He hath fore-ordained whatsoever comes to pass.

1. 'Some preachers near Olney,' says John Newton, 'dwelt on the doctrine of predestination. An old woman said, "Ah, I have long settled that point; for if God had not chosen me before I was born, I am sure He would have seen nothing in me to have chosen me for afterwards!" '

2. A young person, riding one day with a friend, asked him, 'What is

your opinion of election, sir?' His friend judiciously remarked, 'Stephen, you have learned fractions, decimals, etc.; do you understand them?' 'Yes, sir.' 'Do you think when you were learning addition you could?' 'No, sir.' 'Neither can you, my dear boy, at present comprehend the deep things of God.' The youth appeared much interested, and during the remainder of the journey he seemed to be absorbed in his own reflections.

3. Cornelius Winter was once in company with an Arminian who spoke violently against the doctrine of election. 'You believe election,' said Winter, 'as firmly as I do.' 'I deny it,' answered the other, 'on the contrary, it is a doctrine I detest.' 'Do you believe that all men will be saved on the last day, or some only?' 'Only some.' 'Do you imagine that these some will be found to have saved themselves?' 'No, certainly; God in Christ is the only Saviour of sinners.' 'But God could have saved the rest, could He not?' 'No doubt.' 'Then salvation is peculiar to the saved?' 'To be sure.' 'And God saves them designedly, and not against His will?' 'Certainly.' 'And willingly suffers the rest to perish, though He could easily have hindered it?' 'It should seem so.' 'Then is not this election?' 'It amounts to the same thing.'

4. A person in the lower ranks, at Lochwinnoch, in Scotland, whose life and practice had not been consistent with that of a genuine Christian, was nevertheless a great speculator on the high points of divinity. Even on his death-bed he was wont to perplex and puzzle himself and his visitors with knotty questions on the divine *decrees*, and such other topics. Thomas Orr, a person of very different character, was sitting at his bedside, endeavouring to turn his attention to what more immediately concerned him: 'Ah, William,' said he, 'this is the *decree* you have at present to do with, "He that believeth and is baptised shall be saved; but he that believeth not shall be damned" .' (Mark 16. 16).

Q. 8. *How doth God execute His decrees?*

A. God executeth His decrees in the works of creation and providence.

1. The master of an Infant school, having directed a little fellow to move a stool, but so as not to be himself seen, thus endeavoured to instruct his infant charges: 'You cannot see any one moving the stool, is it not alive?' 'Oh no, master, it's not alive, never was alive; some one must be moving it.' 'But, my little fellows, you cannot see any body; perhaps it moves itself?' 'Oh no, sir, though we do not see any body, that does not make any odds; it *does not* move itself.' He then told them of the sun, and moon, and stars; and that although we did not see any one move them, yet it was certain they were moved, and no other could do so but God Himself, but we could not see Him. 'Yes, master, it must be God.' 'But then, my little folks, you cannot see Him?' 'Please, sir, we must believe it.' 'Well, then, you believe it?' 'Yes.' 'This then is *faith*.' 'Please, sir, then little faith is better than no faith.' 'If you have little faith, what will you do?' Little James said, 'I'll shut myself

up in a corner, and I'll pray, "Lord, I believe; help Thou my unbelief." '

2. Julian, usually styled the *Apostate*, one of the Roman emperors, with the view of invalidating the truth of our Saviour's prophecies respecting the desolation of the Jews, made an attempt to rebuild the temple of Jerusalem; but, from the breaking out of terrible balls of fire near the foundations, the workmen were obliged to abandon the impious attempt. 'Who hath hardened himself against God, and hath prospered?' (Job 9. 4). 'My counsel shall stand, and I will do all My pleasure.' (Is. 46.10).

3. In the seventeenth century when, from time to time, outbreaks of what was then called the plague visited various cities of Britain, the city of Chester was troubled in this way. In all such cases the godly of the city doubtless prayed for the special protection and deliverance of the Lord, and it is on record that a gracious answer to such a prayer led a certain citizen, when he rebuilt his house at a later date, to inscribe in clear bold letters across the front of his house, 'God's Providence is my inheritance'. The house is still to be seen with its inscription: it is known as God's Providence House.

4. Alexander Peden, a Scottish Covenanter, with some others had been at one time pursued by both horse and foot soldiers for a considerable way. At last, getting some little height between them and their persecutors, he stood still and said to the little company, 'Let us pray here, for if the Lord hear not our prayer and save us, we are all dead men'. He then prayed, saying, 'Lord, this is the hour and the power of Thine enemies; they may not be idle. But hast Thou no other work for them than to send after us? Send them after them to whom Thou wilt give strength to flee, for our strength is gone. Twine them about the hill, O Lord, and cast the lap of Thy cloak over thir puir things, and save us this ae time, and we will keep it in remembrance, and tell it to the commendation of Thy guidness, Thy pity and compassion, what Thou didst for us at sic a time.' In this he was heard, for a cloud of mist immediately intervened between them and their persecutors, who also received orders from their commander to go to another part of the land.

5. An ancient philosopher used to bless the gods for three privileges: That he was made, not a brute, but a rational creature—That he was born, not in barbarous climes, but in Greece—That he lived, not in the more uncultivated ages, but in the time, and under the tuition of Socrates. How much better reason have we to bless God that, in His providence, we were born in Britain, in a time of gospel light.

6. 'Who would have thought,' says Saurin, 'that King Henry VIII, a cruel and superstitious king, the greatest enemy the Reformation ever had— he who, by the fury of his arms, and by the productions of his pen, opposed this great work, refuting those whom he could not persecute, and persecuting those whom he could not refute—who would have thought that this monarch should first serve the work he intended to subvert, clear the way for reformation, and by shaking off the yoke of the Roman pontiff, execute the plan of Providence, while he seemed to do nothing but satiate his voluptuousness and ambition?'

7. 'It was a special providence of God,' says Samuel Clarke, 'that the

same day that Pelagius, the heretic, was born in Britain, St Augustine, the great confuter of the heresy, was born in Africa. Divine Providence so disposed it, that the poison and the antidote should come into the world together.'

8. John Brotherton was a soldier who fought at the battle of Minden (1759). When he left home, he took a small Bible, which he determined always to carry with him. When going to the battle, he put his Bible between his coat and his waistcoat, over his breast. It was the means of saving his life; for one of the enemy thrust at him with a bayonet, and the point of the weapon pierced through his belt and coat, and about fifty leaves of the Bible.

9. Thomas Charles of North Wales had a remarkable escape in one of his journeys to Liverpool. His saddle-bag was by mistake put into a different boat from that in which he intended to go. This made it necessary for him to change his boat, even after he had taken his seat in it. The boat in which he meant to go, went to the bottom, and all in it were drowned. Thus did God, in a wonderful way preserve His servant—'immortal till his work was done.' God had a great work for His servant to do, and He supported and preserved him till it was completed.

10. A pious old man who had served God for many years, was sitting one day with several persons, eating a meal upon a bank, near the mouth of a pit, in the neighbourhood of Swansea. While he was eating, a pigeon, which seemed very tame, came and fluttered in his breast, and slightly pecked him. It then flew away, and he did not think much about it; till, in five minutes, it came again, and did the same. The old man then said, 'I will follow thee, pretty messenger, and see where thou comest from.' He rose up to follow the bird and, whilst he was doing so, the banks of the pit fell in, and his companions were all killed.

Q. 9. *What is the work of creation?*

A. The work of creation is God's making all things of nothing, by the word of His power, in the space of six days, and all very good.

1. Sir Isaac Newton said, a little before his death, 'I do not know what I may appear to the world; but to myself, I seem to have been only like a boy playing on the sea-shore, and diverting himself in now and then finding a smoother pebble, or a prettier shell than ordinary, while a great ocean of truth lay all undiscovered before me.'

2. A native of Griqualand West in South Africa, stated that the first thing which led him to think of religion, was observing the Hottentots, who belonged to Zak river mission, giving thanks when eating. 'I went,' said he, 'afterwards to that settlement, where I heard many things, but felt no interest in them. But one day, when alone in the fields, I looked very seriously at a mountain, as the work of that God of whom I had heard; then I looked to my two hands, and for the first time noticed, that there was the same

number of fingers on each. I asked why there are not five on this hand, and three on that?: it must be God that made them so. Then I examined my feet, and wondered to find my soles both flat; not one flat and the other round. God must have done this, said I. In this way I considered my whole body, which made a deep impression on my mind, and disposed me to hear the Word of God with more interest till I was brought to trust that Jesus died for my sins.'

3. Dr Beattie of Aberdeen, wishing to impress on the mind of his son, a little boy about six years of age, the important truth that God made him, used the following method: 'In the corner of a little garden,' says the doctor, 'without informing any person of the circumstance, I wrote in the mould, with my finger, the three initial letters of his name, and sowing garden cress in the furrows, covered up the seed, and smoothed the ground. Ten days after this, he came running to me; and, with astonishment in his countenance, told me that his name was growing in the garden. I laughed at the report, and seemed inclined to disregard it, but he insisted on my going to see what had happened. "Yes," said I, carelessly, on coming to the place, "I see it is so: but what is there in this worth notice? is it not mere chance?" and I went away. He followed me, and taking hold of my coat, said with some earnestness, "It cannot have happened by chance—somebody must have contrived matters so as to produce it." "So you think," said I, "that what appears as the letters of your name, cannot be by chance?" "Yes," said he with firmness, "I think so." "Look at yourself," I replied, "and consider your hands and fingers, your legs and feet, and other limbs; are they not regular in their appearance, and useful to you?" He said they were. "Came you then hither," said I, "by chance?" "No," he answered, "that cannot be; something must have made me." "And who is that something?" I asked. He said, "I do not know." I had now gained the point I aimed at, and saw that his reason taught him (though he could not express it) that what begins to be must have a cause; and that what is formed with regularity must have an *intelligent* cause. I therefore told him the name of the Great Being who made him, and all the world; concerning whose adorable nature, I gave him such information as I thought he could in some measure comprehend. The lesson affected him greatly, and he never forgot either it or the circumstance that introduced it.'

4. A gentleman being invited by an honourable personage to see a stately building erected by Sir Christopher Hatton, he desired to be excused, and to sit still, looking on a flower, which he held in his hand: 'For,' said he, 'I see more of God in this flower, than in all the beautiful edifices in the world.'

Q. 10. *How did God create man?*

A. God created man male and female, after His own image, in knowledge, righteousness, and holiness, with dominion over the creatures.

1. When Galen, a celebrated Greek physician, but atheistically inclined, had anatomized the human body, and carefully surveyed the frame of it, viewed the fitness and usefulness of every part of it, and the many several intentions of every little vein, bone, and muscle, and the beauty of the whole, in a rapture of devotion he wrote a hymn to the honour of his Creator.

2. In the reign of Theodosius the Great, a Roman Emperor of the East, a violent sedition arose at Antioch, because he had exacted a new kind of tribute from the people. In the heat of the commotion, the populace broke down the statue of the deceased Empress Flacilla. The Emperor in a great rage, sent forces against the city to sack it. When the herald came and told this to the citizens, one Macedonius, a wise monk, sent to the herald an answer after this manner:—'Tell the Emperor these words—that he is not only an emperor, but also a man, therefore let him look not only on his empire, but also on himself; for he, being a man, commands also those who are men; let him not, then, use men so barbarously, who were made in the image of God. He is angry, and that justly, because the brazen image of his wife has been contumeliously used; and shall not the King of heaven be angry to see His glorious image in man contumeliously handled? O what a difference there is betwixt the reasonable soul and the brazen image! We, for this image, are able to set up an hundred; but he is not able to set up a single hair of these men again, if he kill them.' These words being told the Emperor, he suppressed his anger, and drew back his forces.

3. The Rev. James Armstrong was once preaching in Indiana (United States of America), when a doctor of that State, a professed deist, or infidel, called on his associates to accompany him while he attacked the Methodists, as he said. At first, he asked Mr Armstrong:—'If he followed preaching to save souls?' He answered in the affirmative. He then asked Mr Armstrong—'If he ever saw a soul?' 'No.' 'If he ever heard a soul?' 'No.' 'If he ever tasted a soul?' 'No.' 'If he ever smelled a soul?' 'No.' 'If he ever felt a soul?' 'Yes, thank God,' said Mr Armstrong. 'Well,' said the doctor, 'there are four of the five senses against one that there is a soul.' Mr Armstrong then asked the gentleman if he was a doctor of medicine; and he also answered in the affirmative. He then asked the doctor—'If he ever saw a pain?' 'No.' 'If he ever heard a pain?' 'No.' 'If he ever tasted a pain?' 'No.' 'If he ever smelled a pain?' 'No.' 'If he ever felt a pain?' 'Yes.' Mr Armstrong then said—'There are also four senses against one to evidence that there is a pain; yet, sir, you know that there is a pain, and I know there is a soul.' The doctor appeared confounded, and walked off.

4. Some of the courtiers of the Emperor Sigismund (of the Holy Roman Empire) having no taste for learning, inquired why he so honoured and respected men of low birth on account of their science. The emperor replied —'In one day I can confer knighthood or nobility on many, in years I cannot bestow genius on one. Wise and learned men are created by God only. No advantage of education, no favourable combination of circumstances, can produce talents, where the Father of spirits has not dropt the seeds of them in the souls which He hath made.'

5. Isaac Watts, though in person below the ordinary stature, yet had a certain dignity in his countenance, and such a piercing expression in his

eyes, as commanded attention and awe. Being once in a coffee-room with some friends, he overheard a gentleman asking, rather contemptuously: 'What? is that the great Dr Watts?' Turning round suddenly, and in good humour, he repeated a stanza from his Lyric Poems, which produced silent admiration:

> Were I so tall to reach the pole,
>   Or grasp the ocean with a span,
> I must be measured by my soul;
>   The mind's the standard of the man.

6. A British officer in India, having once rambled into a jungle adjoining the military encampment, suddenly encountered a royal tiger; the rencontre appeared equally unexpected on both sides, and both parties made a dead halt, earnestly gazing on each other. The gentleman had no firearms, and was aware that a sword would be no effective defence in a struggle for life with such an antagonist. But he had heard that even the Bengal tiger might be sometimes checked by looking him firmly in the face. He did so: in a few minutes the tiger, which appeared preparing to take his fatal spring, grew disturbed, shrunk aside, and attempted to creep round upon him behind. The officer turned constantly upon the tiger, which still continued to shrink from his glance; but darting into a thicket, and again issuing forth at a different quarter, it persevered for above an hour in this attempt to catch him by surprise, till at last it fairly yielded the contest, and left the gentleman to pursue his walk, who, as may be easily believed, in all haste took a straight direction to the tent.

Q. 11. *What are God's works of providence?*

A. God's works of providence are, His most holy, wise, and powerful preserving and governing all His creatures, and all their actions.

1. The punctuality of John Newton, while tide-surveyor at Liverpool, was particularly remarked. One day, however, some business had detained him, and he came to his boat much later than usual, to the surprise of those who had observed his former punctuality. He went out in the boat as heretofore, to inspect a ship, but by some accident the ship blew up just before he reached it; and it appears, that if he had left the shore a few minutes sooner, he must have perished with the rest on board.

2. *Inscription on a Tomb-stone in Jamaica.* 'Here lies the body of Lewis Galdy, Esq., who departed this life at Port-Royal, the 22nd of December 1736, aged eighty. He was born at Montpelier, in France; but left that country for his religion, and came to settle in this island, where he was swallowed up in the great earthquake, in the year 1692, and by the providence of God, was by another shock thrown into the sea, and saved by swimming, until a boat took him up. He lived many years after, in great reputa-

tion, beloved by all who knew him, and much lamented at his death. God is a God of providence, as well as a God of grace. "Are not two sparrows sold for a farthing? and one of them shall not fall to the ground without your Father. But the very hairs of your head are all numbered. Fear ye not, therefore, ye are of more value than many sparrows." '

3. There is at Bristol a charitable institution called 'Colston's School,' from the name of its founder. The scholars wear on their breasts the figure of a dolphin in brass, the reason for which is as follows: Edward Colston, a rich West India merchant, was coming home with a ship which contained all his treasure: she sprung a leak, and after having pumped for a long time, day and night, the people on board were every moment expecting to go to the bottom. At once, to their great astonishment, the leak was stopped. On examination, it was found that a dolphin had providentially squeezed itself into the hole, and thus saved them from destruction. Colston, therefore, ordered this emblem of a dolphin to be worn as a signal both of his deliverance and gratitude.

4. Sir Thomas Gresham, who built the Royal Exchange in London, was the son of a poor woman, who, while he was an infant, abandoned him in a field. By the providence of God, however, the chirping of a grasshopper attracted a boy to the spot where the child lay; and his life was by this means preserved. After Sir Thomas had, by his unparalleled success as a merchant, risen to the pinnacle of commercial wealth and greatness, he chose a grasshopper for his crest; and becoming, under the patronage of Queen Elizabeth, the founder of the Royal Exchange, his crest was placed on the walls of the building in several parts, and a vane or weathercock, in the figure of a grasshopper, was fixed on the summit of the tower.

5. John Craig, a distinguished minister, and colleague of John Knox, having gone to reside in Bologna, in a convent of Dominicans, found a copy of Calvin's Institutes, which God made the means of his conversion to the Reformed Faith. He was seized as a heretic soon after, and carried to Rome, where he was condemned to be burnt; but on the evening preceding the day of execution, the reigning pontiff died, and, according to custom, the doors of all the prisons were thrown open. All others were released; but heretics, after being permitted to go outside the walls, were re-conducted to their cells. That night, however, a tumult was excited, and Craig and his companions escaped. They had entered a small inn at some distance from Rome, when they were overtaken by a party of soldiers sent to recapture them. On entering the house, the captain looked Craig steadfastly in the face, and asked him if he remembered having once relieved a poor wounded soldier in the neighbourhood of Bologna. Craig had forgotten it. 'But,' said the captain, 'I am the man; I shall requite your kindness; you are at liberty; your companions I must take with me, but for your sake I shall treat them with all possible lenity.' He gave him all the money he had, and Craig escaped. His money soon failed him; yet God, who feeds the ravens, did not. Lying at the side of a wood, full of gloomy apprehensions, a dog came running up to him with a purse in its teeth. Suspecting some evil, he attempted to drive the animal away, but in vain. He at length took the purse, and found in it a sum of money, which carried him to Vienna.

6. The providence of God has been often remarkably displayed in the discovery of murder. A Basle publication relates the following instance: A person who worked in a brewery quarrelled with one of his fellow-workmen, and struck him in such a manner, that he died upon the spot. No other person was witness to the deed. He then took the body, and threw it into a large fire under a boiling vat, where it was in a short time so completely consumed, that no traces of its existence remained. On the following day, when the man was missed, the murderer observed very coolly, that he had perceived his fellow-servant to have been intoxicated, and that he had probably fallen from a bridge, which he had to cross on his way home, and been drowned. For the space of seven years after, no one entertained any suspicion of the suggested explanation. At the end of this period, the murderer was again employed in the same brewery. He was then induced to reflect on the singularity of the circumstance, that his crime had remained so long concealed. Having retired one evening to rest, one of the other workmen who slept with him, hearing him say in his sleep, 'It is now full seven years ago,' asked him, 'What was it you did seven years ago?' 'I put him,' he replied, still speaking in his sleep, 'under the boiling vat.' As the affair was not entirely forgotten, it immediately occurred to the man, that his bed-fellow must allude to the person who was missing about that time; and he accordingly gave information of what he had heard to a magistrate. The murderer was apprehended, and though at first he denied that he knew anything of the matter, a confession of his crime was at length obtained from him, for which he suffered condign punishment.

7. Queen Mary Tudor having dealt severely with the Protestants in England, about the end of her reign signed a commission to take a similar course with them in Ireland, and, to execute the same with greater force, she nominated Dr Cole one of the commissioners. The doctor coming with the commission to Chester, the Mayor of that city, hearing that her Majesty was sending a messenger into Ireland, waited on the doctor, who, in discourse with the Mayor, took out of a cloakbag, a leather box, saying, 'Here is a commission that shall lash the heretics of Ireland,' calling the Protestants by that title. The good woman of the house, being well-affected to the Protestant religion, and also having a brother in Dublin named John Edmunds, of the same religious profession, was much troubled at the doctor's words; but watching her convenient time, while the Mayor took his leave, and the doctor accompanied him down stairs, she opened the box, took the commission out, and placed in lieu of it, a sheet of paper with a pack of cards wrapped up in it, the knave of clubs being faced uppermost. The doctor, coming up to his chamber, and suspecting nothing of what had been done, put up the box as formerly. The next day, going to the water side, wind and weather serving him, he sailed towards Ireland, and landed on the 7th of October 1558, at Dublin. When he arrived at the castle, the Lord Fitz-Walter, being Lord Deputy, sent for him to come before him and the privy council. He came accordingly, and after he had made a speech, relating on what account he had come over, he presented the box to the Lord Deputy, who causing it to be opened, that the secretary might read the commission, there was nothing, save a pack of cards, with the knave of

clubs uppermost; which not only startled the Lord Deputy and council, but also the doctor, who assured them that he had a commission, but knew not how it was gone. The Lord Deputy made answer, 'Let us have another commission, and we will shuffle the cards in the meanwhile.' The doctor, being troubled in his mind, went away, and returned to England, and, coming into the court obtained another commission; but staying for the wind on the water side, news came to him that the Queen was dead. Thus God preserved the Protestants of Ireland. Queen Elizabeth was so delighted with this story, which was related to her by Lord Fitz-Walter on his return to England, that she sent for Elizabeth Edmunds, and gave her a pension of £40 a year during her life.

Q. 12. *What special act of providence did God exercise towards man in the estate wherein he was created?*

A. When God had created man, He entered into a covenant of life with him, upon condition of perfect obedience; forbidding him to eat of the tree of the knowledge of good and evil upon the pain of death.

1. In the reign of Charles I, the goldsmiths of London had a custom of weighing several sorts of their precious metals before the privy council. On one occasion they made use of scales, poised with such exquisite nicety, that the beam would turn, the master of the company affirmed, at the two-hundredth part of a grain. William Noy, the attorney-general, standing by and hearing this, replied, 'I shall be loath, then, to have all my actions weighed in these scales.' 'With whom I heartily concur,' says James Hervey, 'in relation to myself. And since the balances of the sanctuary, the balances in God's hand, are infinitely exact, O what need have we of the merit and righteousness of Christ, to make us acceptable in *His* sight, and passable in *His* esteem!'

2. As man at first broke the law of God, notwithstanding the dreadful penalty annexed to disobedience, so sinners, from the depravity of their nature, the pernicious influence of erroneous principles, and the uncontrolled force of bad habits, still proceed in their evil courses, in opposition to threatened misery both in a present and future world.

A gentleman of a very amiable disposition, and justly popular, contracted habits of intemperance; his friends argued, implored, remonstrated; at last he put an end to all importunity in this manner. To a friend, who was addressing him in the following strain: 'Dear Sir George, your family are in the utmost distress on account of this unfortunate habit; they perceive that business is neglected; your moral influence is gone; your health is ruined; and, depend upon it, the coats of your stomach will soon give way, and then a change will come too late', the poor victim, deeply convinced of the hopelessness of his case, replied thus: 'My good friend, your remarks are just, they are indeed too true; but I can no longer resist temptation: if a bottle of brandy stood at one hand, and the pit of hell yawned on the other, and if I were convinced that I would be pushed in as surely as I took one glass more, I could not refrain. You are very kind; I ought to be very grateful for so many kind, good friends; but you may spare yourself the trouble of trying to reform me—the thing is impossible.'

3. A servant who had drawn conclusions which might be expected from hearing the irreligious and blasphemous conversation continually passing at the table upon which he waited, took an opportunity to rob his master. Being apprehended, and urged by his master to give a reason for this infamous behaviour, 'Sir,' said he, 'I have heard you and your friends so often talk of the impossibility of a future state, and that after death there was no reward for virtue, nor punishment for vice, that I was tempted to commit the robbery.' 'Well,' replied the master, 'but had you no fear of that death which the laws of your country inflict upon the crime?' 'Sir', rejoined the servant, looking sternly at his master, 'what is that to you, if I had a mind to venture it? you and your wicked companions had removed my greatest terror, why should I fear the less?'

Q. 13. *Did our first parents continue in the estate wherein they were created?*

A. Our first parents, being left to the freedom of their own will, fell from the estate wherein they were created, by sinning against God.

1. 'Many have puzzled themselves,' says John Newton, 'about the origin of evil. I observe there *is* evil, and that there is no way to *escape* it; and with this I begin and end.'

2. When the physicians told Theotimus, that except he abstained from drunkenness and licentiousness, he would lose his eyes, his heart was so wedded to his sins, that he answered, 'Then farewell, sweet light.' He had rather lose his eyes than leave his sins. So a man bewitched with sin had rather lose God, Christ, heaven, and his own soul, than part with it.

3. Colonel Gardiner having received a challenge to fight a duel, made the following truly noble and Christian reply: 'I fear *sinning*, though you know, sir, I do not fear fighting.'

Q. 14. *What is sin?*

A. Sin is any want of conformity unto, or transgression of, the law of God.

1. The last words that Archbishop Usher was heard to express, were, 'Lord, forgive my sins, especially my sins of *omission*.'

2. A minister explaining the distinction between sins of omission and

sins of commission, made use of the following simile by way of illustration: 'Behold yonder fire which lately burnt with so much brightness; it is now dull; let it alone, and it will soon go out; but if you pour water on it, you will put it out. The first is an act of omission, the second of commission.'

3. Count Gondomar, Spanish ambassador to Britain in the reign of James I, often professed, in his declining years, when death and the eternal world seemed near, 'That he feared nothing in the world more than *sin*; and whatever liberties he had formerly taken, he would rather now submit to be torn to pieces by wild beasts, than knowingly or willingly commit any sin against God.'

4. Phoebe Bartlet, a very little girl, went with some other children to gather plums in a neighbouring orchard. When she brought some of the fruit home, her mother mildly reproved her, and said she ought not to have gathered the plums without leave, because it was *sin*: God had commanded her not to steal. The child, not being sensible of the evil before, seemed greatly surprised, and bursting into tears, cried out, 'I won't have these plums!' and turning to her sister Eunice, very earnestly said to her, 'Why did you ask me to go to that plum tree? I should not have gone, if you had not asked me.' The other children did not seem much concerned; but there was no pacifying Phoebe. Her mother mentioned the circumstance to the owner of the tree, and requested of him that she might have the plums; but still she was deeply affected; and being asked what it was that troubled her now, she said that she wept, *because it was sin*. She declared, that if Eunice were to ask her a hundred times, she would not go again, and she retained an aversion to that fruit for a long time after.

Q. 15. *What was the sin whereby our first parents fell from the estate wherein they were created?*

A. The sin whereby our first parents fell from the estate wherein they were created, was their eating the forbidden fruit.

1. John Thomas, one of the missionary brethren of Serampore, Bengal, was one day, after addressing a crowd of the natives on the banks of the Ganges, accosted by a Brahmin as follows: 'Sir, don't you say that the devil tempts men to sin?' 'Yes' answered Thomas. 'Then,' said the Brahmin, 'certainly the fault is the devil's; the devil, therefore, and not man, ought to suffer punishment.' While the countenances of many of the natives revealed their approbation of the Brahmin's inference, Thomas, observing a boat, with several men on board, descending the river, with that facility of instructive retort for which he was so much distinguished, replied, 'Brahmin, do you see yonder boat?' 'Yes.' 'Suppose I were to send some of my friends to destroy every person on board, and bring me all that is valuable in the boat—who ought to suffer punishment? *I* for intructing them, or *they* for doing this wicked act?' 'Why,' answered the Brahmin, with emotion, 'you ought *all* to be put to death together.' 'Ay, Brahmin,' replied Thomas,

'and if you and the devil sin together, the devil and you will be punished together.'

2. 'There is,' says one, 'a tree, called the manchineel, which grows in the West Indies; its appearance is very attractive, and the wood of it peculiarly beautiful; it bears a kind of apple, resembling the golden pippin. This fruit looks very tempting, and smells very fragrant; but to eat of it is instant death. Its sap or juice is so poisonous, that if a few drops of it fall on the skin, it raises blisters and occasions great pain. The natives dip their arrows in the juice that they may poison their enemies when they wound them. Providence has so appointed it that one of these trees is never found, but near it there also grows a *white wood*, or a fig tree, the juice of either of which, if applied in time, is a remedy for the diseases produced by the manchineel.

'Sin, like this poisonous apple, looks pleasant to the eye, and men desire it, —eat of it, and die. We may think there is no harm in such a thing—it is only a little sin. But who would eat only a little poison? The least sin, if not forgiven, will ruin our souls for ever. This is fruit that must not be tasted; yea, it ought not to be looked upon, or thought of. It is sin that gives to the darts of Satan all their fiery qualities; and to the arrow of death all its bitterness. Now, all who have looked upon the fruit of this tree have desired it and have eaten of it; and if not delivered from its fatal effects, will surely die; but there is a remedy at hand: it is the precious blood of the Son of God, which soothes the troubled conscience, and cleanses it from all sin.

> "Not balm, new bleeding from the wounded tree,
>   Not blessed Arabia with his spicy grove,
>   Such fragrance yields".
>   (*Nicholas Rowe*)

'Apply, therefore, to this means of cure! fly to a crucified Saviour! there is no time to be lost!—the poison works within!—the disease every moment is increasing. Go to the great Physician without delay, and say, "Lord if Thou wilt, Thou canst make me whole." '

Q. 16. *Did all mankind fall into Adam's first transgression?*

A. The covenant being made with Adam, not only for himself, but for his posterity; all mankind, descending from him by ordinary generation, sinned in him, and fell with him in his first transgression.

1. A gospel minister, having preached on the doctrine of original sin, was afterwards waited on by some persons who stated their objections to what he had advanced. After hearing them, he said, 'I hope you do not deny actual sin too'. 'No,' they replied. The good man expressed his satisfaction at their acknowledgement; but to show the folly of their opinions in denying a doctrine so plainly taught in Scripture, he asked them, 'Did you ever see a tree growing without a root?'

2. When Melancthon was converted, he thought it impossible for his hearers to withstand the evidence of the truth in the ministry of the gospel. But after preaching a while, he complained, 'That old Adam was too hard for young Melancthon.'

3. 'I overheard a discourse,' says one, 'something like altercation, between a deacon, his son, and servants.' Some one had informed him that the cattle had broken into the corn field, and were making great ravages. His servants were ordered to make haste and to turn them out, and repair the breach. 'How came they in there?' says one; 'Which way did they get in?' cries another; 'It is impossible, the fences are good,' says a third. 'Don't stand here talking to no purpose,' cries the deacon, with increased earnestness, 'they are in the field destroying the corn. I see them with my own eyes. Out with them speedily, and put up the fence.' As I approached him he began to be more calm. 'Your pardon, sir; these fellows have quite vexed me. They make one think of our pastor's sermon on the origin of sin, spending his time needlessly, inquiring *how* it came *into* the world, while he ought to be exhorting us to *drive it out*.' 'Your observation is just,' said I, 'and your directions to your servants contain sound orthodox doctrine—a good practical improvement to the discourse we have heard to-day.'

4. 'What shall we principally aim to teach our children?' said some Sabbath school teachers to a venerable minister. 'That they are sinners,' answered he. 'And what in the next place?' 'The same: tell it them over and over again; make it the first part of your instructions, and the last; because it is all-important.'

5. Massilon was once asked, how a man who lived so retired could so well describe human nature, to which he replied, 'That he only studied his own heart.' Supposing that all hearts were alike, from this model the illustrious Frenchman portrayed the hearts of others.

Q. 17. *Into what estate did the fall bring mankind?*

A. The fall brought mankind into an estate of sin and misery.

1. The Rev. Dr Ives, whose house was on the road by which the criminals were carried weekly in carts to Tyburn, used to stand at his window and say to any young friends who might be near him, pointing out any of the most notorious malefactors, 'There goes *Dr Ives!*' If an explanation was asked, he took occasion to expound the innate corruption of the heart; and appealed to the *experience* of his auditors, 'whether they had not often felt the movements of those very passions, errors, prejudices, lusts, revenge, covetousness, etc., whose direct tendency was to produce the crimes for which these offenders satisfied the claims of public justice, and which were solely prevented from carrying them to the same dreadful fate, by the restraining grace of God.'

2. 'I have this evening,' says Mrs Housman, in her diary, 'had my dear child with me in my room, conversing with her, endeavouring to awaken

her, and convince her of her sin and misery by nature and practice. The child was seemingly affected, and melted into tears. So greatly was she distressed, that I was obliged to turn my discourse, and tell her God was good, and willing to pardon and receive sinners, especially those children that were desirous to be good betimes, and in their younger days set themselves to love God and serve Him. I told her she must pray to God to pardon her, and give her grace to serve Him. The child seemed willing to pray, but lacked words to express herself. I asked her if I should help her, and teach her to pray?' The pious mother adds, 'O Lord, may this dear offspring rise and call Thee blessed!'

3. A minister of the gospel once made use of the following illustration to show the awful nature of sin. 'Suppose,' he said, 'a person went to a blacksmith and said to him, "Sir, I wish you to make me a very long and heavy chain; have it ready by such a day and I will pay you cash for it." The blacksmith is pressed with other and more important work, but for the sake of the money he commences to make the chain. After toiling hard many days he finishes it. The individual calls. "Have you made the chain?" "Yes, sir, here it is." "That is very well done; a good chain, but it is not long enough." "Why, it is just the length you told me to make it." "Oh, yes, yes, but I have decided to have it much longer than at first; work on another week, I will then call and pay you for it." Thus flattered with praise, and encouraged with the promise of full reward for his labour, the blacksmith toils on, adding link to link, till the appointed time when his employer calls again, and as before praises his work. But still he insists that the chain is too short. "But," says the blacksmith, "I can do no more; my iron is used up, and so is my strength. I need the pay for what I have done, and can do no more till I have it." "Oh, never mind; I think you have the means of adding a few links more, and then the chain will answer the purpose for which it is intended, and you will be fully rewarded for all your toil." With his remaining strength and a few scraps of iron he adds the last link of which he is capable. Then says the man to him, "The chain is a good one; you have toiled hard and long to make it; I see that you can do no more, and now you shall have your wages." But instead of paying him the money, he takes the chain, binds the workman hand and foot, and casts him into a furnace of fire!' 'Such,' said the preacher, 'is a course of sin! It promises much, but its reward is death; and each sin is an additional link to that chain which will confine the transgressor in the prison-house of hell.' 'Now therefore, be ye not mockers, lest your bands be made strong' (Is. 28. 22). Providentially, there was in the congregation that day a blacksmith, who had lived a very wicked life. He was much excited, and declared at the close of the meeting that the whole discourse had been directed to him. He wished to know 'who had been telling the preacher all about him?' The preacher had never even heard that there was such a man. It is recorded that the blacksmith was soundly converted.

4. Cyrus the Great, King of Persia, after he had long been attended by armies and vast trains of courtiers, ordered this inscription to be engraved on his tomb, as an admonition to all men of the approach of death, and the desolation that follows it: 'O man, whosoever thou art, and whencesoever

thou comest, I know thou wilt come to the same condition in which I now am. I am Cyrus, who brought the empire to the Persians: do not envy me, I beseech thee, this little piece of ground which covers my body.'

Q. 18. *Wherein consists the sinfulness of that estate whereinto man fell?*

A. The sinfulness of that estate whereinto man fell, consists in the guilt of Adam's first sin, the want of original righteousness, and the corruption of his whole nature, which is commonly called Original Sin; together with all actual transgressions which proceed from it.

1. Dr Milne, the missionary, in speaking of his conversion, says, 'The book which God made use of more especially for convincing me of my sin and misery, was Boston's *Fourfold State*, which I read with the deepest attention. It conducted me into my own heart, discovered the evil which before lay hid in the chambers of imagery, the monstrous ingratitude to God which marked all my conduct, and the pollution of original and actual sin with which my soul was contaminated. I saw that I was necessarily under the strongest and most righteous obligations to God, and had never for one hour of my life discharged these, but lived in rebellion against the Author of my life; so I was justly under the curse of God's righteous law, and exposed to everlasting misery.' Under the tormenting fears of *eternal wrath*, he sometimes wished himself transformed into a stone, or into one of the birds he saw flying over his head in the fields. He was frequent and fervent in prayer, and was, in the mercy of God, led to those means by which he learned how even a vile and guilty creature, such as he was, might be for ever saved.

2. 'It is a very singular fact,' says a country paper, 'that a hare, that was opened a few days ago at Sheffield, was found to have two hearts. They were joined together by a thin membrane.' An African heathen, after having heard the missionaries for some time, declared seriously to one, that he had now got two hearts within him. The one heart said, Do good; the other said, Do evil. Many, besides this heathen, feel within them two opposing principles.

3. Socrates was once accused by a person who claimed that he could read a man's character in his face, of having a base and lewd disposition. His disciples, knowing his character to be altogether the reverse, were much enraged, and would have beaten the offender; but Socrates interposed, and modestly acknowledged, 'I was once naturally the character he describes, but I have been regenerated by philosophy.' Every Christian will acknowledge that he is by nature a child of disobedience and wrath, and that by the grace of God he is what he is.

4. James Hervey being in company with a person who was paying him compliments on account of his writings, replied, laying his hand on his

C

breast, 'Oh! sir, you would not strike the sparks of applause, if you knew how much corrupt tinder I have within.'

5. A certain Italian having his enemy in his power, told him there was no possible way to save his life, unless he would immediately deny and renounce his Saviour. The timorous wretch, in hopes of mercy, did so, when the other forthwith stabbed him to the heart, saying, 'That now he had a noble revenge, for he had at once killed both his soul and his body!'

6. The beginning of the Emperor Nero's reign was marked by acts of the greatest kindness and condescension—by affability, complaisance, and popularity. The object of his administration seemed to be the good of his people; and when he was desired to sign his name to a list of malefactors that were to be executed, he exclaimed, 'I wish to heaven I could not write!' He was an enemy to flattery; and when the senate had liberally commended the wisdom of his government, Nero desired them to keep their praises till he deserved them. Yet this was the wretch who assassinated his mother, set fire to Rome, and destroyed multitudes of men, women, and children, throwing the odium of that dreadful action on the Christians. The cruelties he exercised towards them were beyond description. 'The heart is deceitful above all things, and desperately wicked; who can know it?' (Jer. 17. 9).

Q. 19. *What is the misery of that estate whereinto man fell?*

A. All mankind by their fall lost communion with God, are under His wrath and curse, and so made liable to all the miseries of this life, to death itself, and to the pains of hell for ever.

1. Some of the natives of South America, after listening a while to the instructions of the popish missionaries, gave them this cool answer: 'You say that the God of the Christians knows everything, that nothing is hidden from Him, that He is everywhere, and sees all that is done below. Now, we do not desire a God so sharp-sighted; we choose to live in freedom in our woods, without having a perpetual observer of our actions over our heads.'

2. 'I am credibly informed,' says Job Orton, in his *Sermons on Old Age*, 'that a person who had lately a large sum of money left him to distribute in charity, had applications made to him for a share of it from no fewer than thirty persons who had rode in their own carriages.'

3. 'I have seen,' says a nobleman, once well known in the gay world, 'the silly round of business and pleasure, and have done with it all. I have enjoyed all the pleasures of the world, and consequently known their futility, and do not regret their loss. I appraise them at their real value, which in truth is very low; whereas those who have not experienced, always overrate them. They only see their gay outside, and are dazzled with their glare; but I have been behind the scenes. I have seen all the coarse pulleys and dirty ropes which exhibit and move the gaudy machine; and I have seen

and smelt the tallow candles which illuminate the whole decoration, to the astonishment and admiration of the ignorant audience. When I reflect on what I have seen, what I have heard, and what I have done, I can hardly persuade myself that that frivolous hurry of bustle and pleasure of the world had any reality; but I look on all that is past as one of those romantic dreams which opium commonly occasions, and I do by no means wish to repeat the nauseous dose for the sake of the fugitive dream. Shall I tell you that I bear this melancholy situation with that meritorious constancy and resignation that most men boast? No, sir, I really cannot help it; I bear it because I must bear it, whether I will or not. I think of nothing but killing time the best way I can; now that time has become my enemy, it is my resolution to sleep in the carriage during the remainder of the journey.'

4. Some time ago, a gentleman in London, when on his death-bed, felt so strong an aversion to dying, and leaving behind him all his hard-earned wealth, that he hastily rose from his bed, went out and walked in his yard, calling out that he would not die. But the unhappy man's strength being soon exhausted, he was brought back to his bed by his affrighted friends, where he expired, for his hour was come. It is observed by one, that death comes always too soon to a bad man, even though he be far advanced in years, because it comes before he is ready.

5. It is said of Cesar Borgia, that in his last moments he exclaimed, 'I have provided in the course of my life, for everything except death; and now, alas! I am to die, although entirely unprepared.'

6. A boy went from a retired country hamlet to be apprenticed to a shop-keeper in a large city. The shop was in a street leading to the principal churchyard. Not having formerly seen a funeral above once in a year or two, he was alarmed to witness two or three funerals pass the shop the first day he was there; still more, by observing as many the second day: and finding not fewer on the third, he resolved to remain no longer in what he conceived to be so hazardous a place. By sunrise, on the fourth morning, he packed up his little bundle of clothes, and having escaped by the window of his chamber, he fled home in great haste to his mother. Being surprised at this unexpected visit, she naturally inquired into the cause of his return. 'Mother,' said he, 'a person is not sure of his life for a minute in that town, for they are burying the people as fast as they can.' It is to be feared that, from the frequency of the occurrence, the sight of a funeral makes but little impression on the minds of the generality of those who inhabit large towns.

7. 'Ah! Mr Hervey,' said a dying man, 'the day in which I ought to have worked is over, and now I see a horrible night approaching, bringing with it the blackness of darkness for ever. Woe is me! when God called, I refused. Now I am in sore anguish, and yet this is but the beginning of sorrows. I shall be destroyed with an *everlasting* destruction.'

8. A young girl, eighteen years of age, a native of New York, was brought up by her parents in all the gaiety and follies of youth; by them encouraged to ornament her person, and engage in every vain amusement. When she was taken ill, three physicians were sent for immediately, who pronounced her speedy dissolution. No sooner was their opinion made known to her, than she requested as a favour, that all her gay companions might be collected

with haste. They were soon around her bed, when she told them she was going to die—described the awful manner in which they spent their precious time, and in a very affecting manner, exhorted them all to repentance before it was too late. Turning next to her father and mother, she addressed to them, in the presence of her acquaintances, these heart-rending words: 'You have been the unhappy instruments of my being; you fostered me in pride, and led me in the paths of sin; you never once warned me of my danger, and now it is too late. In a few hours you will have to cover me with earth; but remember, while you are casting earth upon my body, my soul will be in hell, and yourselves the miserable cause!' Shortly afterwards she died.

9. Some years ago, an individual, well known and highly respected in the religious world, in early life, was making a tour on the continent with a college companion. At Paris his friend was seized with an alarming illness. A physician of great celebrity was speedily summoned, who stated that the case was a critical one, and that much would depend on a minute attention to his directions. As there was no one at hand upon whom they could place much reliance, he was requested to recommend some confidential and ex-perienced nurse. He mentioned one, but added—'You may think yourself happy indeed should you be able to secure her services; but she is so much in request among the higher circles here, that there is little hope of finding her disengaged.' The gentleman at once ordered his carriage, went to her residence, and much to his satisfaction found her at home. He briefly stated his errand, and requested her immediate attendance. 'Before I consent to accompany you,' she said, 'permit me to ask you a singular question. Is your friend a Christian?' 'Yes,' he replied, 'indeed he is—a Christian in the best and highest sense of the term, a man who lives in the fear of God. But I should like to know your reason for such an inquiry.' 'Sir,' she answered, 'I was the nurse that attended Voltaire in his last illness, and, for all the wealth of Europe, I would never see another infidel die.'

Q. 20. *Did God leave all mankind to perish in the estate of sin and misery?*

A. God having, out of His mere good pleasure, from all eter-nity, elected some to everlasting life, did enter into a covenant of grace, to deliver them out of the estate of sin and misery, and to bring them into an estate of salvation by a Redeemer.

1. Lord Bolingbroke, the celebrated infidel, was one day reading Cal-vin's *Institutes*, when a clergyman of his acquaintance came on a visit to him. Bolingbroke said to him, 'You have caught me reading John Calvin; he was indeed a man of great parts, profound sense and vast learning. He handles the doctrines of grace in a very masterly manner.' 'Doctrines of grace!' re-plied the clergyman; 'the doctrines of grace have set all mankind together by the ears.' 'I am surprised to hear you say so,' was the reply, 'you who

profess to believe and to preach Christianity. Those doctrines are certainly the doctrines of the Bible, and if I believe the Bible, I must believe them; and let me tell you seriously, that the greatest miracle in the world is the survival of Christianity, and its continued preservation as a religion, when the preaching of it is committed to the care of such unchristian wretches as you.'

2. A good man, who had been for a long time perplexed about the doctrine of election, as fearing he was not among the number chosen, resolved one day to fall down upon his knees, and give thanks to God for having elected *some* to everlasting life, though *he* should be passed by. He did so, and the happy consequence was, that while thus engaged, he obtained assurance of his own personal election, and was freed from his perplexity.

3. When George Whitefield was in the zenith of his popularity, Lord Clare, who knew that his influence was considerable, applied to him by letter, requesting his influence at the ensuing general election at Bristol. Mr Whitefield replied, that in *general elections* he never interfered, but he would earnestly entreat his lordship to use diligence to make his own particular calling and election sure.

4. The late John Newton, rector of St Mary Woolnoth, London, when his memory was nearly gone, used to say, that forget what he might, he never forgot two things—firstly, That he was a great sinner; secondly, That Jesus Christ was a great Saviour.

5. 'I remember, a few years ago,' says George Burder of London, in his sermon on the Value of the Soul, 'that a boy, who was sent upon some errand on a cold winter evening, was overtaken by a dreadful storm. The snow fell so thick, and drifted in such a manner, that he missed his way; and, continuing to wander up and down for several hours, was ready to perish. About midnight, a gentleman in the neighbourhood thought he heard a sound, but he could not imagine what it was, till opening his window, he distinguished a human voice, at a great distance, pronouncing in a piteous tone, "*Lost! lost! lost!*" Humanity induced the gentleman to send in search of the person from whom the voice proceeded, when the boy, at length, was found and preserved. Happy for him that he perceived his danger, that he cried for help, and that his cry was heard! So will it be happy for us, if, sensible of the value of our souls, and their danger of perishing in hell, we now cry out for mercy and help, to that dear and gracious Friend of sinners, that great and generous Deliverer, who "came to seek and to save that which was lost." But if this be neglected, the soul will be lost indeed, lost without remedy, lost for ever.'

Q. 21. *Who is the Redeemer of God's elect?*

A. The only Redeemer of God's elect is the Lord Jesus Christ, who, being the eternal Son of God, became man, and so was, and continueth to be, God and man, in two distinct natures, and one person, for ever.

1. A minister who resided at Bedford, taking a ride one afternoon by way of relaxation, overtook a decent-looking woman on the road, to whom, after a little conversation on other subjects had passed, he said, 'Good woman, you seem to be an intelligent person, pray, do you know anything of the Lord Jesus Christ?' She replied, 'No, sir; there is no such nobleman living hereabouts that I know of!'

2. A girl, seventeen years of age, the daughter of a respectable Jewish merchant at Ohio, in America, being near death, said to her father, 'I know but little about Jesus, for I was never taught; but I know that He is a Saviour, for He has manifested Himself to me since I have been sick, even for the salvation of my soul. I believe He will save me, although I never before loved Him; I feel that I am going to Him—that I shall be ever with Him. And now, my father, do not deny me; I beg that you will never again speak against this Jesus of Nazareth; I entreat you to obtain a New Testament, which tells of Him.' The father afterwards became a humble follower of the once despised Saviour.

3. A poor man, unable to read, who obtained a livelihood by mending old shoes, was asked by an Arian minister, how he knew that Jesus Christ was the Son of God? 'Sir,' he replied, 'I am sorry you have put such a question to me before my children, although I think I can give you a satisfactory answer. You know, sir, when I first became concerned about my soul, and unhappy on account of my sins, I called upon you to ask for your advice, and you told me to get into company, and spend my time as merrily as I could, but not to go to hear the Methodists.' 'I did so,' answered the ungodly minister. 'I followed your advice,' continued the illiterate cobbler, 'for some time; but the more I trifled, the more my misery increased; and at last I was persuaded to hear one of those Methodist ministers who came into our neighbourhood, and preached Jesus Christ as the Saviour. In the greatest agony of mind, I prayed to Him to save me, and to forgive my sins; and now I feel that He has freely forgiven them—and by this I know that He is the Son of God.'

4. ' I have sometimes heard of Christ,' said an Indian girl, seven years old, 'and now I experience Him to be just such a Saviour as I want. I have often heard people undertake to tell of the excellency that is in Christ; but their tongues are too short to express the beauty and love which are contained in this lovely Jesus! I cannot tell my poor relations how lovely Christ is! I wonder my poor playmates will choose that dreadful place *hell*, when here stands that beautiful person, Jesus, calling upon sinners, and saying, "Come away, sinners, to heaven!" Come, O do come to my Saviour! Shut Him out no longer, for there is room enough in heaven for all of you to be happy for evermore. It causes much joy at times that I delight to serve Him, and by the help of God I mean to hold out to the end of my days.'

5. As a tutor and his pupil toured the shores of the Mediterranean, they slept one night at the little town where Bonaparte landed, and in the very room in which he rested on his return from Elba. About day-break, the pupil heard his companion thus speaking in an audible, distinct, and deliberate tone, 'Took upon Himself the form of a servant. Now, every creature is, by the mere fact of his creation, the servant of his Maker. Not

so our Lord Jesus Christ, for He *took upon Himself* the form of a servant; therefore He is, He can be, no creature—therefore He is *the Creator*—therefore He is *God over all, blessed for ever.*' And then followed, in expressions of the deepest fervour, and of the most elevated sublimity, a solemn dedication to this Lord Jesus Christ, as his Maker, Redeemer, and ever-blessed God and portion, of himself, of his person, of his ministry, of his all. The pupil was electrified, and rivetted; but he thought it to be the morning meditation of his reverend companion, unconsciously uttered aloud, and would not intrude on so hallowed an exercise. As they rode along, however, in the course of the day, he could not refrain from saying, 'I was deeply interested, sir, in your reflections this morning.' 'What reflections?' asked the tutor. 'The reflections you uttered before you rose to-day.' 'I remember none, what were they?' The pupil repeated them. As he was doing so, the tutor's mind seemed caught by the novelty of the conception, and powerfully struck also by the weight and conclusiveness of it. 'Perfectly new!' he exclaimed, 'I never saw the passage in that light before—it is a finishing stroke. It cuts them up (the Socinians and Arians) root and branch. But—*I remember nothing of the morning.*'

6. Sometimes there were more kings than one in Sparta, who governed by joint authority. A king was occasionally sent to some neighbouring senate in the character of a Spartan ambassador. Did he, when so sent, cease to be a king of Sparta, because he was also an ambassador? No; he did not divest himself of his regal dignity, but only added to it that of public deputation. So Christ, in becoming man, did not cease to be God; but though He ever was, and still continued to be, King of the whole creation, He acted as the voluntary servant and messenger of the Father.

7. When a certain Mr Kirkland was a missionary to the Oneidas, a tribe of North American Indians, being unwell, he was unable to preach on the afternoon of a certain Sabbath, and told Peter, one of the head men of the Oneidas, that he must address the congregation. Peter modestly and reluctantly consented. After a few words of introduction, he began to discourse on the character of the Saviour. 'What, my brethren,' said he, 'are the views which you form of the character of Jesus? You will answer, perhaps, that He was a man of singular benevolence. You will tell me, that He proved this to be His character, by the nature of the miracles which He wrought. All these, you will say, were kind in the extreme. He created bread to feed thousands, who were ready to perish. He raised to life the son of a poor woman, who was a widow, and to whom his labours were necessary for her support in old age. Are these, then, your only views of the Saviour? I will tell you they are lame. When Jesus came into the world, He threw His blanket around Him, but the God was within.'

8. Among the many whom George Whitefield was honoured to be the means of converting to the knowledge and love of the truth, and who will be a crown of joy to him in the day of the Lord, it is perhaps not generally known that the celebrated James Hervey is to be mentioned. In a letter to Whitefield, Hervey expresses himself thus: 'Your journals, dear sir, and sermons, especially that sweet sermon on *What think ye of Christ?* were the means of bringing me to the knowledge of the truth.'

Q. 22. *How did Christ, being the Son of God, become man?*

A. Christ, the Son of God, became man, by taking to Himself a true body, and a reasonable soul, being conceived by the power of the Holy Ghost, in the womb of the Virgin Mary, and born of her, yet without sin.

1. When a certain Mr Hunt was preaching one Sabbath morning at his meeting-house, Horsleydown (London), on 'The Mystery of Godliness,' he challenged the audience to explain how God assumed human nature; when a little boy in the gallery rose, and with much simplicity repeated the above answer from the Assembly's Catechism. Mr Hunt then inquired if he could give the Scripture proofs, which, after a short pause, he did correctly. The venerable minister was much affected, publicly thanked him, called him his young tutor, and invited him into the vestry after the service, where several persons handsomely rewarded his diligence.

2. A sick woman said to Richard Cecil, 'Sir I have no notion of God, I can form no notion of Him. You talk to me about Him, but I cannot get a single idea that seems to contain anything.' 'But you know how to conceive of Jesus Christ as a man.' replied Cecil; 'God comes down to you in Him, full of kindness and condescension.' 'Ah! sir, that gives me something to lay hold on. *There* I can rest. I understand God in His Son.' 'God was *in Christ*, reconciling the world to Himself, not imputing their trespasses unto them.' (2 Cor. 5. 19).

3. John Brown of Haddington, in his last illness, having heard the bells ringing, and understanding it to be the King's birthday, said: 'O, blessed be God, however worthy our Sovereign be, we have a better King's birthday to celebrate. Unto us was born, in the city of David, a Saviour who is Christ the Lord! On account of that event the gospel bells have been sounding for ages past, and they will ring louder and louder still. O the Saviour! the Son of God our Saviour! O His kindness, His kindness! A Saviour, a husband to sinners, to me!'

4. Henry Martyn the missionary, when at Dinapore in India, wrote thus: 'Upon showing the Moonshee the first part of John 3, he instantly caught at those words of our Lord, in which He first describes Himself as having *come down* from heaven, and then calls Himself "the Son of man which is *in* heaven." He said that this was what the philosophers called "nickal" (impossible)—even for God to make a thing to be in two different places at the same time. I explained to him, as soon as his heat was a little subsided, that the difficulty was not so much in conceiving how the Son of man could be, at the same time, in two different places, as in comprehending that union of the two natures in Him, which made this possible. I told him that I could not explain this union, but showed him the design and wisdom of God in effecting our redemption by this method. I was much at a loss for words, but I believe that he collected my meaning and received some information which he did not possess before.'

5. William Greenfield was once in company, at the house of a friend,

with a person of deistical principles, a stranger to him, who asked why Jesus
Christ is called the Word? 'What is meant by the Word? It is a curious
term.' Greenfield, ignorant of the sceptical motive of the inquirer, replied
with the mild simplicity and decision by which his character was marked,
'I suppose, as words are the medium of communication between us, the
term is used in the sacred Scriptures to demonstrate to us that Christ is the
only medium between God and man; I know no other reason.' To this the
deist could make no reply.

Q. 23. *What offices doth Christ execute as our Redeemer?*

A. Christ, as our Redeemer, executeth the offices of a
prophet, of a priest, and of a king, both in His estate of humiliation and exaltation.

1. A trader once endeavoured to persuade an Indian Christian named
Abraham, that the Moravian brethren were not privileged teachers.
Abraham replied, 'They may be what they will; but I know what they have
told me, and what God has wrought within me. Look at my poor countrymen there, lying drunk before your door. Why do you not send privileged
teachers to convert them, if they can? Four years ago I also lived like a beast,
and not one of you troubled himself about me; but, when the brethren
came, they preached the cross of Christ, and I have experienced the power
of His blood, according to their doctrine, so that I am freed from the dominion of sin. Such teachers we want.'

2. Gideon, a converted Indian, was one day attacked by a savage, who,
presenting his gun to his head, exclaimed, 'Now, I will shoot you, for you
speak of nothing but Jesus.' Gideon answered, 'If Jesus does not permit
you, you cannot shoot me.' The savage was so struck with this answer,
that he dropped his gun, and went home in silence.

3. In 1596, when the design of recalling the popish lords was ascertained,
Andrew Melville accompanied a deputation of the clergy to Falkland, Fife-
shire, where James VI then resided. They were admitted to a private
audience, when he thus addressed the king: 'Sir, we will always humbly
reverence your majesty in public; but since we have this occasion to be with
your majesty in private, and since you are brought into extreme danger,
both of your life and crown, and along with you the country and the Church
of God are like to go to wreck, for not telling you the truth and giving you
faithful counsel, we must discharge our duty, or else be traitors both to
Christ and you. Therefore, sir, as diverse times before I have told you, so
now again I must tell you, there are two kings and two kingdoms in Scotland: there is King James, the head of the commonwealth, and there is
Christ Jesus, the King of the Church, whose subject James the Sixth is,
and of whose kingdom he is not a king, nor a lord, nor a head, but a member.
We will yield to you your place, and give you all due obedience; but again,
I say, you are not the head of the Church; you cannot give us that eternal

life which we seek for even in this world, and you cannot deprive us of it. Permit us then freely to meet in the name of Christ, and to attend to the interests of that Church of which you are a chief member.'

4. A laborious and successful gospel minister in Wiltshire used to say, he considered three things when he preached: '1*st*, I have immortal souls to deal with. 2*nd*, There is a free and full salvation for such. 3*rd*, All the blessings of the gospel are treasured up in the Lord Jesus.' Happy would it be, if every minister were constantly impressed with the same important truths.

Q. 24. *How doth Christ execute the office of a prophet?*

A. Christ executeth the office of a prophet, in revealing to us, by His word and Spirit, the will of God for our salvation.

1. The comfortable influence of the precious truths of the Bible at a dying hour was manifested in the case of a soldier who was mortally wounded at the battle of Waterloo. His companion conveyed him to some distance, and laid him down under a tree. Before he left him, the dying soldier entreated him to open his knapsack, and take out his pocket Bible, and read to him a small portion of it before he died. When asked what passages he should read, he desired him to read John 14. 27: 'Peace I leave with you; my peace I give unto you; not as the world giveth, give I unto you. Let not your heart be troubled, neither let it be afraid.' 'Now,' said he, 'I die happy. I desire to have peace with God, and I possess the peace of God, which passeth all understanding.' A little while after, one of his officers passed him, and seeing him in such an exhausted state, asked him how he did. He said, 'I die happy, for I enjoy the peace of God, which passeth all understanding,' and then expired. The officer left him, and went into the battle, where he was soon after mortally wounded. When surrounded by his brother officers, full of anguish and dismay, he cried out, 'Oh! I would give ten thousand worlds, if I had them, that I possessed that peace which gladdened the heart of a dying soldier, whom I saw lying under a tree; for he declared that he possessed the peace of God, which passeth all understanding. I know nothing of that peace! I die miserable! for I die in despair.'

2. Robert Aitken, a bookseller in Philadelphia, was the first person who printed a Bible in that city. He was a Scotch Seceder, and a very godly man. While he kept a book store, a person called on him, and inquired if he had Tom Paine's *Age of Reason* for sale. He told him he had not; but having entered into conversation with him, and found he was an infidel, he told him he had a better book than Paine's *Age of Reason*, which he usually sold for a dollar, but would lend it to him, if he promised to read it; and if, after he had actually read it, he did not think it worth a dollar, he would take it again. The man consented, and Aitken put a Bible into his hands. He smiled when he found what book he had engaged to read; but he said he would perform his engagement. He did so; and when he had finished

the perusal, he came back to the bookseller, and expressed the deepest gratitude for his recommendation of the book, saying it had made him what he was not before—a happy man; for he had found in it a Saviour, and the way of salvation. Aitken rejoiced in the event, and had the satisfaction of knowing that this reader of the Bible, from that day onwards lived a consistent Christian life, and died with a hope full of immortality.

3. 'Give me' says Lactantius, 'a man of a passionate, abusive, headstrong temper. With a few only of the words of God, I will make him as gentle as a lamb. Give me a greedy, covetous, selfish wretch, and I will teach him to distribute his riches with a liberal and unsparing hand. Give me a cruel and blood-thirsty monster, and all his rage will be changed into love. Give me a man guilty of injustice, full of ignorance, and lost in wickedness; he shall soon become just, prudent, and holy. In the single laver of regeneration he shall be cleansed from all his malignity.'

4. Dr John Owen, when a young man, having been for a considerable time in distress of mind, went one Lord's day, with a cousin of his, to hear Edmund Calamy, a celebrated preacher in London. From some occurrence, Mr Calamy was prevented from preaching that day. Being uncertain whether there would be any sermon at all, Dr Owen was solicited by his relation to go and hear another eminent minister. Being indisposed to go farther, however, he kept his seat, resolving, if no minister came, to return to his lodgings. After he had waited some time, a country minister came up to the pulpit, a stranger not only to Dr Owen, but to the congregation. Having prayed earnestly, he took for his text these words, 'Why are ye fearful, O ye of little faith?' (Matt. 8. 26). The very reading of the words surprised Dr. Owen; on which he secretly put up a prayer, that God would be pleased by the minister to speak to his case. His prayer was heard; for in that sermon the minister was directed to answer those very objections which he had commonly formed against himself; and though he had formerly given the same answers to himself without effect, yet now the time was come when God designed to speak peace to his soul; and the sermon (though otherwise a plain familiar discourse) was blessed for the removing of all his doubts, and laid the foundation of that solid peace and comfort, which he afterwards enjoyed as long as he lived.

A. 25. *How doth Christ execute the office of a priest?*

A. Christ executeth the office of a priest, in His once offering up of Himself a sacrifice to satisfy divine justice, and reconcile us to God; and in making continual intercession for us.

1. Xenophon mentions an Armenian prince, taken captive, together with his queen, by Cyrus, King of Persia, who, on being asked if he desired the restoration of his liberty, his kingdom, and his queen, answered, 'As for my liberty and my kingdom, I value them not; but if my blood would redeem my wife, I would cheerfully give it.' Cyrus having generously re-

stored him all, he asked his queen what she thought of Cyrus's person; she replied, 'I really did not observe him, my mind was so occupied with the man who offered to give his life for my ransom, that I could think of no other.' Jesus Christ has actually done what this prince offered to do, and has abundantly exceeded that generous action. May we feel a similar regard for Him, so as to overlook all other objects.

2. A poor girl, after having been educated in the Hibernian Female School in Sligo, was apprenticed to a dressmaker. A lady, who had formerly taken charge of her, and had been very kind to her, going one Sabbath into the chapel before service, found the girl sitting by herself, reading her Testament. The lady inquired where she was reading. She said, 'In the 5th chapter of the Epistle to the Romans.' 'Why do you choose that chapter?' She replied, 'Oh! I delight in it much.' 'On what account?' 'It just meets my case: see, is not that delightful?'—pointing to the 6th verse—'For when we were yet without strength, in due time Christ died for the ungodly;' and then added, 'I am indeed a sinner, and without strength; but here is the blessed remedy, "Christ died for the ungodly." '

3. Christmas Evans, a Welsh minister, preaching on the depravity of man by sin, and of his recovery by the death of Christ said—'Brethren, if I should compare the natural state of man, I should conceive of an immense grave-yard, filled with yawning sepulchres and dying men. All around are lofty walls and massive iron gates. At the gate stands Mercy, sad spectatress of the melancholy scene. An angel flying through the midst of heaven, attracted by the awful sight, exclaims, "Mercy, why do you not enter, and apply to these objects of compassion the restoring balm?" Mercy replies, "Alas! I dare not enter; Justice bars the way." By her side a form appeared like unto the Son of Man. "Justice," He cried, "what are thy demands that Mercy may enter and stay the carnival of death?" "I demand," said Justice, "pain for their ease; degradation for their dignity; shame for their honour; death for their life." "I accept the terms: now, Mercy, enter." "What pledge do you give for the performance of these conditions?" "My word, my oath." "When will you fulfil them?" "Four thousand years hence, on the hill of Calvary." The bond was sealed in the presence of attendant angels, and committed to patriarchs and prophets. A long series of rites and ceremonies, sacrifices and oblations, was instituted to preserve the memory of that solemn deed; and at the close of the four thousandth year, behold at the foot of Calvary the incarnate Son of God! Justice too was there, presenting the dreadful bond to the Redeemer, and demanding the fulfilment of its awful terms. He accepted the deed, and together they ascended to the summit of the mount. Mercy was seen attendant at His side, and the weeping church followed in His train. When He had reached the top, what did He with the bond? Did He tear it in pieces, and scatter it to the winds of heaven? Oh! no, He nailed it to His cross. And when the wood was prepared, and the devoted willing sacrifice stretched on the tree, Justice sternly cried, "Holy fire, come down from heaven and burn this sacrifice." Holy fire replied, "I come, I come, and when I have consumed this sacrifice, I will burn the universe." The fire descended and rapidly consumed His humanity; but when it touched His

Deity, expired! Then did the heavenly hosts break forth in rapturous strains, "Glory to God in the highest, and on earth peace, good will toward men." '

4. The price paid for the ransom of the soul shows its infinite worth.— A converted Jew pleading the cause of the Society through whose instrumentality he had been brought to a knowledge of Christianity, was opposed by a learned gentleman, who spoke very lightly of the objects of the Society, and of its effects, and said, 'I do not suppose they will convert more than a hundred altogether.' 'Be it so,' replied the Jew, 'you are a skilful calculator, —take your pen now, and calculate the worth of one hundred immortal souls!'

> "Knowest thou the value of a soul immortal?
> Behold the midnight glory; worlds on worlds!
> Amazing pomp! redouble this amaze;
> Ten thousand add, and twice ten thousand more,
> Then weigh the whole,—*one soul* outweighs them all!"

5. History informs us of two brothers, one of whom, for capital crimes, was condemned to die; but on the appearance of the other, who had lost an arm in the successful defence of his country, and on his presenting the remaining stump, the judges were so affected with a grateful recollection of past services, as fully, for his sake, to pardon the guilty brother. Thus the Redeemer, in interceding for His people, appears as a 'lamb that had been slain,' presenting the merits of His sufferings and death on their behalf, nor does He thus appear in vain.

Q. 26. *How doth Christ execute the office of a king?*

A. Christ executeth the office of a king, in subduing us to Himself, in ruling and defending us, and in restraining and conquering all His and our enemies.

1. It has been said of Edward the Black Prince, that he never fought a battle which he did not win; and of the great Duke of Marlborough, that he never besieged a city which he did not take. Shall that be said of men, which we deny concerning the Most High God? Is He less successful than some human generals? Shall these invincibly prevail, and grace be liable to defeat? *Impossible!* The former of these, having conquered and taken prisoner King John of France, nobly condescended to wait on his royal captive the same night at supper. Christ, having first subdued His people by His grace, waits on them afterwards to the end of their lives.

2. One day, when the Emperor Napoleon was reviewing his troops, the bridle of his horse slipped from his hand and his horse galloped off. A common soldier ran, and holding the bridle brought back the horse to the Emperor's hand, when he addressed him and said, 'Well done, Cap-

tain.' The soldier immediately inquired, 'Of what regiment, Sir?' 'Of the Guards,' answered Napoleon, pleased with the instant belief in his word. The Emperor rode off, the soldier threw down his musket, and though he had no epaulets on his shoulders, no sword by his side, nor any other mark of his advancement than the word of the Emperor, he ran and joined the staff of commanding officers. They laughed at him, thinking him to be out of his senses, and said, 'What have you to do here?' He replied, 'I am Captain of the Guards.' They were amazed, but he said, 'The Emperor has said so and therefore I am.' In like manner we are to take Christ at His word! 'Where the word of a king is, there is power' (Eccles. 8. 4.).

3. The Roman Emperor Julian, a determined enemy of Christianity, was mortally wounded in a war with the Persians. In this condition, we are told that he filled his hand with blood, and casting it into the air, said, 'O Galilean! Thou hast conquered.' During this expedition, one of Julian's followers asked a Christian of Antioch, 'what the carpenter's son was doing?' 'The Maker of the world,' replied the Christian, 'whom you call the carpenter's son, is employed in making a coffin for the emperor.' A few days after, news came to Antioch of Julian's death.

4. The day before John Hooper, Bishop of Gloucester, was burned at the stake, in front of his cathedral, in the days of Mary Tudor, a well-wisher came to him in prison and urged him to change from his Protestant beliefs and accept the Romish doctrine which was being enforced by the Queen and Parliament. 'Consult your safety,' he said, 'life is sweet and death is bitter, and your life hereafter may do good.' Said the good bishop, 'I thank you for your friendly counsel. True it is that death is bitter and life is sweet, but consider that the death to come is more bitter and the life to come is more sweet. Therefore, for the desire and love I have to the one, and the terror and fear I have of the other, I do not so much regard this death nor esteem this life; but have settled myself, through the strength of God's Holy Spirit, patiently to pass through the torments and extremities of the fire now prepared for me, rather than to deny the truth of His Word.'

Q. 27. *Wherein did Christ's humiliation consist?*

A. Christ's humiliation consisted in His being born, and that in a low condition, made under the law, undergoing the miseries of this life, the wrath of God, and the cursed death of the cross; in being buried, and continuing under the power of death for a time.

1. As a poor but godly man was sitting by his fire, one cold evening, with his wife and children, he said to them, 'I have been thinking a great deal to-day about that part of Scripture: "The Son of Man hath not where to lay His head." (Matt. 8.20). How wonderful it is, that we who are so sinful, unworthy, and helpless, should be more favoured than He was!' 'It is wonderful, indeed, father,' said the eldest girl; 'for though our house is

mean, and our victuals scanty, compared with the houses and way of living of great folks, yet it seems that Jesus Christ was not so well provided for as we are.' 'I am right glad to hear you speak in that way, Sarah,' said the wife. 'How happy we all are in our little dwelling this cold night, and as soon as we wish, we have beds to rest ourselves upon; *there*, sharp and piercing as the frost is, and bleak and stormy as the wind blows, we shall be comfortable and warm; and yet the Son of Man, as your father has just told us, "had not where to lay His head." O that this thought may make us thankful for our many mercies!' 'Tommy,' said the father, 'reach that hymn which our minister gave you last Sabbath at the Sabbath School; and, as our hearts are in a good frame, let us try to keep them so by singing it.' The whole company, father, mother, and children, then, with a glow of sacred ardour and pleasure, sang the hymn, entitled, "The Son of Man had not where to lay His head."

2. A little boy, between four and five years old, was one day reading to his mother in the New Testament; and, when he came to these words, 'The foxes have holes, and the birds of the air have nests, but the Son of Man hath not where to lay His head,' His eyes filled with tears, his breast heaved, and at last he sobbed aloud. His mother inquired what was the matter; but for some time he could not answer her. At length, as well as his sobs would let him, he said, 'I am sure, mother, if I had been there, I would have given Him my pillow.'

3. A poor, but pious man in a workhouse, said to a visitor, 'I am as full of pain as my poor body can bear, but I find the truth of the promise, "As thy days are, so shall thy strength be."' (Deut. 33. 25). Then pointing to an orange which was near his bed, he said, 'I, a poor man, have an orange to refresh me, while my Saviour had only vinegar mixed with gall to quench His thirst.'

4. The first wife of a certain Dr Grosvenor was a most devout and amiable woman. The Sabbath after her death, the doctor expressed himself from the pulpit in the following manner: 'I have had an irreparable loss; and no man can feel a loss of this consequence more sensibly than myself; but the cross of a dying Jesus is my support; I fly from *one* death for refuge to *another*.' How much superior was the comfort of the Christian minister to that of the heathen philosopher, Pliny the younger, who says that, in a similar distress, study was his only relief!

5. Louis II of France died of vexation, occasioned by the revolt of his son, Louis of Bavaria. The broken-hearted father said, as he expired, 'I forgive Louis; but let him know he has been the cause of my death.' The sins of God's elect were the cause of the Messiah's death; yet in dying, He declared, 'Father, forgive them, for they know not what they do.'

Q. 28. *Wherein consisteth Christ's exaltation?*

A. Christ's exaltation consisteth in His rising again from the dead on the third day, in ascending up to heaven, in sitting at the right hand of God the Father, and in coming to judge the world at the last day.

1. A little child, when dying, was asked where he was going: 'To heaven,' said the child. 'And what makes you wish to be there?' said one. 'Because Christ is there,' replied the child. 'But,' said a friend, 'what if Christ should leave heaven?' 'Well,' said the child, 'I will go with Him.' Some time before his departure, he expressed a wish to have a golden crown when he died. 'And what will you do,' said one, 'with the golden crown?' 'I will take the crown,' said the child, 'and cast it at the feet of Christ.' Does not such a child—to use the language of prophecy—die a hundred years old?

2. On the morning of the day on which Dr John Owen died, Thomas Payne, an eminent dissenting minister, who had been entrusted with the publication of the doctor's work, entitled, *Meditations on the Glory of Christ*, called to take his leave, and to inform him that he had just been giving it to the printer. 'I am glad to hear it,' said the doctor; and, lifting up his hands and eyes, exclaimed, 'But, O brother Payne, the long-wished-for day is come at last, in which I shall see that glory in another manner than I have ever done, or was capable of doing in this world!'

3. Legh Richmond, in one of his visits to the Young Cottager, found her asleep, with her finger lying on a Bible, which lay open before her, pointing at these words, 'Lord, remember me when Thou comest into Thy kingdom.' 'Is this casual or designed, thought I. Either way is remarkable. But in another moment, I discovered that her finger was indeed an index to the thoughts of her heart. She half awoke from her dozing state, but not sufficiently so to perceive that any person was present, and said in a kind of whisper, "Lord, remember me—remember me—remember—remember a poor child; Lord, remember me." '

4. A Christian king of Hungary being very sad and pensive, his brother, who was a gay courtier, was desirous of knowing the cause of the sadness. 'O, brother,' said the king, 'I have been a great sinner against God, and know not how to die, or how to appear before God in judgment!' The brother, making a jest of it, said, 'These are but gloomy thoughts.' The king made no reply; but it was the custom of the country, that if the executioner came and sounded a trumpet before any man's door, he was presently led to execution. The king in the dead of night, sent the executioner to sound the trumpet before his brother's door; who hearing it, and seeing the messenger of death, sprang into the king's presence, beseeching him to know in what he had offended. 'Alas! brother,' said the king, 'you have never offended me. And is the sight of my executioner so dreadful? and shall not I, who have greatly offended, fear to be brought before the judgment seat of Christ?'

5. 'In January last,' said a godly father, in writing to his friends, 'I dreamed that the day of judgment was come. I saw the Judge on His great white throne, and all nations were gathered before Him. My wife and I were on the right hand; but I could not see my children. I went to the left hand of the Judge, and there found them all standing in the utmost despair. As soon as they saw me, they caught hold of me, and cried, "O, father, we

will never part." I said, "My dear children, I am come to try, if possible, to get you out of this awful situation." So I took them all with me, but when we came near the Judge, I thought He cast an angry look, and said, "What do thy children with thee now? they would not take thy warning when on earth, and they shall not share with thee the crown in heaven; depart, ye cursed." At these words I awoke, bathed in tears. A while after this, as we were all sitting together on a Sabbath evening, I related to them my dream. No sooner did I begin, than first one, and then another, yea, all of them burst into tears, and God fastened conviction on their hearts. Five of them are rejoicing in God their Saviour; and I believe the Lord is at work with the other two, so that I doubt not He will give them also to my prayers.'

6. Not long after the Rev. J. Cooke became a Methodist minister in the town of Maidenhead, the mayor of the town, one Sabbath evening, attended the meeting-house, and heard Mr Cooke preach. The text was, 'Behold, He cometh with clouds, and every eye shall see Him" (Rev. 1. 7). His attention was powerfully arrested: an arrow of conviction entered his heart; he speedily became a changed man, and regularly attended the means of grace. He had been a jovial companion, a good singer, and a most gay and cheerful member of the corporation. The change was soon perceived. His brethren, at one of their social parties, chaffed him upon Methodism. But he stood firm by his principles, and said, 'Gentlemen, if you will listen patiently, I will tell you why I go to meeting, and do not attend your card-table. I went one Sunday evening to hear Mr Cooke. He took for his text, "Behold, He cometh with clouds, and every eye shall see Him." *Your eye* shall see Him!' In short, he gave them so faithful and powerful an epitome of the sermon, and applied it so closely to them individually, marking the words, 'every eye shall see Him,' with such emphasis, and pointing to them, said, 'Your eye,' and 'your eye,' that they were satisfied with his reasons for going, and never again durst speak to him on the subject.

Q. 29. *How are we made partakers of the redemption purchased by Christ?*

A. We are made partakers of the redemption purchased by Christ, by the effectual application of it to us by His Holy Spirit.

1. When Bishop Butler lay on his death bed, he called for his chaplain, and said, 'Though I have endeavoured to avoid sin, and to please God to the utmost of my power, yet, from the consciousness of perpetual infirmities, I am still afraid to die.' 'My lord,' said the chaplain, 'you have forgotten that Jesus Christ is a Saviour.' 'True,' was the answer; 'but how shall I know that He is a Saviour for *me*?' 'My lord, it is written, "Him that cometh unto Me, I will in no wise cast out." ' 'True' said the bishop, 'and I am surprised that, though I have read that Scripture a thousand times over, I never felt its virtue till this moment; and now I die happy.'

2. Several learned men tried to persuade a great scholar to believe in

D

Christianity, but all their labour was in vain. A plain honest person, however, managed the argument in a different manner, by referring not so much to logical reasoning, as to the work of the Divine Spirit, so that at last the scholar exclaimed: 'When I heard no more than human reason, I opposed it with human reason; but when I heard the Spirit, I was obliged to surrender.' Thus it is, the wisest trusting to their own wisdom, are lost; while those who are taught of the Spirit, know the way of God in truth.

3. Mr Guthrie, an eminent minister in Scotland, was one evening travelling home very late. Having lost his way in a moor, he laid the reins on the neck of his horse, and committed himself to the direction of Providence. After long travelling over ditches and fields, the horse brought him to a farmer's house, into which he went, and requested permission to sit by the fire till morning, which was granted. A popish priest was administering extreme unction to the mistress of the house, who was dying. Guthrie said nothing till the priest had retired; he then went forward to the dying woman, and asked her if she enjoyed peace in the prospect of death, in consequence of what the priest had said and done to her. She answered, that she did not; on which he spoke to her of salvation through the atoning blood of the Redeemer. The Lord taught her to understand, and enabled her to believe the message of mercy, and she died triumphing in Jesus Christ her Saviour. After witnessing this astonishing scene the minister mounted his horse, and rode home. On his arrival, he told Mrs Guthrie he had seen a great wonder during the night. 'I came,' said he, 'to a farm-house, where I found a woman in a state of nature; I saw her in a state of grace; and I left her in a state of glory.'

4. John Flavel, in the preface to his *Treatise on the Soul of Man*, speaking of his inattention to his spiritual interests, says, 'I studied to know many other things, but I knew not myself. It was with me, as with a servant to whom the master committed two things: the child, and the child's clothes. The servant is very careful of the clothes; brushes and washes, starches and irons them, and keeps them safe and clean; but the child is forgotten and lost. My body which is but the garment of my soul, I kept and nourished with excessive care; but my soul was long forgotten, and had been lost for ever, as others daily are, had not God roused it by the convictions of His Spirit, out of that deep oblivion and deadly slumber.'

5. An intelligent sceptic, hearing that some devoted Christians were meeting together to offer special prayer for the influences of the Holy Spirit, resolved to go, in order, as he expressed it, to see what these foolish people were about, and to ascertain, if possible, the idea which they attached to such a service. He went; and, while he was listening to their supplications, wakened up as if from a long and dreary dream. Then, for the first time in his life, did he apprehend the plan of human redemption. The very doctrine which he had long regarded as the offspring of the wildest enthusiasm, in one instant approved itself to his understanding, his conscience, and his heart. Forthwith, he himself became a man of prayer; and throughout his subsequent course, he regarded that memorable season as the hour of his conversion.

Q. 30. *How doth the Spirit apply to us the redemption purchased by Christ?*

A. The Spirit applieth to us the redemption purchased by Christ, by working faith in us, and thereby uniting us to Christ in our effectual calling.

1. The wife of William Romaine was once in company with a clergyman at Tiverton, who spoke with no little zeal against what he called 'irresistible grace,' alleging that 'such grace would be quite incompatible with free will.' 'Not at all so,' answered Mrs Romaine; 'grace operates effectually, yet not coercively. The wills of God's people are drawn to Him and to divine things, just as your will would be drawn to a bishopric, if you had the offer of it.'

2. A lady was one evening engaged in dispute with a gentleman, and argued so long and so violently, in defence of the creature's being *first* in the matter of conversion to God, that to her surprise she perceived it was *one o'clock* in the morning. She was startled, and said, 'Well, I did not know it was so late; I see I cannot work upon you, and I am sure all you say will not convince me; so good night.' 'Yes,' said the gentleman, 'it is time to go to rest. Madam, I wish you a good night. I suppose, however, that when you retire, you think to spend a few minutes praying to God.' 'Doubtless, isr, I do.' 'Please, then, madam, to tell God what you have just told me.' 'What is that, sir?' 'Why, madam, that you began with Him, before He began with you.' 'No, I will not,' said she. 'I knew you would not,' replied the gentleman, 'and therefore I reserved this argument to the last, for I never found any person of your opinion, that could address God, in consistency with the language you hold out so confidently to your fellow-mortals.'

3. The Rev. Ebenezer Erskine was once preaching in the open air at Glendevon, in Perthshire, and pressing on his hearers the importance of at once acceding to the terms of salvation. 'You will perhaps tell me', he said, 'that you *cannot* believe. Very true, you cannot; but the offer of Christ to sinners is the means by which they are enabled to receive Him; and if I had a commission from my great Lord and Master, I would offer Him to these rocks, and they would answer me.' He pronounced these last words with a considerable elevation of voice; and, there being an echo in the place, the word *rocks* was immediately reverberated. The people were so struck with this incident, that they all turned their eyes to the rocks behind them.

4. 'I have had six children,' said John Eliot (minister to the Indians of North America), 'and I bless God for His free grace, they are all either with Christ, or in Christ; and my mind is now at rest concerning them. My desire was, that they should have served Christ on earth; but if God will choose to have them rather serve Him in heaven, I have nothing to object to it. His will be done.'

5. One of the missionaries in the East Indies being called to visit the death-bed of one of the native Christians, inquired into the state of her mind. She replied, 'Happy! happy! I have Christ *here*,' laying her hand on the

Bible, 'and Christ *here*,' pressing it to her heart, 'and Christ *there*,' pointing upwards to heaven. Happy Christian! to whatever part of the universe she might be removed, the Lord of the universe was with her, and she was secure of a home.

Q. 31. *What is effectual calling?*

A. Effectual calling is the work of God's Spirit, whereby, convincing us of our sin and misery, enlightening our minds in the knowledge of Christ, and renewing our wills, He doth persuade and enable us to embrace Jesus Christ, freely offered to us in the gospel.

1. Thomas Doolittle, a godly minister of the seventeenth century, used to catechise the members, and especially the young people of his congregation, every Lord's day. One Sabbath evening, after having received an answer in the words of the Assembly's Catechism, to the question, 'What is effectual calling?', and having explained it, he proposed that the question should be answered by changing the words *us* and *our*, into *me* and *my*. Upon this proposal a solemn silence followed; many felt its vast importance; but none had courage to answer. At length a young man rose up, and with every mark of a broken and contrite heart, by divine grace, was enabled to say, 'Effectual calling is the work of God's Spirit, whereby, convincing *me* of *my* sin and misery, enlightening *my* mind in the knowledge of Christ, and renewing *my* will, He *doth* persuade and enable me to embrace Jesus Christ, freely offered to *me* in the gospel.' The scene was truly affecting. The proposal of the question had commanded unusual solemnity. The rising up of the young man had created high expectations, and the answer being accompanied with proofs of unfeigned piety and modesty, the congregation was bathed in tears. This young man had been convicted by being catechised; and to his honour, Doolittle says, 'from being an ignorant and wicked youth, he had become an intelligent professor, to God's glory, and my much comfort.'

2. George Whitefield was preaching once at Exeter. A man was present, who had loaded his pockets with stones, in order to throw them at the minister. He heard his prayer, however, with patience; but no sooner had he named his text, than the man pulled a stone out of his pocket, and held it in his hand, waiting for a fair opportunity to throw it. But God sent a word to his heart, and the stone dropped from his hand. After sermon, he went to Whitefield and told him, 'Sir, I came to hear you this day, with a view to break your *head*, but the Spirit of God, through your ministry, has given me a broken *heart*.' The man proved to be a sound convert, and lived an ornament to the gospel.

3. 'Will you go with me to hear our minister today?' said a serious youth, in humble life, to his younger brother. 'Not to-day,' was the answer; 'certainly not to-day.' 'Why not *to-day*?' asked the other. 'Because next week

is the fair. I am sure Mr—— will preach against it to-day, and then I should not enjoy the fair at all, for I should go with a *sting in my conscience.*'

4. Nathaniel Partridge, one of the English ministers ejected in 1662, having once preached at St Alban's, upon these words, (Rev. 3. 18.), 'Anoint thine eyes with eye-salve, that thou mayest see;' a poor man, who was as blind in mind as he was in body, went afterwards to his house, and asked him very gravely, 'where he might get that ointment to cure his blindness?' It is to be hoped the minister improved the occasion, by saying something to this ignorant creature, with a view to open the eyes of his mind, though we are not informed respecting it.

5. 'I have taken much pains,' says the learned John Selden, 'to know everything that was esteemed worth knowing amongst men; but with all my disquisitions and readings, nothing now remains with me, to comfort me, at the close of life, but this passage of St Paul—"It is a faithful saying, and worthy of all acceptation, that Jesus Christ came into the world to save sinners;" to this I cleave, and herein I find rest' (1 Tim. 1. 15).

6. The excellent and pious James Durham, when on his deathbed, was for sometime under considerable darkness respecting his spiritual state, and said to his friend, William Carstairs; 'For all that I have preached or written, there is but one Scripture I can remember, or dare grip to: tell me if I dare lay the weight of my salvation upon it; "Him that cometh unto Me, I will in no wise cast out." ' Mr Carstairs answered, 'You may depend upon it, though you had a thousand salvations at hazard.'

Q. 32. *What benefits do they that are effectually called partake of in this life?*

A. They that are effectually called do in this life partake of justification, adoption, and sanctification, and the several benefits which in this life do either accompany or flow from them.

1. Thomas Doolittle, at one time having finished prayer, looked round upon the congregation, and observing a young man who had just been put into one of the pews, very uneasy indeed, adopted the following singular expedient to detain him: Turning to one of the members of his church, who sat in the gallery, he asked him this question aloud, 'Brother, do you repent of coming to Christ?' 'No, sir,' he replied, 'I never was happy till I came; I only repent that I did not come to Him sooner.' The minister then turned to the opposite gallery, and addressed himself to an aged member in the same manner: 'Brother, do you repent of coming to Christ?' 'No, sir,' said he, 'I have known the Lord from my youth upwards.' He then looked down upon the young man, whose attention was fully engaged, and fixing his eyes upon him, said 'Young man, are *you* willing to come to Christ?' This unexpected address from the pulpit, drawing the observation of all the

people, so affected him, that he sat down and concealed his face. The person who sat next him encouraged him to rise and answer the question. The minister repeated, 'Young man, are you willing to come to Christ?' With a tremulous voice he replied, 'Yes, sir.' 'But *when*, sir?' added the minister, in a solemn and loud tone. He mildly answered, 'Now, sir.' 'Then stay,' said he, 'and learn the word of God, which you will find in 2 Corinthians 6. 2, "Behold, *now* is the accepted time; behold *now* is the day of salvation." By this sermon he was greatly affected, and came into the vestry after the service, bathed in tears. His earlier reluctance to remain was occasioned, he said, by the strict injunctions of his father, who threatened that if he went to hear the fanatics, he would turn him out of doors. Having now heard the gospel, and being unable to conceal the feelings of his mind, he was afraid to meet his father. The minister sat down and wrote an affectionate letter to him, which had so good an effect, that both father and mother came to hear for themselves. They were both brought to a knowledge of the truth; and, together with their son, were joyfully received into Christian communion.

2. Matthew Henry, a little before his death, said to a friend, 'You have been accustomed to take notice of the sayings of dying men: this is mine, That a life spent in the service of God, and in communion with Him, is the most comfortable and pleasant life that any one can live in this world.'

3. The presence of God renders believers truly happy, even in this world, so that they can say with David, 'Thou hast put gladness in my heart, more than in the time that their corn and their wine increased' (Ps. 4. 7). A godly minister in Scotland, being asked by a friend, during his last illness, whether he thought himself dying, answered, 'Really, friend, I care not, whether I am or not; if I die, I shall be with God, and if I live, God will be with me.'

4. 'The devil,' says Thomas Brooks, 'tempting Bonaventure, suggested to him that he was a reprobate, and persuaded him to drink in the pleasures of this life, because he was excluded from the future joys with God in heaven. Bonaventure's graces being active, he answered, "No, not so, Satan; if I must not enjoy God *after* this life, let me enjoy Him as much as I can *in* this life." '

5. A man who worked in Rowland Hill's garden at Wotton under Edge (Glos.) and was supposed to have forsaken a life of sin, under the influence of religion, was at length discovered to have been the perpetrator of several burglaries, and other daring robberies in the neighbourhood, though, till caught in the act, he had never been suspected. He was tried at Gloucester, condemned, and executed. During Hill's interviews with him there, he confessed the many crimes of which he had been guilty. 'How was it, William,' he inquired, 'that you never robbed me when you have had such abundant opportunity?' 'Sir,' replied he, 'do you recollect the juniper bush on the border against the dining room?—I have many times hid under it at night, intending, which I could easily have done, to get into the house and plunder it; but, sir, I was afraid; something said to me, he is a man of God, it is a house of prayer, if I break in there I shall surely be found out; so I never could pluck up courage to attempt it.' In another conversation, he told him, 'Sir, I well knew that old Mr Rigg (a member of Hill's congregation), was

in the habit of carrying a deal of money in his pocket; times and times have I hid behind the hedge of the lane leading to his house. He has passed within a yard of me, when going home from the prayer meeting, again, and again. I could not stir. I durst not touch so holy a man. I was afraid. I always began trembling as soon as he came near me, and gave up the thought altogether, for I knew he was a holy man.'

Q. 33. *What is justification?*

A. Justification is an act of God's free grace, wherein He pardoneth all our sins, and accepteth us as righteous in His sight, only for the righteousness of Christ imputed to us, and received by faith alone.

1. The first time Andrew Fuller passed through Oxford, he was conducted by a friend to see the principal buildings of the University. He viewed them with little emotion; and on being requested to notice one object of peculiar interest, he said, 'Brother, I think there is one question, which, after all that has been written on it, has not yet been well answered.' His friend desired he would name the subject; he said, 'The question is, What is justification?' It was immediately proposed to return to the fireside and discuss the subject, to which Fuller gladly acceded, saying, 'That inquiry is far more to me than all these fine buildings.'

2. Robert Fleming, in his *Fulfilling of the Scriptures*, relates the case of a man who was a very great sinner, and for his horrible wickedness was put to death in the town of Ayr. This man had been so stupid and brutish, that all who knew him thought him beyond the reach of all ordinary means of grace; but while in prison, the Lord wrought wonderfully on his heart, and in such a measure revealed to him his sinfulness, that after much serious exercise and sore wrestling, a most kindly work of repentance followed, with great assurance of mercy, insomuch that when he came to the place of execution, he could not cease crying out to the people, under the sense of pardon and the comforts of the presence and favour of God—'O, He is a great forgiver! He is a great forgiver!' And he added the following words: 'Now has perfect love cast out fear. I know God has nothing to lay against me, for Jesus Christ has paid all; and those are free whom the Son makes free.'

3. 'I once saw,' says the Rev. William Innes, 'so much joy produced by the good news of deliverance from a great dreaded evil, as may diminish our surprise at the same effect resulting from the first discovery of pardoning mercy. In the town where I resided a reprieve was expected for a man under sentence of death. I requested the chief magistrate to let me know when it arrived, as I should like to be the first messenger of the good news to the criminal. He did so. I went in and communicated to the poor man the glad tidings. He instantly fell on his knees on the cold earthen floor of his dungeon, and clasping his hands, and lifting up his eyes to heaven, while the tears

rushed down his cheeks, he prayed that the seven days of reprieve might be to him as seven thousand years of genuine turning to God. This man afterwards received a pardon.'

4. When the Rev. John Eyre was only four years of age, his mind was powerfully acted upon by an incident, which he ever afterwards regarded as an element in the formation of his religious character. A friend of his family, eminently godly and benevolent, took up young Eyre one day in his arms, and said to him, 'There is such a thing, my dear child, as the pardon of sin, and there is such a thing as knowing it too.' This affectionate appeal, though in no way remarkably adapted to the infant mind, seized on the conscience of Eyre, and left such an abiding impression on his memory and feelings, that in the days of childhood and youth he often reflected on the words of his venerable friend; and at the early age of fourteen began to seek in prayer the blessing of forgiveness, under a deep sense of his sinfulness in the sight of God.

5. When George Burder of London was preaching at Warwick, he was called to attend the execution of three men, one a coiner, and the other two housebreakers. 'One circumstance,' says he, 'affected me very deeply. All the men were on ladders, then the mode of execution, with the ropes about their necks, about to be turned off, when the coiner, endeavouring to fortify his mind in this awful situation, uttered words to this purpose, which I distinctly heard, being at a short distance, "I never killed any body, I never hurt any body—I hope the Lord will have mercy upon me." This poor creature seemed to die nearly in the spirit of the Pharisee, "I thank God, I am not as other men are, or as this publican," for I thought he alluded to the two thieves suffering with him. I was so deeply affected that I could scarcely refrain from crying out to the man, Do not trust in your own righteousness, look to Christ. This has often occurred to me as one of the most glaring instances of a self-righteous spirit that I ever knew.'

6. In the parish where James Hervey preached, when he inclined to Arminian sentiments, there resided a ploughman, who usually attended the ministry of Dr Doddridge, and was well informed in the doctrines of grace. Hervey being advised by his physician, for the benefit of his health, to follow the plough, in order to smell the fresh earth, frequently accompanied this ploughman in his rural employment. Understanding the ploughman was a serious person, he said to him one morning, 'What do you think is the hardest thing in religion?' To which he replied, 'I am a poor illiterate man, and you, sir, are a minister: I beg leave to return the question.' 'Then,' said Hervey, 'I think the hardest thing is to deny sinful self;' and applauded at some length this instance of self-denial. The ploughman replied, 'Mr Hervey, you have forgot the greatest act of the grace of self-denial, which is to deny ourselves of a proud confidence in our own obedience for justification. You know I do not come to hear you, Sir, but I take my family every Sabbath to Northampton to hear Dr Doddridge. We rise early and have prayers and walk there and back. I enjoy it, but to this moment I find it very hard not to be proud of my Sabbath-keeping.' In repeating this story to a friend, Hervey observed, 'I then hated the righteousness of Christ; I looked at the man with astonishment and disdain, and thought him an old

fool. I have since clearly seen who was the fool: not the wise old Christian, but the proud James Hervey.'

7. A citizen of Bristol named Reynolds being importuned by a friend to sit for his portrait, at last consented. 'How would you like to be painted?' 'Sitting among books.' 'Any book in particular?' 'The Bible.' 'Open at any part?' 'At the fifth chapter of the Romans; the first verse to be legible: "Therefore, being justified by Faith, we have peace with God, through our Lord Jesus Christ." '

Q. 34. *What is adoption?*

A. Adoption is an act of God's free grace, whereby we are received into the number, and have a right to all the privileges of the sons of God.

1. A Kaffir boy, twelve years old, was asked whether he did not repent having come to Guadenthall, the missionary settlement of the Moravian Brethren in South Africa. On his answering in the negative, the missionary observed, 'But in the Kaffir country you had meat in plenty, and excellent milk, and here you can get neither.' To this the boy replied, 'It is very true; but I wish to become a child of God; and I hear in this place how I may attain it, whilst in my own country I hear nothing of it. I rejoice, therefore, that I am come thither, and am satisfied with any thing.'

2. On the evening of December 9, 1710, while Thomas Boston was walking up and down in his study, in heaviness, his little daughter Jane, whom he had laid in bed, suddenly raising up herself, called to him, and thus expressed herself: "Mary Magdalene went to the sepulchre. She went back again with them to the sepulchre; but they would not believe that Christ was risen till Mary Magdalene met Him; and He said to her, "Tell my brethren, they are my brethren yet." ' 'This,' says Boston, 'she pronounced with a certain air of sweetness. It took me by the heart. "His brethren yet" (thought I), and may I think that Christ will own me as one of His brethren yet? It was to me as life from the dead.'

3. A popish priest in Ireland, who was making the Scriptures his daily study, and was an advocate for the schools in that country, which most of the priests opposed, met one of the scholars going to school, and asked him what book it was that he carried under his arm. 'It is a will, sir,' said the boy. 'What will?' rejoined the priest. 'The last will and Testament that Jesus Christ left to me, and to all who desire to claim a title in the property herein bequeathed,' replied the boy. 'What did Christ leave you in that will?' 'A kingdom, sir.' 'Where does the kingdom lie?' 'It is the kingdom of heaven, sir.' 'And do you expect to reign as a king there?' 'Yes, sir; as joint heir with Christ.' 'And will not every person get there as well as you?' 'No, sir; none can get there but those that claim their title to that kingdom upon the ground of the will.' The priest asked several other questions, to which the boy gave such satisfactory answers as quite astonished him. 'In-

deed,' said he, 'you are a good little boy; take care of the book wherein God gives you such precious promises; believe what He has said, and you will be happy here and hereafter.'

4. John Flavel, the Puritan preacher of Dartmouth, tells us (quoting the old writer Plutarch) that when Titus Flamininus, a Roman general, proclaimed liberty to the Greeks after his defeat of the King of Macedon who had subjugated them, the people pressed so closely around the herald of the good news that he was in danger of losing his life at their hands. It took them some little time to apprehend the nature of the proclamation, but when they came to understand that deliverance from long bondage was being announced, they shouted for joy, crying, 'A saviour! a saviour!', so that the very heavens rang again with their acclamations, and the very birds fell down astonished. All that night the Grecians, with instruments of music and songs of praise, danced and sang about the general's tent, extolling him as the one who had brought them deliverance from oppression. 'Surely', said the preacher, 'you have more reason to be exalting the Author of your salvation who, at a dearer rate, has freed you from a more dreadful bondage. O ye that have escaped the eternal wrath of God by the humiliation of the Son of God, extol your great Redeemer, and for ever celebrate His praises.'

5. Robert Glover, one of the English martyrs in Mary Tudor's brief reign, a little before his death had lost the sense of God's favour. This occasioned him no little heaviness and grief. But when he came within sight of the stake at which he was to suffer, he experienced such abundant comfort and heavenly joy, that, clapping his hands together, he cried out, 'He is come, He is come,' and died in triumph.

6. A Polish prince was accustomed to carry the picture of his father always in his bosom; and on particular occasions used to take it out and view it, saying, 'Let me do nothing unbecoming so excellent a father.' A suitable reflection for a Christian!

Q. 35. *What is sanctification?*

A. Sanctification is the work of God's free grace, whereby we are renewed in the whole man after the image of God, and are enabled more and more to die unto sin, and live unto righteousness.

1. George Whitefield had formed an acquaintance with Dr Franklin, the American philosopher, who frequently heard him preach, though not, it is to be feared, with the same benefit which so many others had derived from it. 'Not many wise after the flesh are called.' In a letter dated August, 17, 1752, he thus exhorts his philosophical correspondent to still higher pursuits; 'I find you grow more and more famous in the learned world. As you have made a pretty considerable progress in the mysteries of electricity, I would now humbly recommend to your diligent, unprejudiced

pursuit and study, the mystery of the new birth. It is a most important, interesting study, and, when mastered, will richly answer and repay you for all your pains. One, at whose bar we are shortly to appear, hath solemnly declared, that without it we cannot enter into the kingdom of heaven. You will excuse this freedom. I must have something of Christ in all my letters.'

2. Two or three years before John Newton's death, when his sight was become so dim that he was no longer able to read, an aged friend and brother in the ministry called on him to breakfast. Family prayers following, the portion of Scripture for the day was read to him. It was taken from Bogatsky's *Golden Treasury*: 'By the grace of God I am what I am.' It was Newton's custom on these occasions, to make a short familiar exposition on the passage read. After the reading of this text, he paused for some moments, and then uttered the following affecting soliloquy: 'I am not what I *ought* to be. Ah! how imperfect and deficient. I am not what I *wish* to be. I abhor what is evil, and I would cleave to what is good. I am not what I *hope* to be; soon, soon, I shall put off mortality, and with mortality all sin and imperfection. Yet, though I am not what I *ought* to be, nor what I *wish* to be, nor what I *hope* to be, I can truly say, I am not what I *once* was—a slave to sin and Satan; and I can heartily join with the apostle, and acknowledge, "By the grace of God, I am what I am." Let us pray.'

3. A friend of Archbishop Usher repeatedly urged him to write on sanctification, which at length he engaged to do; but a considerable time elapsing, the performance of his promise was importunately claimed. The bishop replied to this purpose: 'I have not written, and yet I cannot charge myself with a breach of promise; for I began to write, but when I came to treat of the new creature which God formeth by His Spirit in every regenerate soul, I found so little of it wrought in myself, that I could speak of it only as parrots, or by rote, without the knowledge of what I might have expressed; and therefore I durst not presume to proceed any further upon it. I must tell you, we do not understand what sanctification and the new creature are. It is no less than for a man to be brought to an entire resignation to the will of God, and to live in the offering up of his soul continually in the flames of love, as a whole burnt-offering to Christ; and oh! how many who profess Christianity, are unacquainted experimentally with this great work upon their souls.'

4. Robert the Bruce, the restorer of the Scottish monarchy, being out one day reconnoitering the enemy, lay at night in a barn, belonging to a loyal cottager. In the morning, still reclining his head on the pillow of straw, he noticed a spider climbing up the beam of the roof. The insect fell to the ground, but immediately made a second attempt to ascend. This attracted the notice of the hero, who, with regret, saw the spider fall a second time from the eminence. It made a third unsuccessful attempt. Not without a mixture of concern and curiosity, the monarch twelve times beheld the insect baffled in its design; but its thirteenth attempt was crowned with success; it gained the summit of the barn. Bruce, starting from his couch, exclaimed, 'This despicable insect has taught me perseverance. I will follow its example. Have I not been twelve times defeated by the enemy's superior force? On one fight more hangs the independence of my country.'

In a few days his anticipations were fully realized, by the glorious result to Scotland of the battle of Bannockburn. Let the Christian learn, both from the insect and the patriot, to persevere in his endeavours to overcome his spiritual enemies, and to gain the crown of glory. Constancy will issue in his reaching these objects of his holy ambition.

Q. 36. *What are the benefits which in this life do accompany or flow from justification, adoption, and sanctification?*

A. The benefits which in this life do accompany or flow from justification, adoption, and sanctification, are assurance of God's love, peace of conscience, joy in the Holy Ghost, increase of grace, and perseverance therein to the end.

1. The celebrated Philip de Mornay, Huguenot statesman, and a most exemplary Christian, being asked a little before his death, if he still retained the same assured hope of future bliss which he had so comfortably enjoyed during his illness, made this memorable reply: 'I am,' said he, 'as confident of it, from the incontestible evidence of the Spirit of God, as ever I was of any mathematical truth from all the demonstrations of Euclid.'

2. Mr Kidd, when minister of Queensferry, a few miles from Edinburgh, was one day very much depressed and discouraged, for want of that comfort which is produced by the faith of the gospel alone. He sent a note to Mr L., minister of Culross, a few miles off, informing him of his distress of mind, and desired a visit as soon as possible. Mr L. told the servant, he was so busy that he could not wait upon his master, but desired him to tell Mr K. to *remember Torwood*! When the servant returned, he said to his master, 'Mr L. could not come, but desires me to tell you, to *remember Torwood*!' This answer immediately struck Mr K., and he cried out, 'Yes, Lord! I will remember *Thee*, from the hill Mizar, and from the Hermonites!' All his trouble and darkness vanished, upon the recollection of a day which he had formerly spent in prayer along with Mr L. in Torwood, where he had enjoyed eminent communion with God.

3. Dr Stonehouse, who attended James Hervey during his last illness, seeing the great difficulty and pain with which he spoke, and finding by his pulse that the pangs of death were then coming on, desired that he would spare himself and refrain from speaking. 'No,' said Hervey, 'Doctor, No: you tell me that I have but a few minutes to live, O let me spend them in adoring our great Redeemer. Though my heart and flesh fail me, yet God is the strength of my heart and my portion for ever.' After saying this, he enlarged in a most striking manner on the words of Paul: 'All things are yours, life and death, things present and things to come, all are yours, and ye are Christ's, and Christ is God's.' 'Here,' said he, 'is the treasure of a Christian, and a noble treasure it is. Death is reckoned in this inventory; how thankful I am for it, as it is the passage through which I get to the Lord and Giver of eternal life, and as it frees me from all the misery

you see me now endure, and which I am willing to endure as long as God sees fit; for I know He will by and by, in His good time, dismiss me from the body. These light afflictions are but for a moment, and then comes an eternal weight of glory. O welcome, welcome death! thou mayest well be reckoned among the treasures of the Christian. To live is Christ but to die is gain.'

4. John Flavel, the Puritan, at one time on a journey, set himself to improve his time by meditation. By degrees his mind grew intent, until at length he had such ravishing tastes of heavenly joy, and such full assurance of his interest in Christ, that he utterly lost the sight and sense of this world and all its concerns so that for a time he did not know where he was. At last, perceiving himself faint from a great loss of blood from his nose, he alighted from his horse and sat down at a spring where he washed and refreshed himself, earnestly desiring, if it were the will of God, that he might leave the world. His spirits reviving, he finished his journey in the same delightful frame of mind. He passed the following night without sleep, the joy of the Lord still overflowing him, so that he all but felt himself to be in a higher world. For many years he called that day one of the 'days of heaven', and professed he understood more of the life of heaven by it than by all the discourses he had heard, or the books he had ever read.

5. When Lord North, prime minister during the war of American Independence, sent to John Fletcher of Madeley (who had written on that unfortunate war, in a manner that had pleased the minister), to know what he wanted, he sent him word, that he wanted but one thing, which it was not in his lordship's power to give him, and that was *more grace*.

6. A person who suspected that a minister of his acquaintance was not truly a Calvinist, went to him and said, 'Sir, I am told that you are against the perseverance of the saints.' 'Not I, indeed,' answered he, 'it is the perseverance of sinners that I oppose.' 'But this is not a satisfactory answer, sir. Do you think that a child of God cannot fall very low, and yet be restored?' He replied, 'I think it will be very dangerous to make the experiment.'

Q. 37. *What benefits do believers receive from Christ at death?*

A. The souls of believers are at their death made perfect in holiness, and do immediately pass into glory; and their bodies, being still united to Christ, do rest in their graves till the resurrection.

1. 'Death,' says one, 'is a subject of deep solemnity, and therefore should always be treated with seriousness. The "assurance of hope" itself will never justify an opposite course. I once knew "an old disciple" who had no patience with Christians that were afraid to die; it was bringing, he said, such a reproach upon religion. For his own part, as he expressed it, he was always looking out for the holidays, and wondering why his Father was so long in sending to take him home. But when the message came, he was filled with

consternation. During the illness which brought him to the grave, he clung to earthly existence, with a tenacity which was perfectly distressing. On the announcement of his decease, a neighbour, who was unprepared to appreciate his religious character, and still less able to understand the lesson which such a circumstance was calculated to impart, remarked concerning him, "Poor old man! he would have given the world to die: and in death, he would have given the world to live." '

2. Joseph Addison, after a long and manly but vain struggle with his distemper, dismissed his physicians, and with them all hopes of life. But with his hopes of life, he dismissed not his concern for the living, but sent for his step-son who was highly accomplished. He came, and, after a decent pause, the youth said, 'Dear sir, you sent for me, I believe: I hope you have some commands; I shall hold them most sacred.' Forcibly grasping the young man's hand, he softly said, 'See in what peace a Christian can die.' He spoke with difficulty, and soon expired.

3. Douglas Cousin, one of the missionaries whom Dr Ebenezer Henderson mentions in his Travels, and whose grave he visited when at Karass, died, as his brethen observed, like a true Christian. Being asked a little before his death, if he wished any thing to be written about him to an old Christian friend in Scotland, whom he greatly loved, he said, after thinking a little, with a peculiar and expressive tone, 'Yes; tell him I died in the faith —full in the Faith.'

4. 'Conversing once,' says a writer, 'with a hardened sinner who was well acquainted with divine truth, I said, "In your present state of mind, have you any hope of going to heaven?" Mark his reply! "In my present state of mind, sir, heaven would be worse to me than hell." Fearful as was this acknowledgment, it was unquestionably true; and should the unconverted reader cherish the persuasion that he is safe for eternity, he knows less of himself, and less of God, and less of heaven, than did that unhappy man.'

5. 'In the article of death,' says the Rev. James Dore, 'the righteous have glorious prerogatives. The truth of this principle is generally admitted. We do not hear men exclaiming, "Let me die the death of the *philosopher!*" in whatever terms they express their admiration of his talents, his experiments, and his discoveries: or, "Let me die the death of the *warrior!*" with whatever ardour they celebrate his martial virtues, and his military achievements; or, "Let me die the death of the *statesman!*" whatever encomium they may be disposed to pass on his political abilities. No, their language is, "Let me die the death of the *righteous,* and my last end be like his." '

6. The Rev. Robert Bruce, the morning before he died, being at breakfast, and having, as he used, eaten an egg, said to his daughter Martha, 'I think I am yet hungry; you may bring me another egg.' But having mused a while, he said, 'Hold, daughter, hold, my Master calls me.' With these words his sight failed him: on which he called for the Bible, and said, 'Turn to the 8th chapter of the Romans, and set my finger on the words—"I am persuaded that neither death, nor life, etc., shall be able to separate me from the love of God, which is in Christ Jesus my Lord." ' When this was done, he said, 'Now, is my finger upon them?' Being told it was, he added,

'Now, God be with you, my dear children: I have breakfasted with you, and shall sup with my Lord Jesus Christ this night.' And then he expired.

7. 'I am just returned,' says Legh Richmond, in a letter to one of his daughters, 'after executing the difficult and affecting task of preaching a funeral sermon for my most excellent and revered mother, at her parish church. I took my subject from Psalms 115. 1, as best suited to her humble, meek, and believing frame of mind. It was indeed a trying effort; but God carried me through surprisingly. I introduced some very interesting papers, which I found amongst her memoranda, in her own handwriting. Her last message to me was—"Tell my son I am going direct to happiness." '

8. A young girl at Portsea, Hampshire, who died at nine years of age, one day in her illness, said to her aunt, with whom she lived, 'When I am dead I should like Mr Griffin to preach a sermon to children, to persuade them to love Jesus Christ, to obey their parents, not to tell lies, but to think about dying and going to heaven. I have been thinking,' said she, 'what text I should like him to preach from—2 Kings 4. 26. You are the Shunammite, Mr Griffin is the prophet, and I am the Shunammite's child. When I am dead, I daresay you will be grieved, though you need not. The prophet will come to see you, and when he says, "How is it with the child?" you may say, "It is well." I am sure it will then be well with me, for I shall be in heaven, singing the praises of God. You ought to think it well too.' Mr Griffin accordingly fulfilled the wish of this pious child.

9. A little girl in Yorkshire, about seven years of age, went, accompanied by a brother younger than herself, to see an aunt who lay dead. On their return home, the little boy expressed his surprise that he had seen his aunt, saying, 'I always thought when people were dead, that they went to heaven; but my aunt is not, for I have seen her.' 'Brother,' replied his sister, 'You do not understand it; it is not the body that goes to heaven: the soul is the thing that goes to heaven; the body remains, and is put into the grave, where it sleeps till God shall raise it up again.'

Q. 38. *What benefits do believers receive from Christ at the resurrection?*

A. At the resurrection, believers being raised up in glory, shall be openly acknowledged and acquitted in the day of judgment, and made perfectly blessed in the full enjoying of God to all eternity.

1. A man in Scotland who had some years before buried his wife and several of his children, one day stood leaning over a low wall, intently gazing on the spot in the churchyard where their bodies lay. A person who observed his thoughtful attitude asked him what occupied his mind. 'I am looking,' he said, 'at the dust that lies there, and wondering at the indissoluble union betwixt it and the Lord Jesus Christ, who is in glory.'

2. A visit to a paper-mill suggested to a seventeenth-century writer in Germany the following thoughts. And so paper, that article so useful in human life, that repository of all arts and sciences, that minister of all Governments, that broker in all trade and commerce, that second memory of the human mind—takes its origin from vile rags! The rag dealer trudges on foot, or drives his cart through towns and villages, and his arrival is the signal for searching every corner and gathering every old and useless shred. These he takes to the mill, and there they are picked, washed, mashed, shaped and sized—in short, formed into a fabric beautiful enough to venture, unabashed, into the presence of monarchs and princes. This reminds me of the resurrection of the body. When deserted by the soul, I know not what better the body is than a worn and rejected rag. Accordingly it is buried in the earth and there gnawed by worms, reduced to dust and ashes. If, however, man's art and device can produce so pure and white a fabric as paper from filthy rags, what should hinder God, by His mighty power, to raise from the dead this vile body of mine, and fashion and refine it like the glorious body of the Lord Jesus Christ.

3. It is related of Dr William Leechman of Glasgow, that upon his death-bed he thus addressed the son of a nobleman who had been under his care: 'You see, my young friend, the situation in which I now am. I have not many days to live, and am happy that you witness the tranquillity of my last moments; but it is not tranquillity alone, it is joy and triumph; nay, it is complete exultation.' His features brightened, and his voice rose in energy as he spoke. 'And whence,' said he, 'does this exultation spring? From that book, too much neglected indeed, but which contains invaluable treasures—treasures of bliss and rejoicing; for it makes us certain that this mortal shall put on immortality.'

4. 'I remember,' says the writer of John Janeway's Life, 'once there was a great talk that one had foretold that doomsday should be on such a day. Although he blamed their daring folly that could pretend to know that which was hid, yet, granting their suspicion to be true, "what then?" said he; "what if the day of judgment were come, as it will most certainly come shortly? If I were sure the day of judgment were to come within an hour, I should be glad with all my heart. If at this very instant, I should hear such thundering, and see such lightning, as Israel did at Mount Sinai, I am persuaded my very heart would leap for joy. But this I am confident of, through infinite mercy, that the very meditation of that day hath even ravished my soul; and the thought of the certainty and nearness of it is more refreshing to me than the comforts of the whole world." '

5. An infidel and profligate youth, who had formerly disregarded all the pious injunctions of his parents, on one occasion went with them to hear a popular minister, who had come to the town where they dwelt. The subject of discourse was, *the heavenly state;* and the minister describing, in glowing language, the nature of the happiness, employment, and company of the spirits of just men made perfect. On his return home, the youth expressed his admiration of the speaker's talents; 'but,' said he, turning to his mother, 'I am surprised, that while pleasure was visible in the faces of all around me, you and my father appeared gloomy and sad, and more than once were in

tears. I am surprised,' continued the youth, 'because I thought, that if any could claim an interest in the subject, you were the happy persons.' 'Ah! my son,' replied the anxious mother, 'I did weep; but it was not because I feared my own personal interest in the subject, or that of your affectionate and godly father. I wept when I thought of you: it was the fear that *you*, the son of my womb, and the son of my vows, would be banished at last from the delights of the celestial paradise, which caused my bursting heart to seek vent in tears.' 'I supposed,' said the father, turning to his wife, 'those were your reflections. The thought of the spiritual condition of our son forcibly impressed my own heart, and made me weep too.' The pointed, yet cautious and tender admonition of the mother, wisely sanctioned by her husband, found its way to the youthful heart of her child, and terminated in his saving conversion to God.

6. A minister, in the early part of the 17th century was preaching before an assembly of his brethren; and in order to direct their attention to the great motive from which they should act, he represented to them something of the great day of judgment. Having spoken of Christ as seated on His throne, he described Him as speaking to His ministers; examining how they had preached, and with what views they had undertaken and discharged the duties of the ministry. 'What did you preach for?' 'I preached, Lord, that I might keep a good living that was left me by my father; which, if I had not entered the ministry, would have been wholly lost to me and my family.' Christ addresses him, 'Stand by, thou hast had thy reward.' The question is put to another, 'And what did you preach for?' 'Lord, I was applauded as a learned man, and I preached to keep up the reputation of an excellent orator, and an ingenious preacher.' The answer of Christ to him also is, 'Stand by, thou hast had thy reward.' The Judge puts the question to a third. 'And what did you preach for?' 'Lord,' saith he, 'I neither aimed at the great things of this world, though I was thankful for the conveniences of life which Thou gavest me; nor did I preach that I might gain the character of a wit, or of a man of parts, or of a fine scholar; but I preached in compassion to souls, and to please and honour Thee; my design, Lord, in preaching, was that I might win souls to Thy blessed Majesty.' The Judge was now described as calling out, 'Room, men; room, angels! let this man come and sit with me on my throne; he has owned and honoured me on earth, and I will own and honour him through all the ages of eternity.' The ministers went home much affected; resolving, that through the help of God, they would attend more diligently to the motives and work of the ministry than they had before done.

Q. 39. *What is the duty which God requireth of man?*

A. The duty which God requireth of man, is obedience to His revealed will.

1. A person who had been at public worship, having returned home,

E

perhaps somewhat sooner than usual, was asked by another of the family, who had not been there, 'Is all done?' 'No,' replied he, 'all is *said*, but all is *not done*.'

2. Antonio Guevara used to say, 'That heaven would be filled with such as *had done good works*, and hell with such as *intended* to do them.' A very suitable hint to those who put off their convictions to what they think will be a more convenient season.

3. 'I remember,' says Dr Cotton Mather, 'what Calvin said when the order of his banishment from ungrateful Geneva was brought to him: "Most assuredly, if I had merely served man, this would have been a poor recompense; but it is my happiness that I have served Him who never fails to reward His servants to the full extent of His promises." '

4. 'When you see a dog following two men,' says Ralph Erskine, in one of his sermons, 'you know not to which of them he belongs while they walk together; but let them come to a parting road, and one go one way, and the other another way, then you will know which is the dog's master. So at times, religion and the world go hand in hand. While a man may have the world and a religious profession too, we cannot tell which is the man's master, God or the world; but stay till the man come to a parting road: God calls him this way, and the world calls him that way. Well, if God be his master, he follows religion, and lets the world go; but if the world be his master, then he follows the world and the lust thereof, and lets God, and conscience, and religion go.'

5. When a gentleman once presented a Bible to a prisoner under sentence of death, he exclaimed, 'Oh, sir, if I had had this book, and studied it, I should never have committed the crime of which I am convicted.' So it is said of a native Irishman, when he read for the first time in his life a New Testament which a gentleman had put into his hands, he said, 'If I believe this, it is impossible for me to remain a rebel.'

6. In 1817, about a month before the death of Princess Charlotte, grand-daughter of George III, as she was walking with her husband, Prince Leopold (later King of the Belgians), in the pleasure-grounds at Claremont (Surrey), she addressed the gardener; and among many other questions, asked him if he could read. 'Yes, Madam,' was the reply (for she never suffered her domestics to address her with any higher title); 'Have you a Bible?' 'No, Madam.' 'Then,' said the Princess, 'I'll give you one.' She immediately went to the house, and returned with a Bible, which she presented to the poor fellow, having written his name in it, with these words, 'From his Friend, Charlotte.'

Q. 40. *What did God at first reveal to man for the rule of his obedience?*

A. The rule which God at first revealed to man for his obedience, was the moral law.

1. A follower of Pythagoras had bought a pair of shoes from a cobbler, for which he promised to pay him on a future day. On that day he took the money; but, finding the cobbler had died in the meanwhile, returned, secretly rejoicing that he could retain the money, and get a pair of shoes for nothing. His conscience, however, says Seneca, would allow him no rest, till, taking up the money, he went back to the cobbler's shop, and casting in the money, said, 'Go thy way, for though he is dead to all the world besides, yet he is alive to me.'

2. A clergyman once travelling in a stage coach, was asked by one of the passengers, if he thought that pious heathens would go to heaven. 'Sir,' answered the clergyman, 'I am not appointed *judge* of the world, and consequently cannot tell; but if ever you get to heaven, you shall either find them there, or a good reason why they are not.' A reply well fitted to answer an impertinent question, dictated by idle curiosity.

3. A certain preacher in the west of England, remarkable for his opposition to the moral law as a rule of life to believers, was preaching on a week-day evening at a village, in a cottage full of poor people; when, declaiming in his usual way against the law, and seemingly at a loss for expressions sufficient to degrade it, he said, 'The law is dead; it is fallen; it is done with.' Having just then occasion to use his handkerchief, he spread it out, and holding a corner in each hand, said, 'The law, my friends, has fallen down before the believer like this handkerchief'; then letting it go from his hands, it unfortunately fell on the candles, and extinguished them, leaving the preacher and all his hearers in darkness; a very just, though accidental, representation of that mental and practical darkness which such preaching is likely to produce.

Q. 41. *Wherein is the moral law summarily comprehended?*

A. The moral law is summarily comprehended in the ten commandments.

1. Archbishop Usher, being once on a visit to Scotland, heard a great deal of the piety and devotion of Samuel Rutherford. He wished much to witness what had been told him, but was at a loss how to accomplish his design. At length it came into his mind to dress himself like a pauper; and on a Saturday evening, when turning dark, he called at Rutherford's house, and asked if he could get quarters for a night. Rutherford consented to give the poor man a bed for a night, and desired him to sit down in the kitchen, which he cheerfully did. Mrs Rutherford, according to custom on Saturday evening, that her servants might be prepared for the Sabbath, called them together and examined them. In the course of the examination, she asked the stranger how many commandments there were. To which he answered, Eleven. On receiving this answer, she replied, 'What a shame is it for you! a man with grey hairs, in a Christian country, not to know how many commandments there are! There is not a child of six years old

in the parish, but could answer this question properly.' She troubled the poor man no more, thinking him so very ignorant, but lamented his condition to her servants; and after giving him some supper, desired a servant to show him up stairs to a bed in a garret. Rutherford, on discovering who he was next morning, requested him to preach for him that day, which the bishop consented to do, on condition that he would not discover him to any other. Rutherford furnished the bishop with a suit of his own clothes, and early in the morning he went into the fields: the other followed him, and brought him in as a strange minister passing by, who had promised to preach for him. Mrs Rutherford found that the poor man had gone away before any of the family were out of bed. After domestic worship and breakfast, the family went to the church, and the bishop had for his text, John 13. 34, 'A new commandment I give unto you, that ye love one another.' In the course of his sermon, he observed that this might be reckoned the eleventh commandment: upon which Mrs Rutherford said to herself, 'That is the answer the poor man gave me last night;' and looking up to the pulpit, said, 'It cannot be possible that this is he!' After public worship, the strange minister and Samuel Rutherford spent the evening in mutual satisfaction; and early on Monday morning, the former went away in the dress in which he came, and was not discovered.

2. Ralph Erskine composed the following ode on the death of his first wife, Margaret Dewar, who died November 22, 1730, aged thirty-two, after having borne ten children:

> The law brought forth her precepts ten,
>   And then dissolved in grace:
> This vine as many boughs, and then
>   In glory took her place.
> Her dying breath triumphantly
>   Did that sweet anthem sing,
> Thanks be to God for victory:
>   O Death! where is thy sting?

Q. 42. *What is the sum of the ten commandments?*

A. The sum of the ten commandments is, To love the Lord our God with all our heart, with all our soul, with all our strength, and with all our mind; and our neighbour as ourselves.

1. 'Father,' said a little boy, 'what is the meaning of the words *cherubim* and *seraphim*, which we find in the Holy Scriptures?' 'Cherubim,' replied his father, 'is a Hebrew word, signifying knowledge; Seraphim is another word of the same language, and signifies flame. Whence it is supposed, that the cherubim are angels who excel in knowledge; and that the seraphim are angels likewise who excel in loving God.' 'I hope, then,' said the

little boy, 'when I die I shall be a seraph; for I would rather love God than know all things.'

2. 'I see God will have all my heart, and He shall have it,' was a fine saying of a lady, when news was brought of two of her children, whom she tenderly loved, being drowned.

3. A martyr was asked, whether he did not love his wife and children, who stood weeping by him. 'Love them? Yes,' said he: 'if all the world were gold, and at my disposal, I would give it for the satisfaction of living with them, though it were in prison. Yet, in comparison of Christ, I love them not.'

4. A boy, called Abraham, not quite four years old, was not only remarkably patient and resigned during his last illness, but his conversation proved an abiding blessing to his father, who happened then to be in an unhappy state of mind. On the day before he died he asked him, 'Father, do you love me?' The father replied, 'Yes, I do.' Upon repeating his question, he received the same answer. 'But then,' added he, 'do you love our Saviour?' 'No,' replied the father, 'I am just now very poor and miserable.' 'Ah!' said the child, 'if you do not love our Saviour, you cannot love me as you ought.'

5. An orphan boy, of peculiar vivacity and uncommon talents, and who had been a favourite comic performer in worldly sports, was sent by his relations to New Hernhuth, a settlement of the Moravian missionaries. His agreeable and engaging manners gained him the affection of one of the wealthiest Greenlanders, in whose family he was placed, who had no son, and whose presumptive heir he was. At the first catechetical meeting at which he was present, being asked whether he would wish to be acquainted with our Saviour, and be converted, 'O yes!' replied he gaily, 'I shall soon be converted;' on which another, who had been lately baptized, gravely told him he little knew what conversion meant—that it was to yield the heart wholly to our Saviour, and to make a surrender of every evil inclination. This he found a hard saying, and would rather have thrown up his prospects among the brethren, and returned to his amusements; till, after considerable mental conflict, he at last ceased contending with his Maker, and yielded a willing and cheerful obedience.

6. During the retreat of Alfred the Great, at Athelney in Somersetshire, after the defeat of his forces by the Danes, a beggar came to his camp there, and requested alms. The queen informed him that they had only one small loaf remaining, which was insufficient for themselves and their friends, who were gone in quest of food, though with little hope of success. The king replied, 'Give the poor Christian one half of the loaf. He who could feed five thousand men with five loaves and two small fishes, can certainly make that half of the loaf suffice for more than our necessities.' Accordingly, the poor man was relieved, and this noble act of charity was soon recompensed by a providential store of fresh provisions, with which his people returned.

7. Louis IX, on his return to France with his queen and his children, was very near being shipwrecked, some of the planks of the vessel having started; and he was requested to go into another ship, which was in com-

pany with that which carried them. He refused to quit his own ship, and exclaimed, 'Those that are with me, most assuredly, are as fond of their lives as I can possibly be of mine. If I quit the ship, they will likewise quit it; and the vessel not being large enough to receive them, they will all perish. I had much rather entrust my life, and those of my wife and children, in the hands of God, than be the occasion of making so many of my brave subjects perish.'

Q. 43. *What is the preface to the ten commandments?*

A. The preface to the ten commandments is in these words, I am the Lord thy God, which have brought thee out of the land of Egypt, out of the house of bondage.

1. A friend calling on Ebenezer Erskine during his last illness, said to him, 'Sir, you have given us much good advice; pray, what are you now doing with your own soul?' 'I am doing with it,' said he, 'what I did forty years ago: I am resting on that word, *I am the Lord thy God;* and on this I mean to die.' To another he said, 'The covenant is my charter, and if it had not been for that blessed word, *I am the Lord thy God*, my hope and strength had perished from the Lord.' The night on which he died, his eldest daughter was reading in the room where he was, to whom he said, 'What book is that you are reading, my dear?' 'It is one of your sermons.' 'What one is it?' 'It is the sermon on that text, *I am the Lord thy God.*' 'O woman,' said he, 'that is the best sermon I ever preached.' And it was, most probably, the best to his soul. A little afterwards, with his finger and thumb, he shut his own eyes, and laying his hand below his cheek, breathed out his soul into the hands of his living Redeemer. Happy the man that is in such a state! Happy the man whose God is the Lord!

2. A gentleman one day took an acquaintance of his upon the leads of his house to show him the extent of his possessions; waving his hand about, 'There,' says he, 'that is my estate.' Then pointing to a great distance on one side, 'Do you see that farm?' 'Yes.' 'Well, that is mine.' Pointing again on the other side, 'Do you see that house?' 'Yes.' 'That also belongs to me.' 'Then,' said his friend, 'do you see that little village out yonder?' 'Yes.' 'Well, there lives a poor woman in that village, who can say more than all this.' 'Aye! what can she say?' 'Why, she can say, "Christ is mine!"' He looked confounded, and said no more.

Q. 44. *What doth the preface to the ten commandments teach us?*

A. The preface to the ten commandments teacheth us, That because God is the Lord, and our God, and Redeemer, therefore we are bound to keep all His commandments.

1. Cardinal Wolsey, a great minister of state under King Henry VIII, having fallen under the displeasure of that monarch, made the following sad reflection a little before his death: 'Had I but served my God as diligently as I have served my king, he would not have forsaken me now in my grey hairs. But this is the just reward that I must receive for my indulgent pains and study, not regarding my service to God, but only to my prince.'

2. When Polycarp, the early Christian martyr, was exhorted to swear, and blaspheme Christ, in order to save his life, he replied, 'Fourscore years have I served Christ, and have ever found Him a good master, how then can I blaspheme my Lord and Saviour?' When he came to the stake at which he was to be burnt, he desired to stand untied, saying, 'Let me alone; for He that gave me strength to come to the fire, will give me patience to undergo the fire without your tying.'

3. Henry Venn, an evangelical and faithful minister of Christ, was one day addressed by a neighbouring clergyman, in nearly the following words: 'Mr. Venn, I don't know how it is, but I should really think your doctrines of *grace* and *faith* were calculated to make all your hearers live in *sin*, and yet I must own that there is an astonishing reformation wrought in your parish; whereas I don't believe I ever made one soul the better, though I have been telling them their *duty* for many years.' Venn smiled at the clergyman's honest confession, and frankly told him, 'he would do well to burn all his old sermons, and try what preaching Christ would do.'

4. Isaac James, speaking of the nature of true religion, says, 'Until the mind is rightly affected towards God, there is no religion, because *He* is the direct and primary object of it. It is something perfectly independent, as to essence, of all the social relations. If a man was wrecked, like Alexander Selkirk, on an uninhabited island, where there would be no room, of course, for loyalty, honesty, kindness, mercy, justice, truth, or any of the *relative* virtues, the claims of piety would still follow him to this dreary and desolate abode; and even there, when he should never hear "the sweet music of speech," nor look on "the human face divine," he would still be under the obligations of piety; even there one voice would be heard breaking the silence around him, with the solemn injunction of Scripture, "Thou shalt love the Lord thy God." God, as He is revealed in His word, is the direct and primary object of all true piety; and the most exemplary discharge of the social duties can be no substitute for that reverence, and love, and gratitude, and obedience, which we owe to Him.'

Q. 45. *Which is the first commandment?*

A. The first commandment is, Thou shalt have no other gods before me.

Q. 46. *What is required in the first commandment?*

A. The first commandment requireth us to know and acknowledge God to be the only true God, and our God; and to worship and glorify Him accordingly.

1. A poor Arabian of the desert was one day asked how he came to be assured that there was a God? 'In the same way,' he replied, 'that I am able to tell by the print impressed on the sand, whether it was a man or a beast that passed that way.'

2. James Hervey, for some years before his death, visited very few of the principal persons in his neighbourhood. Being once asked why he so seldom went to see the neighbouring gentleman, who yet showed him all possible esteem and respect, he answered, 'I can hardly name a polite family where the conversation ever turns upon the things of God. I hear much frothy and worldly chitchat, but not a word of Christ; and I am determined not to visit those companies where there is not room for my Master as well as myself.'

3. Anthony Collins, the deist, met one day with a plain countryman going to church. He inquired where he was going. 'To church, sir.' 'What to do there?' 'To worship God.' 'Pray, whether is your God a great or a little God?' 'He is both, sir.' 'How can He be both?' 'He is so great, sir, that the heaven of heavens cannot contain Him: and so little that He can dwell in my heart.' Collins declared, that the simple answer by the countryman had more effect upon his mind, than all the volumes which the learned doctors had written against him.

4. An atheist being asked by a professor of Christianity, 'how he could quiet his conscience in so desperate a state' replied, 'As much as I am astonished at yourself, who, believing the Christian religion to be true, can quiet your conscience in living so much like the world. Did I believe what you profess, I should think no care, no diligence, no zeal enough.' Alas! that there should still be so much cause given by Christians, for the astonishment of atheists!

5. On the evening of the day on which his father died, the Rev. Dr Balmer (later, Professor of Theology to the United Secession Church), then about ten years of age, brought the books for family worship, as he had been used to do when his father was alive, and quietly placed them before his mother. This occasioned an irrepressible burst of sorrow. Robert, on seeing his mother so overcome, reminded her that God, who had taken away his father, would be a father to them, and had promised to hear their prayers: 'And,' said he, 'we must not go to bed to night without worshipping Him.' His mother then took the books, and conducted the worship of the family, and from that time continued to do so, till Robert, a few years afterwards, took her place in this exercise.

Q. 47. *What is forbidden in the first commandment?*

A. The first commandment forbiddeth the denying, or not worshipping and glorifying the true God, as God, and our

God; and the giving of that worship and glory to any other which is due to Him alone.

1. Lord Rochester was one day at an atheistical meeting in the house of a person of quality. He undertook to manage the discussion, and was the principal disputant against God and religion, and for his performance received the applause of the whole company: 'Upon which,' says he, 'my mind was terribly struck, and I immediately replied thus to myself; Good God! that a man that walks upright, that sees the wonderful works of God, and has the use of his senses and reason, should use them to the defying of his Creator!'

2. The famous German mathematician, Athanasius Kircher, having an acquaintance who denied the existence of the Supreme Being, took the following method to convince him of his error upon his own principles. Expecting him upon a visit, he procured a very handsome globe of the starry heavens, which being placed in a corner of the room in which it could not escape his friend's observation, the latter seized the first occasion to ask from whence it came, and to whom it belonged. 'Not to me,' said Kircher, 'nor was it *ever made by any person*, but came here by *mere chance*.' 'That,' replied his sceptical friend, 'is absolutely impossible; you surely jest.' Kircher, however, seriously persisting in his assertion, took occasion to reason with his friend upon his own atheistical principles. 'You will not,' said he, 'believe that this small body originated in *mere chance; and yet you will contend that those heavenly bodies, of which it is only a faint and diminutive resemblance, came into existence without order and design.' Pursuing this chain of reasoning, his friend was at first confounded, in the next place convinced, and ultimately joined in a cordial acknowledgment of the absurdity of denying the existence of a God.

3. 'It is much to be feared,' says William Innes, 'that the language which Dr Johnson applied to Foote, the comedian, is too applicable to many. When Boswell asked him if Foote was not an infidel, he replied, "Foote was an infidel, sir, as a dog is an infidel; he never thought on the subject." '

4. Nichols, Potter, and Wilson of Westminster, preaching one after another before his Majesty George III, bedaubed the king, who, as Lord Mansfield told Bishop Warburton, expressed his offence publicly, by saying that he came to the chapel to hear the praises of God, and not his own.

5. A gentleman in England who had a chapel attached to his house, was visited by a person from London, to whom he showed the chapel. 'What a glorious kitchen this would make!' said the visitor. 'When I make a god of my belly,' replied the gentleman, 'I will make a kitchen of my chapel.'

6. One morning a little girl came, as usual, into her parent's room, to kneel down at her mother's knee and repeat her prayers. Before she could do so, her father held up the picture of a Hindoo god, and said, 'See, Mary, what a *god* the poor heathen pray to!' It was very ugly, and looked very ill-natured. She gave it but one look, which said, 'What an ugly god!' and immediately dropped on her knees at her mother's side, and began saying in a sweet voice, 'Our Father which art in heaven,' etc. Her parents wept for joy, because she evidently thought God *lovely*.

7. There lived at one time in Perugia, Italy, a man of the loosest morals and the worst conceivable disposition. He had given up all religion, he loathed God, and had arrived at such a desperate state of mind that he had conceived an affection for the devil and endeavoured to worship the evil one, desiring to be considered a devil himself. On one occasion when a Protestant missionary had been in Perugia preaching, a priest happened to say in this man's hearing that the city of Perugia was being defiled by heretics, and, said the priest, Protestants are those who have renounced Christ and who worship the devil. Such a lie answered far other ends than its author meant. 'Oh, then, I will go and meet with these Protestant heretics, for I am much of their mind,' said the man on hearing this, and away he went to the Protestant meeting in the hope of finding an assembly who propagated lawlessness and worshipped the devil. He there heard the gospel and was saved.

Q. 48. *What are we specially taught by the words 'before me' in the first commandment?*

A. These words 'before me' in the first commandment, teach us, That God, who seeth all things, taketh notice of, and is much displeased with, the sin of having any other god.

1. Thomas Scott, the expositor of the Bible, speaking of his early years, says, 'A hymn of Dr Watts, entitled, "The all-seeing God," at this time fell in my way. I was much affected by it, and having committed it to memory, was frequently repeating it, and was thus continually led to reflect on my guilt and danger.' 'Parents,' he adds, 'may from this inconsiderable circumstance be reminded, that it is of great importance to store their children's memories with useful matter, instead of suffering them to be furnished with such corrupting trash as is commonly taught them. They know not what use God may make of these early rudiments of instruction in future life.'

2. A profane coachman, pointing to one of the horses he was driving, said to a godly traveller, 'That horse, sir, knows when I swear at him.' 'Yes,' replied the traveller, 'and so does *One above.*' The coachman seemed to feel the reproof, and immediately became silent.

3. God's best servants are distinguished by their cleaving closely to His Word. Among them was John Rogers of Dedham in Essex in the early part of the seventeenth century. He was at first so addicted to vice that, when he was sent to study at Cambridge, he sold his books and spent the money. Notwithstanding his base ingratitude, his kinsman procured him a fresh stock of books and sent him again to Cambridge. Still continuing a profligate, he repeated the same evil behaviour. The same kind benefactor furnished him with books for a third time and, the grace of God this time changing his heart, he became an ornament to his college and eminent for true godliness of life. In time he became famous as a preacher of the gospel,

and was even called 'the Enoch of his day.' A bishop said of him that England hardly ever brought forth a man who walked more closely with God. He was remarkable for gravity and seriousness in company. On one occassion a gentleman of rank said to him, 'Mr Rogers, I like you and your company well enough, but you are too precise.' 'Oh, sir,' replied John Rogers, 'I serve a precise God!'

4. A youth, who projected a crime of great magnitude, attracted one evening by the light, strolled into a little chapel at the moment the minister was reading the text from Numbers 32. 23, 'Be sure your sin will find you out.' Conscience became alarmed, the violated law of God, with its consequences, was portrayed, and bore a terrifying aspect to the listening sinner, who believed detection must ensue, if the intended sin were committed. The impression remained, and a holy and consistent life resulted.

5. A minister having an only child, his affections were too much set upon it. The Lord in His providence took the child from him by death. The child's portrait was in the minister's possession, which he often took from its case and admired, whilst the object represented was mouldering in the dust. A godly old woman in the minister's congregation, came to him, a short while after the death of his little one, and said, 'Sir, there is something wrong either with you or me, for I have not been enjoying the same benefit from your sermons as I used to get.' He said to her, 'Go home and pray for me.' She did so, and returned after a time, stating that things continued as they had been with her; and always as she prayed for him the passage was brought home to her: He is 'joined to his idols; let him alone;' upon which he went and took out his idol, and burnt it before her.

6. A lady who once heard William Romaine preach, expressed herself mightily pleased with his discourse, and told him afterwards that she thought that she could comply with his doctrine, and give up every hindrance to godliness but one. 'And what is that, madam?' 'Cards, sir,' 'You think you could not be happy without them.' 'No, sir; I know I could not.' 'Then, madam, they are your god, and they must save you.' This pointed and just reply is said to have issued in her conversion.

Q. 49. Which is the second commandment?

A. The second commandment is, Thou shalt not make unto thee any graven image, or any likeness of any thing that is in the heaven above, or that is in the earth beneath, or that is in the water under the earth. Thou shalt not bow down thyself to them, nor serve them: for I the Lord thy God am a jealous God, visiting the iniquity of the fathers upon the children, unto the third and fourth generation of them that hate Me; and showing mercy unto thousands of them that love Me, and keep my commandments.

Q. 50. *What is required in the second commandment?*

A. The second commandment requireth the receiving, observing, and keeping pure and entire, all such religious worship and ordinances as God hath appointed in His Word.

1. In the beginning of the reign of Edward VI of England, Charles V, Emperor of Germany, having requested that leave might be given to the Lady Mary, afterwards Queen Mary, to have mass said in her house, the council sent the Bishops Cranmer and Ridley to the king to entreat him, for certain state reasons, to grant it. The king having heard all that they could say on the matter, gave them such grave and sound answers, supported by Scripture, against any such permission, that the bishops could not reply. However, they continued to press him not to disoblige the Emperor, as such a step might have very bad consequences. The king bade them be satisfied, and told them, 'He was resolved rather to lose his life, and all that he had, than agree to that which he knew with certainty to be against the truth.' The bishops still continuing to urge him, the king at length burst into tears, witnessing his tenderness for the truth, and his zeal for the defence of it, by much weeping, which the bishops no sooner saw, than they wept as fast as he, took their leave, and withdrew. On their return, meeting with Sir John Cheke, the king's tutor, Archbishop Cranmer took him by the hand, and said, 'Ah! Sir John, you may be glad all the days of your life, that you have such a scholar; for he hath more divinity in his little finger, than we have in our whole bodies.'

2. When one of the kings of France solicited M. Bougier, who was a Protestant, to conform to the Roman Catholic religion, promising him in return a commission or a high civil appointment, 'Sire,' replied he, 'if I could be persuaded to betray my God for a marshall's staff, I might be induced to betray my king for a bribe of much less value.'

3. When Nathaniel Heywood, a nonconformist minister of Ormskirk, Lancashire, was quitting his living, in 1662, a poor man came to him, and said, 'Ah! Mr Heywood, we would gladly have you preach still in the church.' 'Yes,' said he, 'and I would as gladly preach as you can desire it, if I could do it with a safe conscience.' 'Oh! sir,' replied the other, 'many a man nowadays makes a great gash in his conscience; cannot you make a little nick in yours?'

4. Bishop John Hooper was condemned to be burnt at Gloucester in Mary Tudor's reign. A gentleman, with a view of inducing him to recant, said to him, 'Life is sweet, and death is bitter.' Hooper replied, 'The death to come is more bitter, and the life to come more sweet. I am come hither to end this life, and suffer death, because I will not gainsay the truth I have here formerly taught you.' When brought to the stake, a box, with a pardon from the queen in it, was set before him. The determined martyr cried out, 'If you love my soul, away with it; if you love my soul, away with it.'

5. Mr Aird, originally a mason, became an eminent minister in the reign of James VI of Scotland. The king, knowing he was in straits, sent

him a purse of gold, in expectation of procuring his vote in one of those packed assemblies in which he endeavoured to bring in bishops. This good man, though he had at that time neither bread, meal, nor money in his house, had the virtue to refuse it as the case stood. Next morning, while he and his family were at prayer, some person in his parish, who knew his straits, sent him several sacks of meal, and set them down at his door and went away, leaving him to admire that Providence and grace which enabled him to preserve the integrity of his conscience, though at the risk of the displeasure of the king.

6. James Hervey, observing an unevangelical sense given by a celebrated expositor, remarks, 'I am sorry to see this and the preceding interpretation in the works of an expositor, whose learning I admire, whose piety I reverence, and whose memory I honour; yet I must say on this occasion, with one of the ancient philosophers, "Plato is my friend, Socrates is my friend, but, above all, *truth* is my friend." '

Q. 51. *What is forbidden in the second commandment?*

A. The second commandment forbiddeth the worshipping of God by images, or any other way not appointed in His Word.

1. The gospel of Christ having spread into Persia, the priests who carried out the sun worship of that land, persuaded the King Sapor to decree the death of all Christians throughout his dominions. Many persons eminent in church and state alike fell martyrs. Usthazares, tutor to the Persian princes, was a Christian. One day the king found him in deep distress. He answered: 'O King, this grieves me, that I am this day alive, who should rather have died long since, and I grieve that I see the sun which, against my heart and mind, for your pleasure and at your decree dissemblingly I appear to worship.' The king accordingly appointed his death. One request he made to the king, that for all the faithful service he had rendered to his father and to him, he would now cause to be proclaimed openly that Usthazares was beheaded, not for any treachery or crime committed against the king or his realm, but only because he was a Christian and would not, at the king's command, deny his God. This request was granted, and many were established in Christianity at his death, as many had been staggered by his apostasy.

2. One day in the spring of 1823, a little girl, about five years old, accompanied her mother to pay a visit to a lady. When alighting from the carriage in the court-yard, she saw a statue of King William III, and immediately addressed her mother in these words: 'Mother, is that a graven image there? If it is, I will not fall down and worship it, I will only worship God Almighty.' This prompt and Christian-like determination of the little girl not only pleased but astonished all present.

3. An Irish boy, when the master of the school was one day teaching his scholars how we are forbidden to worship any image, interrupted him by

saying, 'Please, Sir, there is one image we ought to worship.' 'Indeed!' said the master, 'pray what is that?' The boy replied, 'Why, sir, we are told to worship Christ who is "the image of the invisible God" ' (Col. 1. 15).

4. A missionary in India named Thomas was one day travelling alone through the country when he saw many people entering a temple of an idol. He too entered and, standing in front of the idol, he held up his hand and asked for silence. Putting his fingers over his eyes, he said to them, 'It has eyes but it cannot see; it has ears but it cannot hear, a nose but it cannot smell, hands but it cannot handle, a mouth but it cannot speak; neither is there any breath in it.' The people were taken by surprise. An old Brahmin was so convinced of his folly that he cried out, 'It has feet but cannot run away.' The people raised a shout, but, being ashamed of their stupidity, left the temple and went to their homes.

5. A Protestant who rented a small farm under Alexander, second Duke of Gordon, having fallen behind in his payments, a vigilant steward, in the duke's absence, seized the farmer's stock, and advertised it to be sold by auction on a fixed day. The duke happily returned home in the interval, and the tenant went to him to supplicate for indulgence. 'What is the matter, Donald?' said the duke, as he saw him enter with sad downcast looks. Donald told him his sorrowful tale in a concise natural manner; it touched the duke's heart, and produced a formal acquittance of the debt. Donald, as he cheerfully withdrew, was staring at the pictures and images which he saw in the ducal hall, and expressed to the duke, in a homely way, a wish to know what they were. 'These,' said the duke, who was a Roman Catholic, 'are the saints who intercede with God for me.' 'My lord duke,' said Donald, 'would it not be better to apply yourself directly to God? I went to muckle Sawney Gordon, and to little Sawney Gordon; but if I had not come to your good grace's self, I could not have got my discharge, and both I and my bairns had been turned out from house and home.'

6. Whilst Sir Henry Wotton was in Italy, as ambassador of King James I at the court of Venice, he went, at the request of a Roman Catholic priest, to hear the music at their vespers, or evening service. The priest, seeing Sir Henry stand in an obscure corner of the church, sent to him by a boy of the choir this question, written on a small piece of paper, 'Where was your religion to be found before Luther?' To which question Sir Henry presently underwrote, 'My religion was to be found *then*, where yours is not to be found *now*—in the written word of God.'

7. The Vicar of Bray, in Berkshire, was a papist under Henry VIII, a Protestant under Edward VI, a papist again under Queen Mary, and a Protestant in the reign of Queen Elizabeth. He was reproached, as bringing scandal upon his office. 'I cannot help that,' said the vicar; 'if I changed my religion, I am sure I keep true to my principle, which is, to live and die vicar of Bray.'

8. 'One day,' says a person, 'as I was crossing a meadow, I met with an old man, a Roman Catholic, and entering into conversation with him on his religion, I said to him, "Why do your priests say their prayers in Latin?" The poor man replied with considerable warmth, "Why, to be sure, the devil don't understand the Latin tongue." Well, I thought, here is a mystery

explained in a few words. Here is an importance attached to the Latin tongue that I never before knew. Here the devil is beat outright. Who would not study the Latin tongue?'

Q. 52. *What are the reasons annexed to the second commandment?*

A. The reasons annexed to the second commandment are, God's sovereignty over us, His propriety in us, and the zeal He hath to His own worship.

1. When certain persons attempted to persuade Stephen, king of Poland, to constrain some of his subjects, who were of a different religion, to embrace his, he said to them, 'I am king of men, and not of consciences. Dominion over consciences belongs exclusively to God.'

2. When Dr Rowland Taylor was brought before Gardiner, Bishop of Winchester, the bishop asked him how he durst look him in the face, and if he knew who he (Gardiner) was. 'Yes,' replied the doctor, 'I know who you are, Dr Stephen Gardiner, Bishop of Winchester, and Lord Chancellor, and yet but a mortal man, I trow. But if I should be afraid of your lordly looks, why fear you not God, the Lord of us all? How dare you look any Christian man in the face, since you have forsaken the truth, denied Christ, and done contrary to your oath and writing? With what face will you appear before Christ's judgment seat, and answer to your oath against popery in King Henry VIII's time, and in the reign of King Edward VI, when you both spoke and wrote against it?'

3. Two men of learning were conversing together about the method they should take, in reference to a certain regulation imposed upon them by the higher powers, and against which they had conscientious scruples. One of them thoughtlessly and impiously swore, 'By my faith,' said he, 'I must live.' The other calmly and pleasantly replied, 'I hope to live by my faith too, though I dare not swear by it.' The result was, that the man who resolved by grace to venture his temporal interests for conscience' sake, lived in prosperity to see the other begging, and to contribute to his relief.

4. A Spanish boy who was a Roman Catholic, having a silver crucifix hanging round his neck, was asked by a person to sell it for half a dollar, at which he shook his head. He was then offered a dollar, to which he answered in broken accents, 'No, not for *tousand* of *tousands*.' Is not this a keen reproof to children in Protestant countries, who live in the awful neglect of God's 'unspeakable gift?'

5. On one occasion, when the assembly of Divines was convened at Westminster, a long-studied discourse was made in favour of Erastianism, to which none present seemed readily to give any reply. George Gillespie, the Scottish Commissioner, being urged by his brethren, repeated the substance of the whole discourse, and refuted it, to the admiration of all persons who were present. What struck them most was that, though it was common for the members to take notes of what was spoken in the Assembly

as helpful to their memory, and Mr Gillespie appeared to be so employed
during the delivery of that speech to which he afterwards made a reply,
yet the persons who sat next him declared, that upon looking into his note-
book, they found nothing of that speech written, but in different places,
'Lord, send light—Lord, give assistance—Lord, defend Thine own cause.'

Q. 53. *Which is the third commandment?*

A. The third commandment is, Thou shalt not take the
name of the Lord thy God in vain, for the Lord will not hold
him guiltless that taketh His name in vain.

Q. 54. *What is required in the third commandment?*

A. The third commandment requireth the holy and reverent
use of God's names, titles, attributes, ordinances, words and
works.

1. In the year 1796, when the ship *Duff* was preparing to take out the
missionaries from the London Missionary Society, Mr Cox, one of the direc-
tors, was one day walking in the street, where he was met by a very fine-
looking boy, about fourteen years of age, who, stopping him, said, 'Sir,
have not you some management in the ship that is going out with the missionaries?' 'Yes, I have, my young man,' said Mr Cox. 'I should like very
much, sir, to go out with her as a cabin-boy.' 'Would you?' said Mr Cox;
'have you any parents?' 'I have a mother,' said the boy, 'but no father.'
'And is your mother willing you should go?' 'Oh yes, sir, very willing.' Mr
Cox then desired the boy to call at his house, and to bring his mother along
with him, that she might speak for herself. At the time appointed, the boy
and his mother came, and she having declared her willingness that her son
should go, the matter was accordingly settled. In the course of the conversation, a gentleman who was present in order to try the boy, said to him, 'So
you wish to go to sea?' 'Yes, sir, in the missionary ship.' 'And you know
how to swear I suppose?' Shocked at the very idea of such a thing, the
ingenuous little fellow burst into tears, and exclaimed, 'If I thought there
would be swearing aboard at all, I would not go.'
2. A collier who was addicted to a very wicked course of life, going one
Sabbath morning to buy a game-cock for fighting, was met by a good man
on his way to a religious meeting, who asked him where he was going. He
related the whole to him, and after much entreaty, was prevailed on to go
with him to the meeting, where it pleased God to convince him of his
misery. On the Monday morning he went to his work, where he was beset
by the rest of the colliers, who swore at him, told him he was going mad,
and upbraided him, by saying, that before a month was at an end, he

would swear as bad as ever. On hearing this, he kneeled down before them all, and earnestly prayed that God would sooner take him out of the world, than suffer him to blaspheme His holy name; on which he immediately expired. The person who was the instrument of bringing him to a knowledge of the truth, died a few days afterwards.

3. John Howe being at dinner with some persons of fashion, a gentleman expatiated largely in praise of Charles I, and made some disagreeable reflections upon others. Howe observing that he mixed many horrid oaths with his discourse, took the liberty to say that, in his humble opinion, he had omitted one great excellence in the character of that prince; which when the gentleman had pressed him to mention, and waited with impatience to hear it, he told him it was this: 'That he was never heard to swear an oath in common conversation.' The gentleman took the reproof, and promised to break off the practice.

4. One of the teachers of a Sabbath School, coming home from work one day, overtook a boy, whom he knew to be very wicked, and particularly addicted to swearing. The teacher asked him if he still swore? He answered, 'No.' 'What is the reason you have left it off?' 'Because I go to the Sunday School.'

5. A lady, in a letter addressed to the secretary of the Blackburn Religious Tract Society, states the following fact: 'One of our scholars had the *Swearer's Prayer* lent her lately, and returned it; but she thought very much about it, as her father was in the habit of profane swearing. She was at the time in a very bad state of health; but we did not think her dangerously ill, and paid but little attention to her—her parents only were acquainted with the state of her mind, and were not very competent to give her that direction which she then so much needed. Some weeks afterwards, on a Monday evening, her father came home from his work, and finding something wrong in the family, broke out into such an outrageous fit of swearing, as quite to alarm the child, who was gone to bed. She immediately got up, ran down stairs, and throwing her arms around his neck, begged him, in the most pathetic manner, not to swear. But on this, her feelings and weakness so much overcame her, that she fell down, apparently lifeless, at her father's feet, when he raised her, with all the tenderness of a fond parent; when she had recovered her senses, he asked her why she had given herself so much trouble. She replied, "Because, father, you should not swear." The next day she went to a girl in the school, who had a copy of the *Swearer's Prayer*, and borrowed it from her, but did not say for what purpose she wished it. Finding a convenient opportunity when her father was alone in the house, she went to him, saying, "Father, I have got a little book here; will you read it for me?" He took the book; but when he saw the title, would have instantly returned it, had she not entreated him with much tenderness to read it. To please the child he sat down beside her and read it. It pleased God to bless the reading of the tract to his soul; and I am happy to be able to add, that he was never known to swear any more after that time. The child did not long survive; but she lived long enough to see a reformation in her father's conduct, and died happy in the Lord, before she had attained her fourteenth year.'

F

6. 'In my walk this morning,' says the godly James B. Taylor, 'as I was passing a shop, a man swore by the sacred name of God. I passed on. The query arose, "Shall I let this sin go unnoticed?" I stopped. Many excuses entered my mind. At length this Scripture presented itself: "Thou shalt in any wise rebuke thy neighbour, and not suffer sin upon him." I went back, called the person by name, and requested an interview. We walked aside, where I had a serious talk with him; the result so far was favourable.'

Q. 55. *What is forbidden in the third commandment?*

A. The third commandment forbiddeth all profaning or abusing of any thing whereby God maketh Himself known.

1. John Brown of Haddington, once passing the Firth of Forth, between Leith and Kinghorn had for a fellow-passenger one who appeared to be a Highland nobleman. Brown observed with grief that he frequently took the name of God in vain; but suspecting that to reprove him in the presence of the other passengers might tend only to irritate him, he forbore saying any thing till he reached the opposite shore. After landing, and observing the nobleman walking alone, Brown stepped up to him, and said, 'Sir, I was sorry to hear you swearing while on our passage. You know it is written, "Thou shalt not take the name of the Lord thy God in vain." ' On this the nobleman, lifting his hat, and bowing to Mr Brown, made the following reply: 'Sir, I return you thanks for the reproof you have now given me, and shall endeavour to attend to it in future; but,' added he, 'had you said this to me while in the boat, I believe I should have run you through with my sword.'

2. John Maclaurin of Glasgow, well known to the world by his valuable Christian writings, in passing one day along the street, was disturbed by the noise of some disorderly soldiers. One of them, just as Mr Maclaurin approached them, uttered this awful imprecation, 'God damn my soul, for Christ's sake'. The good man, shocked at hearing such blasphemous language, went up to him, and laying his hand on the shoulder of the man, said to him with peculiar mildness and solemnity, 'Friend, God has already done much for Christ's sake: suppose He should do that too, what would become of you?' It was a word in season, and it came with power. The conscience of the soldier sank under the reproof. He was led not only to reform the evil habit of swearing, to which he had long been addicted, but to reflect on his ways, and to turn to the Lord. He became a genuine Christian; and proved the soundness of his conversion, by maintaining to the end of his life a conversation worthy of the gospel.

3. A minister of the gospel one day finding a servant beating his master's horses, and taking the name of God in vain, stood still and reproved him sharply. The servant made no reply; but, prompted by curiosity, came next Lord's-day to hear his reprover preach. 'Swear not at all,' said the preacher, when concluding his discourse, 'is a divine command, that binds both master

and servant. I knew a man who not long ago surprised one of the swearing tribe of servants, in the very act of damning his master's horses. The son of Belial, though challenged, durst not open his mouth for his father's interest; but hung his head like a coward in the devil's service. He passed by, and had not the manners to thank his reprover, or grace to promise amendment. Is he here?—Do I see him?—Shall I name him?' After some pause, he added, 'We shall rather pray for him.' The servant was sitting trembling before him; and it may be proper to add, that he came afterwards to the minister, confessed his fault, gave signs of true penitence, was added to the church, and was never afterwards heard to blaspheme the worthy Name.

4. One evening as the Rev. William Wilson of Perth was passing along the streets of that town, three soldiers then quartered in it happened to walk behind him, who were indulging in the utterance of most profane and blasphemous language. One of them, on some frivolous account, declared it to be his wish that God Almighty might damn his soul in hell to all eternity. The minister turned round and with a look of dignity and pity said, 'Poor man, and what if God should say amen, and answer that prayer?' So saying, he passed on. The man stood as if petrified, and on going to his quarters was in such distraction of mind and feeling that he knew not where he could turn for relief. He was soon afterwards seized with fever and began to suffer the forebodings of eternal misery. His case was so singular that several Christians went to visit him, to whom he invariably said that he was beyond the reach of God's mercy and that an angel had been sent to tell him so. One of them asked him to describe the appearance of the visitor who had pronounced this doom on him. As he did so, the Christian perceived that it must have been William Wilson, and inquired whether he would like to see him again. 'Oh,' said he, 'I should like above everything to see him, but he will not come near a wretch like me.' The minister was soon brought, and as soon told the soldier of the way of salvation through Christ crucified, encouraging him to flee for refuge to lay hold upon the hope set before him. Divine power accompanied the words, the soldier was enabled to believe in Christ, and shortly he found peace and comfort to his troubled soul. Recovering from his sickness, he became an exemplary Christian, and as he felt the army unfavourable to his profession of the Lord, the minister at his request used influence and procured his honourable discharge. He settled in Perth, became a member of the Church, attached himself steadily to the minister, and was through life a comfort to him and an ornament to the Christian profession.

5. A lady on her way from Edinburgh to Glasgow in the stage coach, was very much annoyed by a young military officer, whose conversation was interspersed with oaths. The lady sat very uneasy, till she could no longer keep silence. 'Sir,' said she to the officer, 'can you talk in the Gaelic tongue?' To this he replied in the affirmative, seemingly with great pleasure, expecting to have some conversation with the lady in that dialect. She then politely requested, that if he wished to swear any more, it might be in that language, as the practice of swearing was very offensive to herself and the rest of the company. The officer was quite confounded at the smart reproof,

and no more oaths were heard from him during the remainder of the journey.

6. An officer, much addicted to profane swearing, visited the mines in Cornwall, attended by a godly person who was employed in the works. During his visit the officer uttered many profane and abominable expressions; and as he descended in company with the miner, finding it a long way, he said to him, 'If it be so far down to your work, how far is it to hell?' The miner promptly replied, 'I do not know how far it is to hell, sir; but I believe, that if the rope by which we are descending should break, you would be there in a minute.'

7. A General who was in early life much addicted to profane oaths, dates his reformation from a memorable check he received from a Scottish clergyman. When he was a lieutenant, and stationed at Newcastle, he got involved in a brawl with some of the lowest class in the public street; and the altercation was carried on, by both parties, with abundance of impious language. The clergyman, passing by, was shocked with the profanity, and stepping into the crowd with his cane uplifted, thus addressed one of the leaders of the rabble—'Oh John, John! what is this I hear! you only a poor collier boy, and swearing like any lord in all the land. Oh John! have you no fear of what will become of you? It may do very well for this gallant gentleman (pointing to the lieutenant) to swear as he pleases; but you—but you, John! it is not for you, or the like of you, to take in vain the name of Him in whom ye live and have your being.' Then turning to the lieutenant, he continued, 'Ye'll excuse the poor man, sir, for swearing, he is an ignorant body, and kens no better.' The young officer slunk away in confusion, unable to make any reply. Next day he made it his business to wait on the minister; he thanked him sincerely for his well-timed reproof, and has ever since been an example of the strictest purity of language.

8. When any indecent or profane language was uttered in the presence of the Rev. Jonathan Scott, pointed reproof was sure to be given; but there was at once a peculiar delicacy in the management, as well as singular fidelity in the application of it. An ostler at an inn in Coventry, being about to attend to his horse, used profane language. The animal turned round to look at Mr Scott, who improved the opportunity, and said to the ostler, 'Do you observe how my horse is caused to wonder? He is not used to such bad words at home: he never hears an oath there; and he does not know what to make of it.' Thus the profane sinner was reproved, but could not be offended.

9. 'My lads,' said a naval captain when reading to the crew on the quarter-deck, his orders to take the command of the ship, 'there is one law that I am determined to make, and I shall insist upon its being kept; indeed it is a favour which I ask of you, and which, as a British officer, I expect will be granted by a crew of British seamen—what say you, my lads, are you willing to grant your new captain, who promises to treat you well, one favour?' 'Hi, Hi, sir,' cried all hands, 'please to let's know what it is, sir,' said a rough-looking hoarse-voiced boatswain. 'Why my, lads,' said the captain, 'it is this; that you must allow me to swear the first oath in this ship; this is a law I cannot dispense with; I must insist upon it: I cannot be denied. No man on board must swear an oath before I do; I am deter-

mined to have the privilege of swearing the first oath on board H.M.S.C——.
What say you, my lads, will you grant me this favour?' The appeal seemed
so reasonable, and the manner of the captain so kind and so prepossessing, that
a general burst from the ship's company announced, 'Hi, Hi, sir,' with their
accustomed three cheers, when they left the quarterdeck. The effect was
good, swearing was wholly abolished in the ship.

Q. 56. *What is the reason annexed to the third commandment?*

A. The reason annexed to the third commandment is, That
however the breakers of this commandment may escape punishment from men, yet the Lord our God will not suffer them to
escape His righteous judgment.

1. An elector of Cologne, who was also an archbishop, one day swearing
profanely, asked a peasant, who seemed to wonder, what he was so surprised at. 'To hear an archbishop swear,' replied the peasant. 'I swear,'
replied the elector, 'not as an archbishop, but as a prince.' 'But, my lord,'
said the peasant, 'when the prince goes to the devil, what will become of
the archbishop?'

2. A person who lived in the parish of Sedgley, near Wolverhampton,
having lost a considerable sum by cock-fighting, to which practice he was
notoriously addicted, swore, in the most horrid manner, that he would
never fight another cock as long as he lived; frequently calling upon God
to damn his soul to all eternity if he did, and with dreadful imprecations,
wishing the devil might fetch him if he ever made another bet. It is not
to be wondered at, if resolutions so impiously formed, should be broken.
For a while, however, they were observed; but he continued to indulge
himself in every other abomination to which his depraved heart inclined
him. But about two years afterwards, Satan, whose willing servant he was,
inspired him with a violent desire to attend a cock-fight at Wolverhampton;
and he complied with the temptation. When he came to the place, he stood
up, as in defiance of Heaven, and cried, 'I hold four to three on such a cock.'
'Four what?' said one of his companions in iniquity. 'Four shillings,' replied
he. 'I'll lay,' said the other. Upon which they confirmed the wager, and as
his custom was, he threw down his hat, and put his hand into his pocket for
the money; when, awful to relate, he instantly fell a ghastly corpse to the
ground. Terrified at his sudden death, some who were present for ever
after desisted from this infamous sport; but others, hardened in iniquity,
proceeded in this barbarous diversion as soon as the dead body was removed from the spot.

3. Ebenezer Erskine, when crossing the Forth from Leith to Kinghorn,
had the unhappiness to find himself in the midst of ungodly passengers, who
took the most unhallowed liberties with their Creator's Name. For a time
he was silent, but at last, unable to suppress his concern, and eager to curb
their blaspheming tongues, he rose from his seat, and taking hold of the

mast, uncovered his head, and cried loudly, in the manner of a herald or town-crier, 'O yes, O yes, O yes.' Having thus secured the attention of the astonished passengers and crew, he proceeded in a solemn and impressive manner to proclaim that commandment of the law of God that they were flagrantly violating: 'Thou shalt not take the Name of the Lord thy God in vain, for the Lord will not hold him guiltless that taketh His name in vain.' Without adding a single word, he quitted the mast, put on his hat, and resumed his seat. Soon, however, general talk became as profane and offensive as before. Among the rest, a lady, regardless of all maxims of politeness, seemed to find a malicious pleasure in continuous acts of profanity, accompanied with smiles of derision and contempt. Soon, however, it pleased God to intervene by sending a sudden storm. The heavens became black with clouds, the sea became angry, and the pilot seemed quite unable to control the ship's helm. This unexpected change of circumstances led to a corresponding change in the demeanour of the passengers. Their sportive gaity gave place to consternation and despair. The same lady who had acted so insolent a part towards Erskine now came to his side as if her only hope of safety lay in her nearness to him, and said, 'O Sir, if I die here, I will die with you.' Soon, however, they weathered the storm, reached the harbour in safety, and dispersed to their various destinations. Such is one way of many in which it pleases God to rebuke blasphemy.

4. In the early nineteenth century as men were drinking in a public house at a village near Dundee, two of them agreed to make a trial who should invent the newest and most profane oaths. While one of them was just opening his mouth to make the dreadful attempt, his jaws were suddenly arrested, so that he was unable to close his mouth, or speak a word. He was carried to the Infirmary and died soon after. Let profane swearers tremble for their danger.

5. A certain man in Oliver Cromwell's time complained to a minister of the gospel: 'The squire of the parish is very much offended by some remarks you made in your sermon last Sabbath Day about profane swearing.' 'Well,' said the Puritan preacher, 'is the squire in the habit of swearing?' It had to be admitted that such was the case, and that therefore he thought himself pointed out by the minister. The Puritan replied to the complainant, who was a tenant of the squire, 'If your lord offends my Lord, I shall not fail to rebuke him, and if he is offended, let him be offended.'

6. A citizen of Glasgow named Jack was remarkable for the cheerfulness as well as the fervour of his piety. When he administered a reproof it was frequently accompanied with a kind of pleasantry which fixed the attention and disarmed the resentment of the person rebuked. Being once in company when a gentleman occasionally embellished his speech with the name of the devil, and at last took the name of God in vain, 'Stop, sir,' said Jack, 'I said nothing while you used only freedoms with the name of your own master, but I insist that you shall use no freedoms with the Name of mine.'

Q. 57. *Which is the fourth commandment?*

A. The fourth commandment is, Remember the Sabbath-day to keep it holy. Six days shalt thou labour, and do all thy work; but the seventh day is the Sabbath of the Lord thy God; in it thou shalt not do any work, thou, nor thy son, nor thy daughter, thy man-servant, nor thy maid-servant, nor thy cattle, nor thy stranger that is within thy gates. For in six days the Lord made heaven and earth, the sea, and all that in them is, and rested the seventh day; wherefore the Lord blessed the Sabbath-day, and hallowed it.

Q. 58. *What is required in the fourth commandment?*

A. The fourth commandment requireth the keeping holy to God such set times as He hath appointed in His word, expressly one whole day in seven, to be a holy Sabbath to Himself.

1. Sir Matthew Hale, a famous seventeenth-century judge, thus speaks of the Sabbath: 'I have,' says he, 'by long and sound experience, found that the due observation of this day, and of the duties of it, have been of singular comfort and advantage to me. The observance of this day hath ever had joined to it a blessing upon the rest of my time; and the week that hath so been begun, hath been blessed and prosperous to me; and on the other side, when I have been negligent of the duties of this day, the rest of the week has been unsuccessful and unhappy to my own secular employments; so that I could easily make an estimate of my successes the week following, by the manner of my passing of this day; and this I do not write lightly or inconsiderately, but upon a long and sound observation and experience.'

2. It is said of the godly and learned Thomas Gouge, that as he forbore providing suppers on the evening before the Sabbath, that servants might not be kept up too late, so he would never suffer any person to tarry at home to dress any meat on the Lord's day for any friends, whether they were mean or great, few or many.

3. Samuel Kilpin, on descending from the pulpit one Sabbath morning, was politely requested by a stranger to dine with him at an inn. He replied, 'Dine with you, sir, at an inn in Exeter on a Sabbath-day! No, sir, not if you would give me the city. A minister who has to address souls, on subjects connected with eternity, dine at an inn with company on the Sabbath day! No, sir, except from necessity, I never sit with my family, but at a short meal, on the Sabbath. I have to preach to myself as well as to others—excuse my firmness, I feel obliged by your kindness.'

4. The Roman Catholic clergy of Ireland at one time manifested the greatest hostility to the schools established in that country in which the Bible was read. A gentleman, on expostulating with a young priest on the subject, was told in reply, that he was only obeying the order of his bishop, whom he was bound to obey by the most solemn and binding oaths taken

at his ordination, and of which the bishop frequently reminded him. He added that he did not execute his directions with that severity he ought, for he was positively directed by his bishop to bring together all the children who were sent by their parents to the 'Bible school,' and while he denounced all the curses of the Roman Church against their parents by name, the children were ordered to curse their own parents by pronouncing audibly at the end of each verse the word Amen.

5. A person, known to the author, states that from long observation he has found that, when he has lain long in bed on a Sabbath morning, he has seldom succeeded, though desirous, in getting up early on the other days of the week.

6. In one of the towns of Connecticut, where the roads were extremely rough, Washington, when president of the United States, was overtaken by night on Saturday, not being able to reach the village where he designed to rest on the Sabbath. Next morning about sun-rise, his coach was harnessed, and he was proceeding forwards to an inn near the place of worship which he proposed to attend. A plain man, who was an informing officer, came from a cottage, and inquired of the coachman, whether there was any urgent reason for his travelling on the Lord's-day. The General, instead of resenting this as impertinent rudeness, ordered the driver to stop, and with great civility explained the circumstances to the officer, commended him for his fidelity, and assured him that nothing was farther from his intention than to treat with disrespect the laws and usages of Connecticut, relative to the Sabbath, which met with his most cordial approbation. How many admirers of Washington might receive instruction and reproof from his example!

7. Mr D——, a gentleman engaged in an extensive manufacturing concern in one of the midland counties, was called to London on business. After being engaged till a late hour one Saturday night, he said to a confidential person in his employment, who had come to town with him: 'Well, ——, we cannot settle our account tonight, but must do it early in the morning.' On the Sabbath accordingly, they were occupied in that work, till three o'clock in the afternoon. When dinner was announced, Mr D——said, 'We have been hard at work all morning, let us eat and drink, for to-morrow we die.' 'Not,' added he, 'that I have any thought of dying for years to come.' After taking his dinner and wine a postchaise was ordered, and Mr D——set out for the country. He arrived at home on the Monday night. The next morning (Tuesday), when at breakfast with his wife, and family, a gentleman came into the room, and said, 'Mr D——, have you heard of the death of Mr——?' 'No,' said Mr D——; 'is he dead? It is very different with me; for my part, I am so engaged in business, that I could not find time to die!' Immediately after uttering this sentiment, he rose from the table, and went into the kitchen; and while stooping in the act of drawing on his boot, he fell down on the floor, and expired!

Q. 59. *Which day of the seven hath God appointed to be the weekly Sabbath?*

A. From the beginning of the world to the resurrection of Christ, God appointed the seventh day of the week to be the weekly Sabbath: and the first day of the week, ever since, to continue to the end of the world, which is the Christian Sabbath.

1. Philip Henry used to call the Lord's-day the queen of days, the pearl of the week, and observed it accordingly. His common salutation of his family or friends on the Lord's-day in the morning, was that of the primitive Christians—'The Lord is risen, He is risen indeed—' making it his chief business, on that day, to celebrate the memory of Christ's resurrection; and he would say sometimes, 'Every Lord's-day is a true Christian's Easter day.'

2. John Knox, a little before his death, rose out of his bed; and being asked why he rose, being so sick, he answered, 'That he had had in the night sweet meditations on the resurrection of Jesus Christ; and now he would go into the pulpit, and impart to others the comforts he felt in his soul.'

3. When King George III was having his palace at Kew repaired, one of the workmen was particularly noticed by the King, and he often held conversations with him of some length upon serious subjects. On a certain Monday morning, His Majesty went as usual to watch the progress of the work, and not seeing this man in his customary place, he inquired the reason for his absence. He was informed that, not having been able to complete a particular job on the Saturday night, the workmen had returned to finish it on the Sabbath morning. This one man had refused to comply, because he considered it a violation of the Christian Sabbath and a matter of conscience; accordingly he had been dismissed from his employment for obstinacy. 'Call him back immediately,' said the King; the man who refuses to do his ordinary work on the Lord's Day is the man for me. Let him be sent for.' The man was accordingly brought back and the King ever after showed him particular favour.

4. A godly minister was one day preaching, and earnestly pressing the sanctification of the Sabbath. In his sermon, he had occasion to make mention of that man, who, by the special commandment of God, was stoned to death for gathering sticks on the Sabbath-day. A person in the congregation wickedly rose up and laughed, and made all the haste he could out of the church, and went and gathered sticks, though he had no need of them. But when the people were coming home from church, they found him lying dead, with the bundle of sticks in his arms. These instances of divine vengeance, inflicted on profaners of the Lord's-day, may contribute very much to confirm us in the belief of the divine institution of this holy day; and likewise may serve to warn all ranks and degrees of persons to guard against the contempt and violation of the Lord's-day. The Lord indeed exerciseth great long-suffering and patience towards many notorious Sabbath-breakers, to show us that there is a judgment-day to come. But nevertheless He makes monuments of some, to let us know that *verily there is a God that judgeth in the earth.*

Q. 60. *How is the Sabbath to be sanctified?*

A. The Sabbath is to be sanctified by a holy resting all that day, even from such worldly employments and recreations as are lawful on other days; and spending the whole time in the public and private exercise of God's worship, except so much as is to be taken up in the works of necessity and mercy.

1. It is the universal practice of the Christian natives of the South Sea Islands, to prepare their Sabbath-day's food on the Saturday. Not a fire is lighted, neither flesh nor fruit is baked, not a tree is climbed, nor a canoe seen on the water, nor a journey by land performed, on God's holy day; religion—religion alone—is the business and delight of these simple-minded people on the Sabbath.

2. The Rev. Dr Benedict, once minister of Sluinfield, gave a writer in the Connecticut Observer the following account, a few years before his death: Soon after he left college, he had occasion to travel southward, as far as the State of North Carolina. Being unacquainted with the way, he was desirous to find some one to accompany him. A man who had frequently travelled that road, in the business of a pedlar, was about to commence the journey, and informed him that it would give him pleasure to be his companion and guide. They accordingly set out together. At the close of the week, Dr Benedict remarked to his companion, that the journey thus far had been pleasant to him; but he added, 'I know not how I shall do next week, provided you intend to continue your journey on the Sabbath. I cannot proceed till Monday; and if you leave me, I shall probably lose my way.' The man replied, 'I have not travelled upon the Sabbath for several years, though my business leads me to take long journeys. I formerly did, but I always lost more than I gained by the practice. Some hindrance or accident would occur the following week, which convinced me that it is for *my* interest to rest on the Sabbath.'

3. John Kilpin, long a deacon in the meeting-house at Bedford (where John Bunyan was once minister,) kept a general retail shop, as an iron-monger. A nobleman in the neighbourhood was among his best customers. One Sabbath morning, the steward came to the house, and said, with an insolent sneer, 'Are you afraid of the devil, Mr Kilpin?' 'No,' replied the good man, 'I am not.' 'Will you then sell me some articles to-day?' 'No, I will not; it is the Sabbath-day; and the God of the Sabbath I love and fear. To-morrow I shall feel much obliged by executing his lordship's orders.' 'Very well, if you will not serve me to-day, you shall not to-morrow, or any other day.' The steward then retired in a violent rage; but it is pleasing to be able to add, that the nobleman increased his favours when told of the circumstance.

4. A little boy in London, who attended a Sabbath school, having occasion every Lord's-day to go through a certain court, observed a shop always open for the sale of goods. Shocked at such a profanation, he considered whether it was possible for him to do any thing to prevent it. He

determined to leave a tract, on the 'Lord's-day,' as he passed the shop in the course of the week. He did so; and on the following Sabbath observed that the shop was shut up. Surprised at this, he stopped, and considered whether it would be the effect of the tract he had left. He ventured to knock gently at the door; when a woman within, thinking it was a customer, answered aloud, 'You cannot have any thing, we don't sell on the Sunday!' Encouraged by what he had heard, the little boy still begged for admittance; when the woman recollecting his voice, said, 'Come in, my dear little fellow; it was you that left the tract here, against Sabbath-breaking; and it alarmed me so, that I did not dare to keep my shop open any longer; and I am determined never to do so again while I live.'

5. A young man accustomed to attend divine worship, and, from a child, well acquainted with the Holy Scriptures, was solicited to join in an excursion on the Thames on the Sabbath-day. Conscience remonstrated; but the love of pleasure, and the temptation of entertaining society, silenced the monitor. The day was agreed upon—the weather was unusually fine, and the party, about twelve in number, assembled on the bank to proceed to Richmond. Among the party was this young man. Just as he was stepping into the boat, the happy remembrance of the Word of God spoke powerfully, 'Remember the Sabbath-day to keep it holy.' Conscience instantly added, 'How can I do this great wickedness, and sin against God?' He could proceed no farther; he retired from the company amid their jeers and ridicule. But what were his feelings when the sad tidings came, that as the party returned from their unhallowed amusement, in the neighbourhood of Putney, the boat ran foul of a barge laden with coal; the party, half intoxicated, saw but could not clear the impending danger. The screams of the females were heard on the shore, but, alas! to no effect. Seven of the number perished.

6. A woman who always used to attend public worship with great punctuality, and took care always to be in time, was asked how it was that she could always come so early; she answered very wisely, 'That it was part of her religion not to disturb the religion of others.'

7. The attention of a servant-maid in Edinburgh to the spiritual interests of a little girl committed to her charge, and who died when nine years old, was peculiarly owned of God. The servant was accustomed to attend on the ministry of a certain Mr Pattison, and the child was permitted to accompany her. By degrees, the attention of her young charge was so drawn out to the sermons she heard, that the account she gave of many of the precious truths which fell from the lips of that worthy minister of Christ far exceeded what might have been expected from her tender years. Happening one day, in the course of his family visits, to call at the house where the child and her maid were to be found, Mr Pattison entered into conversation with her, and from her punctual attendance on public ordinances, took occasion to ask her if she recollected his preaching on Isaiah 40. 11, 'He shall feed His flock like a shepherd, He shall gather the lambs with his arm.' 'Yes,' replied the child, 'I remember it very well; for all the time you were preaching, I was wishing with all my heart, that I were one of Christ's lambs.' 'Ah, my dear,' said the good man, not a little affected, 'what a happy day

would it have been in Bristo Street, had all my hearers been employed in a similar manner!'

8. One Lord's-day, as a man was passing through Haworth, Yorkshire, on horseback, his horse lost a shoe; he applied to a blacksmith, who told him, 'That he could not shoe a horse on the Lord's-day, without the minister's permission.' They went together to William Grimshaw, the minister of the place, and the man satisfying him that he was really in haste, going for a midwife, Grimshaw permitted the blacksmith to shoe the horse, which otherwise he would not have done for double pay.

Q. 61. *What is forbidden in the fourth commandment?*

A. The fourth commandment forbiddeth the omission or careless performance of the duties required, and the profaning the day by idleness, or doing that which is in itself sinful, or by unnecessary thoughts, words, or works, about our worldly employments or recreations.

1. A distinguished nobleman, having observed, one Lord's-day at church, that the greater part of his servants were absent, on his return home, inquired the reason. On the butler's stating that it was owing to the wetness of the roads, his lordship replied, 'Well, this shall soon be remedied;' and on the next wet Sabbath-day that occurred, he ordered the servants to take their places in a large covered cart, while he followed them on foot all the way to church. This singular kind of reproof had the desired effect; and the day must have been very bad indeed, if any of his lordship's servants were absent from public worship.

2. It was the frequent and almost constant custom of William Grimshaw, to leave his church whilst the psalm was singing, to see if any were absent from worship, and idling their time in the church-yard, the street, or the ale houses; and many of those whom he so found he would drive into the church before him. 'A friend of mine,' says John Newton, 'passing a public-house in Haworth, on a Lord's-day morning, saw several persons making their escape out of it, some jumping out of the lower windows, and some over a low wall: he was at first alarmed, fearing the house was on fire; but, on inquiring what was the cause of the commotion, he was told that they saw the parson coming. They were more afraid of their parson, than they were of a justice of the peace. His reproofs were so authoritative, and yet so mild and friendly, that the stoutest sinners could not stand before him.'

3. A minister, observing that some of his people made a practice of coming in very late, and after a considerable part of the sermon was over, was determined that they should feel the force of a public reproof. One day, therefore, as they entered the place of worship at their usual late hour, the minister, addressing his congregation, said, 'But my hearers, it is time for us now to conclude, for here are our friends just come to fetch us home.'

We may easily conjecture what the parties felt at this curious but pointed address.

4. 'A native lad,' says a missionary in India, 'about ten or eleven years of age, distinguished for his understanding and general good behaviour, being at chapel on a Lord's-day, went to sleep during the sermon; on returning home, I reproved him for so doing, but not harshly. A short time after, going out into the verandah, I found him sobbing most bitterly. I inquired of the other boys the cause; they replied, "We do not know; he came and sat down, and began to cry, and we cannot pacify him." I then called him, and, taking him aside, asked the reason of his crying. After some effort he said, "Oh, sir, I went to sleep at chapel!" and then sobbed louder than before. I said, "Do you weep because I was angry with you, or because God was angry with you?" His answer was, "Because God is angry with me; for in going to sleep at worship, I sinned against Him." He was then informed, that since he repented of his conduct, there was reason to hope that God would forgive him. After hearing this, and reading a passage from the Scriptures suited to his case, which I pointed out to him (Proverbs 28. 13) he left me much comforted.'

5. An active and skilful young minister, while engaged under circumstances of the most promising kind in the village of J——, was told of a miller, who, with more than usual of the bravery of profaneness, had repelled every attempt to approach him on the subject of religion, and had daunted all the hopes and efforts of the few serious persons in this vicinity. Among other practices of sinful daring, he uniformly kept his windmill, the most striking object in the hamlet, going on the Sabbath. In a little time, the clergyman determined to make an effort for the benefit of the hopeless man. He undertook the office of going for his flour the next time himself. 'A fine mill,' said he, as the miller adjusted his sack to receive the flour; 'a fine mill, indeed, one of the completest I have ever seen.' This was nothing more than just—the miller had heard it a thousand times before; and would firmly have thought it, though he had never heard it once; but his skill and judgment were still gratified by this new testimony, and his feelings conciliated even towards the minister. 'But, O!' continued his customer, after a little pause, 'there is one defect in it!' 'What is that?' carelessly asked the miller. 'A very serious defect too.' 'Eh,' replied the miller, turning up his face. 'A defect that is likely to counterbalance all its advantages.' 'Well what is it?' said the miller, standing straight up, and looking the clergyman in the face. The minister went on: 'A defect which is likely to ruin the mill!' 'What is it?' rejoined the miller. 'And will one day, no doubt, destroy the owner.' 'And can't you say it out?' exclaimed the impatient miller. 'It goes on the Sabbath!' pronounced the minister, in a firm, and solemn, and monitory tone. The astonished man stood blank and thunderstruck, and remained meek and submissive under a remonstrance and exhortation of a quarter of an hour's length, in which the danger of his state and practice, and the call to repentance towards God, and faith in our Lord Jesus Christ, were fully proposed to him.

6. It is to be regretted that public vehicles are so frequently used without necessity in conveying persons to and from church on Sabbath. The drivers

of these vehicles must either be kept from public worship altogether, or attend at a late hour. One Sabbath morning, a lady stepping into a hackney coach, in order to ride to a place of worship, asked the driver, if he ever went to church on the Lord's-day? She received the following reply: 'No madam; I am so occupied in taking others there, that I cannot possibly get time to go myself!'

7. 'After preaching a sermon,' says James Sherman, 'in which I exhorted every one to do something for Jesus Christ, a little girl, aged eight years, came to me the next morning, and said, "I think, sir, I can do something for Jesus Christ." "And what do you think you can do for your Saviour, my dear child?" said I. "If, sir," she replied, "you would enclose some of those little tracts—(Nothing lost by serving God)—in half sheets of writing paper, and direct them to tradesmen who keep open their shops on the Lord's-day, I do not think they would refuse to take them of a little girl, when they did not appear as tracts, but like letters nicely directed to them." I adopted her suggestion, and put the letters into the dear little one's hands, and acting as a missionary in the district, she has been the instrument of shutting up six shops which were formerly kept open on God's day.'

8. One Sabbath-day, two sons of a poor widow in Derbyshire, the elder sixteen, and the younger thirteen years of age, went to slide on some ice at a short distance from home. Before they left their home, they had been requested by their mother to accompany her to the house of God, and, whilst on the ice, were warned of their danger by a person who passed by, and knew the depth of the water. But, alas! their mother's request, and the seasonable warning of their neighbour were both in vain. In a little time the ice gave way, and both were drowned. Thus were these youthful Sabbath-breakers called to stand before the judgment-seat of the Almighty, who has said, 'Remember the Sabbath-day to keep it holy.'

9. In the year 1809, a youth about seventeen years of age, the son of a respectable tradesman in London, went out for the purpose of shooting birds on a Lord's-day in the afternoon. He had done so more than once before, which coming to the knowledge of his father, he expressly enjoined him never to do the like again. But the lad, disregarding his command, and taking advantage of his father's absence, borrowed a gun from a person in the neighbourhood, and went out as usual. While he was watching the birds, the gun, by some accident, went off, and killed him on the spot.

10. At the village of Ampleforth, in Yorkshire, two young men were playing at fives on the Lord's-day morning. A godly man reproved them, and warned them of the impropriety and danger of their conduct, as they might draw down God's judgment upon them. The reproof, however, had not the desired effect, as the elder of them swore, by the God that made him; and at the same time added, that if he lived until the following Sabbath, he would call three or four of his companions together, to play near the chapel-wall at the time of service. On Sabbath morning he was taken dangerously ill, and in spite of all medical aid, expired in the course of the day!

11. Many years ago the following narrative appeared in a London magazine concerning the death of a cab driver: ' "I'm dying, I feel I'm dying;

fetch some one to pray for me," exclaimed the cabman, who like others of his calling had long neglected spiritual concerns. "Run, George, as fast as you can," said the weeping wife to the poor lad, who had buried his face in the bed on which his dying father was laid: "Run and tell Mr——that your father has got nearly killed, and wants him to come directly and pray for him."

'The medical attendant had done all that was practicable to alleviate the bodily pains of the sufferer; but these were light compared with the horror of death which overwhelmed him. The minister of the parish now arrived.

' "I've been a wicked man," the sufferer said. "O that I had lived a different life! It's too late now."

'The words of mercy were then spoken. He listened, but seemed not to comprehend their meaning. A convulsive struggle ensued; his half-closed eyes were once more opened, when, with an expiring effort, he exclaimed, in a hoarse whisper, and with a look of anguish which no pen can describe, "*I've had no Sundays!*" They were his last words.'

Q. 62. *What are the reasons annexed to the fourth commandment?*

A. The reasons annexed to the fourth commandment are, God's allowing us six days of the week for our own employments, His challenging a special propriety in the seventh, His own example, and His blessing the Sabbath-day.

1. 'I now beg permission,' says a missionary, 'to relate the simple argument of a pious poor man with a Sabbath-breaker. I had it from the poor old man a few weeks since, in the course of a conversation with him, which very much interested me; he is a member of our church at Mattishall (Norfolk). In reasoning with the Sabbath-breaker, he said, "Suppose now, I had been at work hard all the week, and earned seven shillings; suppose now I met a man, and gave six shillings out of the seven, what should you say to that?" "Why, I should say that you were very kind, and that the man ought to be thankful." "Well, but suppose he was to knock me down, and rob me of the other shilling; what then?" "Why, then he would deserve hanging." "Well, now, this is your case; thou art the man: God has freely given you six days to work in, and earn your bread, and the seventh He has kept to Himself, and commands us to keep it holy; but you, not satisfied with the six days God has given, rob Him of the seventh; what then do you deserve?" The man was silenced.'

2. On the Jura mountains in Switzerland, where the winter is very long, and the summer very short, it is of great consequence for men to preserve their hay, and put it up in good order, for if they run out, their cattle must starve, as the snow lies so long and so deep, they cannot go to their neighbours to get any, even if they had sufficient to spare. In this area lived an old man who had the love of Jesus and the fear of God in his heart, and kept

the Lord's-day as the Lord commands His people to keep it. One Lord's-day, when the hay was just in the finest order for putting up, his sons came to him, and proposed to him to go and put up the hay: but he said, 'Not so, my sons; this is the Lord's-day.' However, his sons were tempted by the value of the hay, and the fineness of the weather, to prepare themselves for work, but the moment they put their forks into it, a storm broke over their heads, and the rain poured upon them in torrents—one of the most violent storms they ever had—and the hay was completely destroyed. The old man addressed his sons: 'Thou shalt do no work on the Sabbath-day. Six days shalt thou labour, and do all thy work; but the seventh day is the Sabbath of the Lord thy God; in it thou shalt not do any work, thou, nor thy son, nor thy daughter, thy man-servant, nor thy maid-servant, nor thy cattle, nor thy stranger that is within thy gates. My sons,' continued the old man, 'you have done a work to save your hay, and the rain has destroyed it. Learn from this to respect the commandments of the Lord.' His sons never forgot this lesson; and they never again did common work on the Lord's-day.

3. On a Lord's-day, at the time of a great frost in the year 1634, fourteen young men were playing at football on the river Trent, near Gainsborough. While thus engaged, in the open violation of God's command, they met together in a scuffle; the ice suddenly broke, and they were all drowned!

4. When a minister of the gospel was spending a few weeks in Edinburgh, there came, on business, to the house where he was, a man of the world—one of those modern scoffers who are so constantly fulfilling Peter's prediction, 2 Peter 3. 3. He was introduced to the preacher in the following manner: 'This is Mr ——, an acquaintance of mine, who, I am sorry to add, though young and healthy, never attends public worship.' 'I am almost tempted to hope,' replied the minister, 'that you are bearing false witness against your neighbour.' 'By no means,' said the infidel, 'for I always spend my Sunday in settling accounts.' The minister immediately replied, 'You will find, sir, that the day of judgment will be spent in exactly the same manner.'

5. It is remarkable, wrote Dr William Scoresby in his account of a voyage to Greenland in 1820, 'that during the whole of the voyage, no circumstance ever occurred to prevent us engaging in public worship on the Sabbath Day. In a few instances, the hour of worship could not be easily kept, but opportunity was always found of having each of the services in succession on a plan adopted at the commencement of the voyage. And it is worthy of observation that in no instance, when on fishing stations, was our refraining from the ordinary duties of our profession on the Sunday ever supposed, eventually, to have been a loss to us; for we in general found, that if others who were less regardful, or had not the same view of the obligatory nature of the command respecting the Sabbath Day, succeeded in their endeavours to promote the success of the voyage, we seldom failed to procure a decided advantage in the succeeding week. Independently, indeed, of the divine blessing on honouring the Sabbath Day, I found that the restraint put upon the natural inclinations of the men for pursuing the fishery at all opportunities, acted with some advantage, by proving an

extraordinary stimulus to their exertions when they were next sent out after whales . . . I could relate several instances in which, after our refraining to fish upon the Sabbath while others were thus successfully employed, our subsequent labours succeeded under circumstances so striking, that there was not, I believe, a man in the ship who did not consider it the effect of the divine blessing.'

6. In the city of Bath, during the eighteenth century, lived a barber, who made a practice of following his ordinary occupation on the Lord's-day. As he was pursuing his morning's employment, he happened to look into some place of worship, just as the minister was giving out his text, 'Remember the Sabbath-day to keep it holy.' He listened long enough to be convinced, that he was constantly breaking the laws of God and man, by shaving and otherwise attending his customers on the Lord's-day. He became uneasy, and went with a heavy heart to his Sabbath task. At length he took courage, and opened his mind to the minister, who advised him to give up Sabbath work and worship God. He replied that beggary would be the consequence; he had a flourishing trade, but it would almost all be lost. At length, after many a sleepless night spent in weeping and praying, he was determined to cast all his care upon God, as the more he reflected, the more his duty became apparent. He discontinued Sabbath work, went constantly and early to the public services of religion, and soon enjoyed that satisfaction of mind, which is one of the rewards of doing our duty, and that peace of God, which the world can neither give nor take away. The consequence which he foresaw actually followed. His genteel customers left him, as he was nicknamed a Puritan or Methodist. He was obliged to give up his fashionable shop; and in the course of years became so reduced, as to take a cellar under the old market house, and shave the common people. One Saturday evening, between light and dark, a stranger from one of the coaches, asking for a barber, was directed by the ostler to the cellar opposite. Coming in hastily, he requested to be shaved quickly, while they changed horses, as he did not like to violate the Sabbath. This was touching the barber on a tender chord: he burst into tears, asked the stranger to lend him a halfpenny to buy a candle, as it was not light enough to shave him with safety. He did so, revolving in his mind the extreme poverty to which the poor man must be reduced. When shaved, he said, 'There must be something extraordinary in your history, which I have not now time to hear. Here is half-a-crown for you: when I return, I will call and investigate your case. What is your name?' 'William Reed,' said the astonished barber. 'William Reed!' echoed the stranger: 'William Reed! by your dialect you are from the west?' 'Yes, sir; from Kingston, near Taunton.' 'William Reed, from Kingston, near Taunton! What was your father's name?' 'Thomas.' 'Had he any brothers?' 'Yes, sir, one, after whom I was named; but he went to the Indies, and as we never heard from him, we suppose him to be dead.' 'Come along, follow me,' said the stranger; 'I am going to see a person, who says his name is William Reed of Kingston, near Taunton. Come and confront him. If you prove to be indeed the man whom you say you are, I have glorious news for you; your uncle is dead and has left an immense fortune, which I will put you in possession of, when all

G

legal doubts are removed.' They went by the coach, saw the pretended William Reed, and proved him to be an impostor. The stranger, who was a godly attorney, was soon legally satisfied of the barber's identity, and told him that he had advertised for him in vain. Providence had now thrown him in his way, in a most extraordinary manner, and he had much pleasure in transferring a great many thousand pounds to a worthy man, the rightful heir of the property. Thus was man's extremity God's opportunity. Had the poor barber possessed one halfpenny, or even had credit for a candle, he might have remained unknown for years; but he trusted God, who never said, 'Seek ye my face in vain.'

7. The Rev. J. Scott of Hull, in his funeral sermon for the distinguished William Wilberforce, observes, when speaking of his high veneration for the Sabbath: 'On each returning Sabbath, his feelings seemed to rise, in proportion to the sanctity of the day, to a higher degree of spirituality and holy joy, which diffused a sacred cheerfulness to all around him. I have often heard him assert, that he never could have sustained the labour and stretch of mind required in his early political life, if it had not been for the rest of the Sabbath; and that he could name several of his contemporaries in the vortex of political cares, whose minds had actually given way under the stress of intellectual labour, so as to bring on a premature death, or the still more dreadful catastrophe of insanity and suicide, who, humanly speaking, might have been preserved in health, if they would but have conscientiously observed the Sabbath.'

Q. 63. *Which is the fifth commandment?*

A. The fifth commandment is, Honour thy father and thy mother, that thy days may be long upon the land which the Lord thy God giveth thee.

Q. 64. *What is required in the fifth commandment?*

A. The fifth commandment requireth the preserving the honour and performing the duties, belonging to every one in their several places and relations, as superiors, inferiors, or equals.

1. The judicious Richard Hooker used to say, 'If I had no other reason and motive for being religious, I would earnestly strive to be so for the sake of my aged mother, that I might requite her care of me, and cause the widow's heart to sing for joy.'

2. The danger occasioned by one of the awful eruptions of Mount Etna obliged the inhabitants of the adjacent country to flee in every direction for safety. Amidst the hurry and confusion of this scene, every one carrying

away whatever he deemed most precious, two sons, the one named Ana-
phias, the other Amphonimus, in the height of their solicitude for the preservation of their wealth and goods, recollected their father and mother,
who, being very old, were unable to save themselves by flight. Filial tenderness overcame every consideration: —'Where,' exclaimed the generous
youths, 'shall we find a more precious treasure than our parents?' This
said, the one took up his father on his shoulders, the other his mother, and
so made their way through the surrounding smoke and flames.

3. A boy was once tempted by his companions to pluck some ripe cherries
from a tree which his father had forbidden him to touch. 'You need not
be afraid,' said they, 'for your father will not know anything about it, and
even if he finds out, he is so kind that he will not hurt you.' 'For that very
reason,' replied the boy, 'I ought not to touch them, for though my father
may not punish me, my disobedience would hurt my father.'

4. When Richard Cecil, the noted minister, was but a small boy, his
father had occasion to go to India House, and took his son with him. While
he was transacting his business, the little fellow was dismissed but told to
wait for his father at one of the doors. His father, on finishing his business,
went out at another door and, lost in thought, entirely forgot his son. In
the evening, his mother, missing the boy, inquired where he was; on which,
his father suddenly remembered that he had instructed him to wait at
a certain door. 'You may depend upon it.' he added, 'he is still waiting
where I appointed him.' Such indeed proved to be the case, for the father
returned with all speed to India House and found the lad on the very spot
where he had ordered him to remain. He knew that his father expected
him to wait, and therefore he would not disappoint him.

5. A young man, whose air at once indicated a well-cultivated mind,
and commanded respect, came to a recruiting officer, desiring to be en-
listed into his company. As he appeared to be greatly embarrassed, the
officer asked the cause of it. He replied, 'I tremble lest you should deny
my request.' 'No,' said the officer, 'I accept your offer most heartily; but
why should you imagine a refusal?' 'Because the bounty which I expect
may perhaps be too high.' 'How much, then, do you demand?' said the
officer. 'It is no unworthy motive, but an urgent claim, that compels me
to ask ten guineas; and I shall be the most miserable of mankind if you
refuse me.' 'Ten guineas!' said the officer, 'that indeed is very high; but
I am pleased with you: I trust to your honour for the discharge of your
duty, and will strike the bargain at once. Here are ten guineas: tomorrow
we depart.' The young man, overwhelmed with joy, asked leave to return
home, and promised to be back within an hour. The officer gave permission,
and, induced by curiosity, followed him at some distance. He went to the
town prison, where he knocked and was admitted. The officer, while standing at the door of the prison, overheard the young man say to the jailer,
'Here is the money for which my father is imprisoned, I put it into your
hands, and I request you to conduct me to him immediately, that I may
release him from misery.' The jailer did as he was requested. After a delay
of a few minutes, the officer followed him. What a scene! He saw the son
in the arms of a venerable and aged father, who, without uttering a word,

pressed him to his heart, and bedewed him with tears. The officer approached them, and said to the old man, 'Compose yourself, I will not deprive you of so worthy a son. Permit me to restore him to you, that I may not regret the money which he has employed in so virtuous a manner.' The father and son fell upon their knees at his feet. The young man refused at first to accept of this proffered freedom; but the worthy officer insisted that he should remain with his father. He accompanied them both from the prison, and took his leave, with the pleasing reflection of having contributed to the happiness of a worthy son, and an unfortunate father.

6. I well remember, says a writer on Christian education, being much impressed by a sermon when I was a young father, in which the preacher said, were he to select one word as the most important in education, it should be the word *obey*. My experience since has fully convinced me of the justice of the remark. Without filial obedience everything must go wrong. Is not a disobedient child guilty of a manifest breach of the Fifth Commandment? And is not a parent who suffers this disobedience to continue, an habitual partaker in his child's offence against that commandment? By the disobedience of our first parents sin came into the world, and through the obedience of the second Adam are the gates of heaven opened to true believers. The wicked are emphatically styled *the children of disobedience;* and it is clearly the object of the divine plan of salvation to conquer the rebellious spirit of man, and to bring him into a state of humility and submission. Parental authority is one powerful instrument for effecting the change. It is intended to bend the stubborn will, and by habituating a child to subjection to earthly parents, to prepare him for Christian obedience to his heavenly Father. In proportion as filial obedience is calculated to smooth the way for true religion, filial disobedience must produce the opposite effect. The parent who habitually gives way to it, has appalling reason to apprehend that he is educating his child, not for heaven but for hell.

7. Unnatural and disobedient children are often, in the righteous retributions of Providence, punished for their wickedness. Adolf, son of Arnold, Duke of Guelders, being displeased that his father should live so long, thus preventing him from entering fully into his inheritance, came upon him one night as he was going to bed, took him prisoner, obliged him to go on foot in a cold season of the year, barelegged as he was, and then shut him up in close confinement in a dark dungeon for half a year. Such disobedience and cruelty did not, however, go unpunished; for shortly after, the son himself was arrested, kept for a long time in prison, and after his release, was killed in a battle with the French.

8. A child who had been trained in the ways of religion by a parent, kind but judiciously firm, when dying, affectionately thanked her mother for all her tender care and kindness, and added, 'I thank you most of all for having subdued my self-will.'

9. A boy of seven years of age, in the town of Weser, in Germany, playing one day with his sister of four years old, was alarmed by the cry of some men, who were in pursuit of a mad dog. The child suddenly looking round him, saw the dog running towards him, but, instead of making his escape,

he took off his coat, and wrapping it round his arm, he boldly faced the dog, and holding out the arm covered with the coat, the animal attacked it, and worried the coat till the men came up, who, being armed with clubs, killed the dog. The men reproachfully asked the boy, why he did not run and avoid the dog, which he could so easily have done. 'Yes,' said the little hero, 'I could have run from the dog; but if I had, he would have attacked my sister. To protect her, therefore, I thought of offering him my coat, which he might tear at, till you should come up and kill him.'

10. Frederic the Great of Prussia made it a point to return every mark of respect or civility shown to him in the street by those who met him. He one day commented that whenever he rode through the streets of Berlin, his hat was always in his hand. Baron Polintz, who was present, said that his Majesty had no occasion to notice the civility of every one who pulled his hat off to him in the streets. 'And why not?' said the king in a lively tone, 'are they not all human beings as well as myself?'

Q. 65. *What is forbidden in the fifth commandment?*

A. The fifth commandment forbiddeth the neglecting of, or doing any thing against the honour and duty which belongeth to every one in their several places and relations.

1. An amiable youth was lamenting, in terms of the sincerest grief, the death of a most affectionate parent. His companions endeavoured to console him, by the reflection that he had always behaved to the deceased with duty, tenderness, and respect. 'So I thought,' replied the youth, 'whilst my parent was living; but now I recollect with pain and sorrow many instances of disobedience and neglect, for which, alas! it is too late to make atonement.'

2. 'A friend of mine,' says the Rev. John A. James, 'had a son long since gone to join the immortals, who having one day displeased his father before his younger brothers and sisters, not only meekly submitted to parental rebuke, but when the family were assembled at the dinner table, rose before them all, and after having confessed his fault, and craved his father's forgiveness, admonished the junior branches of the family to take warning by his example, and be cautious never to distress their parents, whom they were under such obligations to love and respect. Nothing could be more lovely or more impressive, than this noble act. He rose, by his apology, to a higher place in the regard and esteem of his parents and the family, than he occupied even before his fault. Sullenness, impertinence, and obstinate resistance are meanness, cowardice, littleness, compared with such an action as this, which combines a heroic magnanimity with the profoundest humility.'

3. A certain man had an only son, to whom he was very kind, and gave every thing that he had. When his son grew up and got a house, he was very unkind to his poor old father, whom he refused to support, and turned out

of his house. The old man said to his grandson, 'Go and fetch the covering from my bed, that I may go and sit by the wayside and beg.' The child burst into tears, and ran for the covering. He met his father, to whom he said, 'I am going to fetch the rug from my grandfather's bed, that he may wrap it round him, and go a-begging.' Tommy went for the rug, and brought it to his father, and said to him, 'Father, cut it in two; the half of it will be large enough for grandfather, and perhaps you may want the other half when I grow a man and turn you out of doors.' The words of the child struck him so forcibly, that he immediately ran to his father, asked forgiveness, and was very kind to him till he died.

4. A poor negress, a slave in the Island of Mauritius, with great labour and long parsimony, had saved as much money as enabled her to purchase her daughter, a slave like herself, from their common owner; being content to remain in bondage for the pleasure of seeing her child walking at large, with shoes on her feet, which were then the badge of freedom among people of colour, no slave being permitted to wear them. Soon after the bargain had been completed, the affectionate mother happening to come into a room, where this daughter was sitting, very naturally and uncon- sciously sat down beside her, as she had been wont to do. A moment or two afterwards, the daughter turned round in a rage, and rebuked her, exclaim- ing, 'How dare you sit down in my presence? Do you not know that I am a free woman, and you are a slave? Rise instantly, and leave the room!'

5. A certain farmer in England had an only son, to whom he was greatly attached, and never could think of chastising him for his faults. When he arrived at the age of twelve years, he bade adieu to his father's house, and went with a band of gipsies. For nearly twenty years he was never heard of. It happened, however, that the old man was under the necessity of taking a journey a considerable way, with a large sum of money. He had to pass a wood, and as he went on, a man rushed from it, seized his horse, and demanded his money. The old man remonstrated with him. He would not hear, but again demanded his money. Most reluctantly he gave it up. The robber, gazing at him, said, 'Do you know me?' 'No,' said the old man. 'Do you not know me?' he repeated. 'No, I do not know you.' 'Well,' said the robber, 'I am your son!' and, returning this money, added, 'Had you corrected me when young, I might have been a comfort to you; but now I am a disgrace to you, and a pest to society!'

6. An undutiful son, who had given his father much trouble and uneasi- ness, and almost brought down his grey hairs with sorrow to the grave, once called on his father on his birthday, to do him honour. 'Ah! my son!' said his father to him, 'the best way to honour me will be to turn from the error of your ways. If you really respect me, learn to respect yourself; till then I can have no faith in your professions, for how can I expect him truly to honour his father on earth, who dishonours his Father who is in heaven?'

7. John Berridge was once invited to meet a loquacious young lady, who, forgetting the modesty of her sex, and the superior gravity of an aged divine, engrossed all the conversation of the interview with small talk concerning herself. When she rose to retire, he said, 'Madam, before you withdraw, I have one piece of advice to give you. When you go into company again,

after you have talked half-an-hour without intermission, I recommend it
to you to stop a while, and see if any other member of the company has
any thing to say.'

8. Once, at a meeting of ministers, a question was put forward for discussion. Upon the first proposal of it, a confident young man said, 'Truly
I hold it so.' 'You hold, sir!' answered a grave minister, 'it becomes you
to hold your tongue.'

9. 'We hear much,' says Richard Cecil, 'of a *decent* pride—a *becoming*
pride—a *noble* pride—a *laudable* pride! Can that be *decent*, of which we
ought to be ashamed? Can that be *becoming*, of which God hath set forth
the deformity? Can that be *noble*, which God resists, and is determined to
debase? Can that be *laudable*, which God calls abominable?'

Q. 66. *What is the reason annexed to the fifth commandment?*

A. The reason annexed to the fifth commandment, is a
promise of long life and prosperity (as far as it shall serve for
God's glory and their own good) to all such as keep this
commandment.

1. Frederic William III, a king of Prussia, having rung his bell one day,
and nobody answering, opened the door, and found the page in waiting
asleep on the sofa. He was just going to awake him, when he perceived the
end of a paper out of his pocket, on which something was written. This
excited his curiosity; he pulled it out, and found it to be a letter from the
mother of the page, thanking him for having sent her part of his wages,
which had proved a very timely assistance to her; and, in conclusion,
beseeching God to bless him for his filial duty. The king stepped softly into
his room, took a quantity of money and slipt it with the letter into the page's
pocket. Returning to his apartment, he rang so violently, that the page
awoke, opened the door, and entered. 'You have been asleep,' said the
king. The page attempted to excuse himself; and, in his embarrassment,
happening to put his hand into his pocket, felt with astonishment the
money. He drew it out, turned pale, and looking at the king, burst into
tears, without being able to speak a word. 'What is the matter?' said the
king; 'what ails you?' 'Ah! sire,' said the young man, throwing himself
at his Majesty's feet, 'somebody wishes to ruin me; I know not how I came
by this money in my pocket.'' 'What God bestows,' resumed the king, 'He
bestows in sleep;* send the money to your mother; salute her in my name,
and assure her, that I shall take care of both her and you.'

2. A clergyman was once asked, when examined for orders by the
bishop's chaplain, whether he had made divinity his study. He replied,
that he had not particularly studied it; 'but,' said he, 'my mother taught
me the Scriptures.' 'Ah!' said the chaplain, 'mothers can do great things.'

* A German proverb.

The young man was examined with respect to the extent of his knowledge, was approved, ordained, and asked to preach before the bishop. The excellent mother alluded to, in writing to another of her sons, on the birth of his eldest child, says, 'Give him an education, that his life may be useful—teach him religion, that his death may be happy.'

3. Philip Henry, speaking once of a wicked son in the neighbourhood, who was very undutiful to his mother, charged some of his children to observe the providence of God concerning him: 'Perhaps,' said he, 'I may not live to see it, but, do you take notice, whether God do not come upon him with some remarkable judgment in this life, according to the threatening implied in the reason annexed to the fifth commandment;' but he himself lived to see it fulfilled not long after, in a very striking providence.

4. Thomas Scott has given us an account of a female servant, belonging to his congregation in London, who was taken ill. With the assistance of kind friends who knew her, he took care of her for many years. She was thus saved from the workhouse, and made comfortable to the day of her death. And who was this servant girl? She was one who in early life spent all her wages as a servant in support of her aged and distressed parents, who confidently believed that God would raise her up friends whenever she might need them; and who gave herself therefore to the duties which her Bible had commanded.

5. The eldest daughter of Dr Philip Doddridge was a most lovely and engaging child. As she was a great favourite with her family and friends, she often received invitations to different places at the same time. Her father once asked her, on such an occasion, what made everybody love her so well? She answered, 'Indeed, father, I cannot think, unless it be because I love every body.'

Q. 67. *Which is the sixth commandment?*

A. The sixth commandment is, Thou shalt not kill.

Q. 68. *What is required in the sixth commandment?*

A. The sixth commandment requireth all lawful endeavours to preserve our own life, and the life of others.

1. A noted physician on his deathbed, gave this advice to a noble friend who asked his counsel for the preservation of health: 'Be moderate in your diet, use much exercise, and little physic.'

2. 'A meek man,' says Matthew Henry, 'escapes many of those perplexities, those woes, and sorrows, and wounds without cause, which he that is passionate, provoking, and revengeful, brings upon his own head.' An instance of this he mentions, taken from Richard Baxter's book on Patience: 'Once as the author was going along the streets of London, a hectoring rude fellow jostled him; he went on his way, and took no notice of it; but

the same man affronting the next person he met in a similar manner, he drew his sword, and demanded satisfaction, on which mischief ensued.'

3. A minister, praying for a child apparently dying, said, 'If it be Thy will, spare this child.' The wretched and distracted mother interrupted him with the words, 'It *must* be God's will; I will have no *ifs*.' The child, to the surprise of many, recovered, but lived to break his mother's heart, and was publicly executed at the age of twenty-two.

4. The power of the Spirit of God in bringing conviction of sin to men who have so long professed innocence that, in some cases, they have almost deceived themselves into believing that they have been wrongly charged with guilt, is sometimes remarkably demonstrated. It is related that a young German who, for the crime of murder, had been long in solitary confinement, was repeatedly visited by a minister of the gospel to whom he made the most positive declarations of his innocence. After six months had elapsed, on leaving him one evening, the minister pointed his attention to three verses in the New Testament about the confession of sin to God and of divine forgiveness for Christ's sake—I John 1. 8-10—and especially urged upon him the importance of the truths which they taught. He promised to read them; he did so; and when he threw himself upon his pallet to rest, he found that sleep had forsaken him; he turned again and again, but still there was no rest. The verses had made a deep impression on his mind, and although for six months he had asserted that he was innocent of the crime for which he was charged, the first words he uttered to the keeper in the morning were, 'I did commit that murder.' Whether he confessed also to God and received the forgiveness and cleansing which the Word of God proclaims is not mentioned.

5. Canute, King of England in the eleventh century, promised to make the man who would kill Edmund Ironside, his rival, the highest man in England. Instead of this, when one had performed the deed and expected his reward, Canute commanded him to be hanged on the highest tower in London. Thus too does Satan deal with his servants and assistants.

6. The Romans had a law, that no person should approach the emperor's tent in the night, upon pain of death; but it once happened that a soldier was found in that situation, with a petition in his hand, waiting an opportunity of presenting it. He was apprehended, and about to be executed; but the emperor having overheard the matter in his pavilion, cried aloud, saying, 'If the petition be for himself, let him die; if for another, spare his life.' Upon inquiry, it was found that the generous soldier was pleading for the lives of his two comrades, who had been taken asleep on the watch. The emperor nobly forgave them all.

7. The following facts concerning a young chief of the Pawnee Indians of North America are highly creditable to his courage, his generosity, and his humanity. At the age of twenty-one, his heroic deeds had acquired for him in his tribe the rank of 'the bravest of the brave.' The savage practice of torturing and burning to death their prisoners, existed in this tribe. An unfortunate female of another tribe, taken in war, was destined to this horrible death. The fatal hour had arrived, the trembling victim, far from her home and her friends, was fastened to the stake, the whole tribe was

assembled on the surrounding plain, to witness the awful scene. Just when the wood was about to be kindled, and the spectators were on the tiptoe of expectation, the young warrior, who sat composedly among the other chiefs, having before prepared two fleet horses, with the necessary provisions, sprang from his seat, rushed through the crowd, loosed the victim, seized her in his arms, placed her on one of the horses, mounted the other himself, and made the utmost speed towards the tribe and friends of the captive. The multitude, dumb and nerveless with amazement at the daring deed, made no effort to rescue their victim from her deliverer. They viewed it as an act of their deity, submitted to it without a murmur, and quietly returned to their village. The released victim was accompanied through the wilderness towards her home, till she was out of danger. He then gave her the horse which he rode, with the necessary provisions for the remainder of her journey, and they parted. On his return to the village, such was the respect entertained for him, that no inquiry was made into his conduct— no censure was passed upon it; and after this transaction, no human sacrifice was offered in this or in any other of the Pawnee tribes.

Q. 69. *What is forbidden in the sixth commandment?*

A. The sixth commandment forbiddeth the taking away of our own life, or the life of our neighbour unjustly, or whatever tendeth thereunto.

1. It is recorded of the Puritan minister John Dod, that one night at a very late hour, he felt strongly moved to visit a gentleman of his acquaintance, who lived at some distance. Not knowing what might be the design of Providence in this, he went. Having come to the house and knocked at the door, the gentleman himself opened it; to whom Dod said, 'I am come to you, I know not why myself, but I was restless in my spirit till I had done it.' The gentleman replied, 'You know not why you came; but God knew why He sent you.' On which he showed him the halter with which he intended to take away his own life, which, by this means, was happily prevented.

2. A young gentleman, who had spent his fortune in riotous living, was reduced to poverty. For a while his friends supported him; but at last they all forsook him. Wandering about as a vagabond, and having no prospect of any further supply, he formed the dreadful resolution of drowning himself. Being then in a strange place, he put lead into his pocket, and went to the river side for this horrid purpose; but waiting till it was dark, he saw a light in a house at no great distance, and went to it. On his arrival, there were people singing psalms; he listened at the door till a chapter of the Bible was read, and a prayer offered up to God. He was surprised to find people assembled there for worship, and wished for admittance, for which purpose he knocked gently at the door. One of the company opened it, and asked what he wanted. He signified his desire to be admitted. He was told it was not customary to admit strangers into their meeting; however,

if he would behave decently, he might enter. In the astonishing kindness of Divine Providence, the passage of Scripture under consideration that evening was, Acts 16. 28; 'Do thyself no harm.' After the several members had made their remarks upon the subject, they concluded as usual with prayer, and they had no sooner done, than the stranger asked them how they came to know his thoughts, for he had not mentioned his intention to any person upon earth. This equally surprised the members of the meeting, who said they had not seen or heard of him till that evening. Upon which the young gentleman told them his design of taking away his life, and how he had been prevented by seeing a light in their window. This remarkable providence struck him to such a degree, that, by the Divine blessing, it was made the means of his conversion.

3. A gentleman, who was very ill, sending for a physician, told him that he felt he must die, and gave him the following account of the cause of his death. He had, about a fortnight before, been riding over Hounslow-heath, where several boys were playing at cricket. One of them striking the ball, hit him just on the toe with it, looked him in the face, and ran away. His toe pained him extremely. As soon as he came to Brentford, he sent for a surgeon, who was for cutting it off. But unwilling to suffer that, he went on to London. When he arrived there, he immediately called another surgeon to examine it, who told him his *foot* must be cut off. But neither would he hear of this. Before the next day, the mortification seized his *leg*, and in a day or two more struck up into his *body*. The physician asked him whether he knew the boy that struck the ball? He answered, 'About ten years ago, I was riding over Hounslow-heath, where an old man ran by my horse's side, begged me to relieve him, and said he was almost famished. I bade him begone. He kept up with me still; upon which I threatened to beat him. Finding that he took no notice of this, I drew my sword, and with one blow killed him. A boy about four years who was with him, screamed out, "My father is killed!" His face I perfectly remember, *That boy it was who struck the ball against me, which is the cause of my death.*'

4. A man and his wife were, a number of years ago, executed at Augsburg for a murder, the discovery of which, after a long lapse of time, strongly manifests the impossibility of eluding the all-seeing eye of Providence. The criminal, whose name was Wineze, was originally of Nuremburg, but removed to Augsburg in 1788, where he followed the law. In this city he became intimate with the family of M. Glegg, to whose daughter he paid his addresses; but the old man not sanctioning his visits, in order to remove the only obstacle to their union, he persuaded the daughter to administer poison to her father. The horrid plan succeeded—no suspicions were entertained, and their union put him in possession of the old man's wealth. During a period of twenty-one years, they lived externally happy, but in secret, a prey to the greatest remorse. At length, unable to endure any longer the weight of guilt, the wife made confession of the particulars of the atrocious crime she had been prevailed upon to commit. The husband was apprehended; and both of them received their due desert in an ignominious death.

5. Laurence Shirley, the fourth Earl Ferrers, was executed at Tyburn

for the murder of his land steward. Many pleas were made to the king, George II, to turn aside the course of justice in favour of this *noble* delinquent; or, if his life might not be spared, that at least he might enjoy the privilege of his peerage, that of being beheaded in the Tower. But the king steadily rejected all applications on his behalf, declaring that justice could own no difference in rank between him and the victim of his passion; that the blood of a peasant demanded the blood of a nobleman, if he had shed it, as much as that of a nobleman would, in like circumstances, demand that of a peasant; and that this crime had degraded him to a level with the very meanest of criminals.

6. A slave-dealer, looking out for a cargo on the African coast, found a trader on the beach, who produced two negro women, each with an infant in her arms. As the slave-dealer declined purchasing, he was asked the reason. He replied that the women would suit him well enough, but their children were an objection. The trader immediately went up to one of the women, and taking the child out of her arms, dashed its head upon a stone. He did the same to the other, and then sold the women!

7. A missionary in Africa mentions that near his station in Kaffirland, a young man left his home for a few days, to visit a village in the neighbourhood. He found there that an infectious disease was prevailing, and immediately returned. His father, selfishly dreading the spread of the infection, instead of pitying his son, went for his gun, loaded it, came into the hut, and while the poor lad was thinking himself safe in his father's house, shot him dead; and to make sure of his death, his two brothers then rushed upon him, and stabbed his dead body with their spears.

Q. 70. *Which is the seventh commandment?*

A. The seventh commandment is, Thou shalt not commit adultery.

Q. 71. *What is required in the seventh commandment?*

A. The seventh commandment requireth the preservation of our own and our neighbour's chastity, in heart, speech, and behaviour.

1. John Newton, as the commander of a slave-ship, had a number of women under his absolute command; and knowing the danger of his situation on that account, he resolved to abstain from flesh in his food, and to drink nothing stronger than water during the voyage, that by abstemiousness he might subdue every improper emotion. Upon his setting sail, the sight of a certain point of land was the signal for his beginning a rule which he was enabled to keep.

2. Zeleucus, prince of the Locrians, enacted a law, by which the person guilty of adultery was to lose both his eyes. His own son became guilty of the crime. The father, to show at once his regard for the law, and his love to his son, ordered one of his son's eyes to be put out, and submitted to lose one of his own.

3. Scipio the Younger, soon after the conquest of Carthage, having retired to his camp, some of his officers brought a young virgin to him of such exquisite beauty, that she drew upon her the eyes and admiration of every person. The young conqueror started from his seat with confusion and surprise. In a few moments, having recovered himself, he inquired of the beautiful captive, in the most civil and polite manner, concerning her country, birth, and connections; and finding that she was betrothed to a Spanish prince, named Allucius, he ordered both him and the captive's parents to be sent for. When the prince appeared in his presence, Scipio took him aside; and to remove the anxiety he might feel on account of the young lady, addressed him thus: 'You and I are young, which admits of me speaking to you with freedom. They who brought me your future spouse, assured me at the same time, that you loved her with extreme tenderness; and her beauty and merit left me no room to doubt of it. Upon which I reflected, that if I were in your situation, I should hope to meet with favour. I therefore think myself happy in the present conjuncture to do you a service. Though the fortune of war has made me your master, I desire to be your friend. Here is your wife; take her, and may you be happy. You may rest assured, that she has been as safe among us, as she would have been in the house of her father and mother. Far be it from Scipio to purchase any pleasure at the expense of virtue, honour, and the happiness of an honest man. No; I have kept her for you, in order to make you a present worthy of you and of me. The only gratitude I require of you for this inestimable gift, is, that you will be a friend to the Roman people.'

4. In the early nineteenth century there was a certain town in North Wales notorious for its immorality and, in particular, for its carelessness with regard to the seventh commandment. Despite regular preaching from the pulpit the situation grew worse until the state of things was mentioned to Thomas Charles of Bala. 'Having considered the subject, he made up his mind to make an attempt to storm this stronghold of Satan in a way different from that of preaching. About two months before the wakes, he sent word to the teachers of their Sunday school, requesting them to get the children to search the Bible for texts which prohibit directly or indirectly such evil practices as dancing, drunkenness, fornication, etc., and to commit them to memory; saying that they might expect him there at the feast to catechise the children. The young people set to work; and there was a great deal of talk in the town and neighbourhood about the subject. When the time arrived, Mr Charles went there; and most of the people of the place, led by curiosity perhaps in a great measure, went to hear what the children had to say on those subjects. The meeting began as usual with singing and prayer. Then Mr Charles began to ask them questions on the points given them to learn. "Is dancing, my dear children, a sin?" "Yes," said one emphatically, "it was owing to dancing that the head of John the Baptist was

cut off." "Is drunkenness set forth as bad and sinful in Scripture?" "Yes," another answered, and repeated these words, "Woe unto them that follow strong drink, that continue until night, till wine inflame them! And the harp and the viol, the tabret and pipe, are in their feasts; but they regard not the work of the Lord, neither consider the operation of his hands." Isa. 5. 11, 12. In this way he proceeded with them concerning the other sins, and the answers were given with great propriety and seriousness. The people began to hold down their heads, and appeared to be much affected. Observing this, he addressed them in the kindest manner and exhorted them by all means to leave off their sinful practices, to relinquish the works of darkness and to attend to the concerns of their never-dying souls; to learn the Word of God after the example of the children, and to try to seek superior pleasures and a better world. The effect was so great that all went home, and the houses of revelling were completely forsaken.'

5. In the conversion of Colonel James Gardiner recorded by Philip Doddridge there is a striking account of how this famous soldier's contempt for the seventh commandment was ended. While in Paris, in July 1719, Gardiner had spent the evening in some gay company and had planned an unhappy association with a married woman whom he was to meet that same night at exactly twelve o'clock. The company broke up about eleven, and not judging it convenient to anticipate the time appointed, he went into his chamber to kill the tedious hour, perhaps with some amusing book. But it accidentally happened that he took up a religious book, which his good mother or aunt had, without his knowledge, slipped into his cases. It was *The Christian Soldier; or, Heaven taken by Storm*, by Thomas Watson. Guessing by the title of it that he should find some phrases of his own pro-fession spiritualized, in a manner which he thought might afford him some diversion, he resolved to dip into it; but he took no serious notice of any-thing he read in it: and yet, while this book was in his hand, an impression was made upon his mind, perhaps God only knows how, which drew after it a train of the most important and happy consequences.

He thought he saw an unusual blaze of light fall on the book while he was reading, which he at first imagined might happen by some accident in the candle; but lifting up his eyes, he apprehended, to his extreme amaze-ment, that there was before him, as it were suspended in the air, a visible representation of the Lord Jesus Christ upon the cross, surrounded on all sides with a glory; and was impressed, as if a voice, or something equivalent to a voice, had come to him, to this effect (for he was not confident as to the very words), 'O sinner! did I suffer this for thee, and are these thy returns?' Struck with so amazing a phenomenon as this, there remained hardly any life in him, so that he sunk down in the armchair in which he sat, and continued, he knew not exactly how long, insensible. Nor did he, throughout all the remainder of the night, once recollect that criminal and detestable assignation which had before engrossed all his thoughts. He rose in a tumult of passions not to be conceived, and walked to and fro in his chamber till he was ready to drop down in unutterable astonishment and agony of heart; appearing to himself the vilest monster in the creation of God, who had all his lifetime been crucifying Christ afresh by his sins, and now saw, as he assuredly believed, by a miraculous vision, the horror of what he had done. With this was connected such a view both of the majesty and goodness of God, as caused him to loathe and abhor himself, and to repent as in dust and ashes.

Q. 72. *What is forbidden in the seventh commandment?*

A. The seventh commandment forbiddeth all unchaste thoughts, words, and actions.

1. A lady of suspected chastity, and who was tinctured with infidel principles, conversing with a minister of the gospel, objected to the Scriptures on account of their obscurity, and the great difficulty of understanding them. The minister wisely and pertinently replied, 'Why, madam, what can be easier to understand than the seventh commandment, *Thou shalt not commit adultery?*'

2. Anthony William Boehm, a German divine, once preached from Exod. 20.14: 'Thou shalt not commit adultery.' A knight, who was one of his hearers, felt himself so much offended and insulted, that he challenged Boehm to fight a duel, because he thought his sermon was designed entirely to offend him. Boehm accepted the challenge, and appeared in his robes, but instead of a pistol, he had the Bible in his hand, and spoke to him in the following manner: 'I am sorry you were so much offended when I preached against that destructive vice; at the time I did not even think of you; here I appear with the sword of the Spirit, and if your conscience condemns you, I beseech you, for your own salvation, to repent of your sins, and lead a new life. If you will, then fire at me immediately; for I would willingly lose my life, if that might be the means of saving your soul.' The knight was so struck with this language, that he embraced him, and solicited his friendship.

3. It is said that Henry IV of France took much pleasure in conversing with an honest and religious man of a low situation in life, who used great freedom with his majesty. One day he said to the king, 'Sire, I always take your part when I hear any man speaking evil of you; I know that you excel in justice and generosity, and that many worthy things have been done by you. But you have one vice for which God will condemn you if you do not repent, I mean the unlawful love of women.' The king, it is said, was too magnanimous to resent this reproof, but he long felt it like an arrow in his bosom. He sometimes said that the most eloquent discourses of the doctors of the Sorbonne, had never made such an impression on his soul as this honest reproof from his humble friend.

4. Grace Bennet was the subject of early religious impressions, which continued till she was sent to a dancing school, which proved a great snare to her, and in a considerable measure destroyed her taste for religion. Having a fine flow of spirits, and being esteemed a good dancer, she became an object of admiration, and her company was much solicited in

circles of gaiety and amusement. 'Dancing,' she observes, 'was my darling sin, and I had thereby nearly lost my life; but God was merciful, and spared the sinner.' Her sense of the danger and evil of this practice was such, that she could never once be prevailed on, after she became truly religious, to join in the most private circle in such amusement; nor did she approve of Christian parents sending their children to dancing schools, though no one had a higher sense of the propriety of instructing them in all the rules of good behaviour.

Q. 73. *Which is the eighth commandment?*

A. The eighth commandment is, Thou shalt not steal.

Q. 74. *What is required in the eighth commandment?*

A. The eighth commandment requireth the lawful procuring and furthering the wealth and outward estate of ourselves and others.

1. A poor family were brought to the last state of want; and seeing nothing but death stare them in the face, the wife said to the husband, 'You must go out and steal what you can.' The husband made many objections, but at last being so closely pressed by his wife, he took up his hat and went out. He soon returned, however, and throwing himself into a chair, he said, 'I can't steal; if we die of hunger, I can't steal.' The wife replied, that she could not bear to see the children famish; and if he would not go she must. She then went out, and a butcher's shop being the first she came to, she snatched a joint of meat and returned home. The butcher saw her; and suspecting the cause, he resolved to follow her, not to bring her to justice, but to learn the truth of his suspicions. He saw her into her house, but did not follow her in for a few minutes. Then, upon opening the door, he actually saw the poor children devouring the mutton in its raw state, and the greater part of it was already gone! The kind butcher not only forgave the theft, but sent the poor family another joint.

2. Two persons who were employed in collecting money for some public charity, knocked at the door of a certain gentleman, intending to solicit his donation. While waiting there, they overheard the master of the house severely reproving his servant for the waste of a small piece of candle. Judging from this appearance of extreme parsimony, that he was a covetous man, one of them proposed that they should lose no more time in waiting there, but go on to another house; the other person, however, thought it best to stay. At length they were introduced, when the gentleman, having read their case, immediately presented them with five guineas. The collectors could not conceal their surprise; which being observed by the donor,

he desired to know why they expressed so much wonder at the gift. 'The reason, sir,' said one of them, 'is this; we happened to hear you severely blaming your servant for losing an inch of candle, and expected nothing from a person, who, we feared, was so parsimonious.' 'Gentlemen,' replied he, 'it is true, I am very exact in the economy of my affairs; I cannot endure the waste of any thing, however small its value; and I do this, that I may save out of a moderate income, something to give to God and religion.'

3. A nobleman lately travelling in Scotland, was asked for alms in the High Street of Edinburgh by a little ragged boy; he said he had no change; upon which the boy offered to procure it. His lordship, in order to get rid of his importunity, gave him a piece of silver, which the boy conceiving was to be changed, ran off for the purpose. On his return, not finding his benefactor, who he expected would have waited, he watched for several days in the place where he had received the money, pursuing his occupation. At length the nobleman happened again to pass that way; he accosted him, and put the change he had procured into his hand, counting it with great exactness. His lordship was so pleased with the boy's honesty, that he placed him at school, and signified his intention of providing for his future advancement in life.

4. There once resided in a country village a poor but worthy clergyman, who, with a small stipend of £40 per annum, supported himself, a wife, and seven children. At one time, walking and meditating in the fields in much distress, from the narrowness of his circumstances, he stumbled on a purse of gold. Looking round in vain to find its owner, he carried it home to his wife, who advised him to employ it, or at least part of it, in extricating them from their present difficulty; but he conscientiously refused, until he had used his utmost endeavours to find out the former owner, assuring her, that honesty is always the best policy. After a short time, it was claimed by a gentleman who lived at some little distance, to whom the clergyman returned it, with no other reward than thanks. On the good man's return, his wife could not help reproaching the gentleman with ingratitude, and censuring the over-scrupulous honesty of her husband: but he only replied as before, honesty is the best policy. A few months after, he received an invitation to dine with the gentleman, who, after hospitably entertaining him, gave him the presentation to a living of £300 per annum, to which he added a gift of £50 for his present necessities. The clergyman, after making suitable acknowledgments to his benefactor, returned with joy to his wife and family, acquainting them with the happy change in his circumstances; and adding, that he hoped she would now be convinced that honesty was the best policy, to which she readily assented.

5. A clergyman was once applied to by a person in his congregation, who had been awakened under his ministry. She had been tempted some years before to steal some trifling articles off the counter of a shop, in a town at some distance. Nothing would satisfy her but an effort to find out the shop, and make restitution. The town was visited, but the same shopkeeper was not there, and every inquiry after him was fruitless; upon which she went to the minister, and gave him a pound for the poor, which was more than fourfold the value of the articles stolen.

H

6. Benjamin Franklin, in his Memoirs, mentions a merchant named Denham, who failed in his business at Bristol, compounded with his creditors, and went to America. In a few years he accumulated a plentiful fortune, returned to England in the same ship with Franklin, called his creditors together to an entertainment, and paid the full remainder of his debts, with interest up to the time of settlement.

7. John Parkhurst, the author of Hebrew and Greek Lexicons, having a tenant who fell behind in the payment of his rent, which was £500 per annum, it was represented to his landlord that it was owing to his being over-rented. A new valuation being made, it was agreed that, for the future, the rent should not be more than £450. Parkhurst justly inferring that if the farm was *then* too dear, it must necessarily have been *always* too dear, unasked, and of his own accord, immediately struck off £50 from the commencement of the lease; and instantly refunded all that he had previously received more than £450 per annum.

8. John Newton relates that a friend of his once dined with Dr Butler, then Bishop of Durham; and though the guest was a man of fortune, and the interview by appointment, the provision was no more than a joint of meat and a pudding. The bishop apologised for this plain fare, saying that it was his manner of living, and that, being disgusted with the fashionable expense of time and money in entertainments, he was determined it should receive no countenance from his example. Nor was his conduct the result of covetousness; for, large as were his revenues, such was his liberality to the poor, that he left at his death little more than enough to discharge his debts and pay for his funeral.

Q. 75. *What is forbidden in the eighth commandment?*

A. The eighth commandment forbiddeth whatsoever doth or may unjustly hinder our own or our neighbour's wealth or outward estate.

1. A gentleman in Surrey held a farm worth £200 a year in his own hands, till he was obliged to sell half of it to pay his debts, and let the other half to a farmer, on a lease of twenty-one years. After a while, the farmer wanted to buy the land. 'How is this,' said the gentleman, 'that I could not live upon the farm, being my own, while you have paid rent, and yet are able to purchase it?' 'Oh,' said the farmer, 'two words make all the difference; you say *go*, and I say *come*; you lay in bed, or took your pleasure, and sent others about your business; and I rise betimes, and see my business done myself.'

2. A blacksmith in the city of Philadelphia, complained to his iron merchant, that such was the scarcity of money, he could not pay his rent. The merchant then asked him how much rum he used in his family in the course of the day. Upon his answering the question, the merchant made a calculation, and showed him, that his rum amounted to more money in

the year than his house-rent. The calculation so astonished the mechanic, that he determined from that day not to buy or drink spirits of any kind. In the course of the next ensuing year, he paid his rent, and bought a suit of new clothes out of the savings of his temperance. He persevered in that habit of temperance through the course of his life; and the consequence was, competence and respectability.

3. A person in Maryland, U.S.A., who was addicted to drunkenness, hearing a considerable uproar in his kitchen one night, felt the curiosity to step without noise to the door, to know what was the matter. He discovered that his servants were indulging in the most unbounded roars of laughter at a couple of Negro boys who were mimicking him in his drunken fits, showing how he reeled and staggered, how he looked and nodded, and hiccupped and tumbled. The pictures which were thus drawn of him, and which filled all the spectators except himself with such merriment, struck him with so salutary a disgust that from that night he became a perfectly sober man, to the great joy of his wife and children. At times the ability to see ourselves as others see us brings our sin home to us with such conviction that it proves sin's cure.

4. Philip, King of Macedon and father of Alexander, having drunk too much wine, judged a cause unjustly, to the hurt of a poor widow, who, when she heard his decision, boldly cried out, 'I appeal from Philip drunk to Philip sober.' The king, struck by this strange appeal, began to recover his senses, heard the cause anew, and finding his mistake, ordered her to be paid, out of his own purse, double the sum she was to have lost.

5. The only sailor who perished in the *Kent* Indiaman, was present in the hold very shortly after the commencement of the fire which destroyed the vessel, when, availing himself of the confusion, he hastened to the cabin of the second mate, forced open a desk, and took from thence 400 sovereigns, which he rolled up in a handkerchief, and tied round his waist; but in attempting to leap into one of the boats, he fell short, and the weight of his spoils caused him immediately to sink.

6. Samuel Kilpin of America, giving an account of his early life, says, 'When seven years old, I was left in charge of the shop. A man passed, crying, "little lambs, and all white and clean, at one penny each." In my eagerness to get one, I lost all self-command, and taking a penny from the drawer, I made the purchase. My keen-eyed, wise mother, inquired how I came by the money. I evaded the question with something like a lie. In God's sight it was a lie, as I kept back the truth. The lamb was placed on the chimney-shelf, and much admired. To me it was a source of inexpressible anguish. Continually there sounded in my ears and heart—"Thou shalt not steal; thou shalt not lie." Guilt and darkness overcame my mind, and in sore agony of soul, I went to a hay-loft, the place is now perfectly in my recollection, and there prayed, and pleaded with groaning that could not be uttered for mercy and pardon. I entreated mercy for Jesus' sake. With joy and transport I left the loft, from a believing application of the text, "Thy sins that are many are all forgiven thee," I went to my mother, told her what I had done, sought her forgiveness, and burnt the lamb, whilst she wept over her young penitent.'

7. One of the teachers in a Sabbath school, going to visit a boy who had been absent, heard the following story related by his mother: 'O mother!' exclaimed the boy, as he entered the house one day, 'something has killed all my rabbits.' Without giving his mother time to reply, he continued, 'It is a judgment of God come upon me, for stealing meat for them; but,' said he, 'I am glad that I have none left, for they would have been a temptation to make me steal again.'

8. Samuel Fairclough, at thirteen years of age, hearing a minister preaching on restitution, from the instance of Zaccheus, and often repeating that the sin was not forgiven unless what was taken were restored, was so touched with remorse for the robbing of an orchard, that after a restless night, he went to a companion of his, who was guilty of the same crime, and told him that he was going to Mr Jude, the owner, to pay him twelve-pence for his three-pence worth of pears, of which he had wronged him. His companion, fearing whipping from his master, answered, 'You talk like a fool, Sam, for God will forgive us ten times sooner than old Jude will forgive us once.' But Sam, being of another mind, went to Jude's house, confessed the injury, and offered the money. Jude pardoned him; but he would take no money. This grieved him more; upon which he made application to the minister and opened to him the whole state of his mind, who received and treated him with great kindness and attention, and gave him suitable counsel. 'This', he wrote, 'contributed to impress me with a special care of exact justice, and the necessity of restitution in the case of things unjustly taken away, being like a burnt child dreading fire.'

9. Thomas Boston states, in his Memoirs, that having been employed, when a young man, for some time, by a notary, his employer failed to pay him for his services. Seeing a neglected book—The Exposition of Matthew's Gospel by David Dickson—lying in the notary's chamber, he secretly took it away, thinking he might lawfully use this method of paying himself: but, on further reflection, he viewed his conduct as sinful, and inconsistent with strict justice, even though he was never paid. Impressed with this conviction, he replaced the book with the same secrecy in which he had taken it away.

10. David Dickson, a minister of the seventeenth century, when riding between Edinburgh and Glasgow, was attacked by robbers. Instead of giving way to his fears, Dickson boldly admonished them of their danger with respect to their souls, and concluded by earnestly exhorting them to try some other profession more safe and creditable than that in which they were engaged. Some years after this, when quietly seated in the College of Edinburgh, he was surprised by receiving the present of a pipe of wine, accompanied with a message that the gentleman who sent it, requested the pleasure of drinking a glass of the wine with him next evening, in his study. The request was granted; and, in the course of conversation, the gentleman, after finding that the minister retained no recollection of having seen him before, informed him that he was one of the robbers who attacked him, that he had been seriously impressed by his admonition, and that, having adopted his advice, he had prospered in foreign trade, and now came to thank his benefactor.

11. Dr George Lawson of Selkirk, when preaching on the eighth com-

mandment, insisted strongly on the duty of restitution. Next morning, a family, from whose house a pair of shoes had been stolen some years before found the price of them lying on the window-sill, placed there by the unknown offender. Ministers draw the bow at a venture, but God directs the arrow to the heart.

12. A widow with a large family was in difficulty over the payment of her rent and her landlord decided to sell her furniture to obtain the sum due to him. George Whitefield learned of her sad plight and gave her the five guineas which she so badly needed. A friend at hand told Whitefield that he could not afford this act of generosity. He replied, 'When God brings a case of distress before us, it is that we may relieve it.' The two men shortly took their journey together, and before long encountered a highwayman who relieved them of their money. Whitefield now turned the tables on his friend, reminding him how much better it was for the widow to have the five guineas than the highwayman. After their loss, the two resumed their journey. Soon, however, the highwayman returned and demanded Whitefield's coat which was so much better than his own. Whitefield of necessity accepted the robber's ragged garment until he could get a better. Presently the same highwayman was for a third time seen galloping furiously towards them, but they spurred on their horses and reached shelter and safety without being overtaken. The robber was doubtless immensely mortified, for when Whitefield took off the tattered coat he found in one of the pockets a small parcel containing a hundred guineas.

Q. 76. *Which is the ninth commandment?*

A. The ninth commandment is, Thou shalt not bear false witness against thy neighbour.

Q. 77. *What is required in the ninth commandment?*

A. The ninth commandment requireth the maintaining and promoting of truth between man and man, and of our own and our neighbour's good name, especially in witness-bearing.

1. Petrarch, a celebrated Italian poet of the fourteenth century, recommended himself to the confidence and affection of Cardinal Colonna, in whose family he resided, by his candour and strict regard to truth. A violent quarrel having occurred in Cardinal Colonna's household, the cardinal, wishing to decide with justice, assembled all his people, and obliged them to bind themselves by a solemn oath on the gospels, to declare the whole truth. Every one, without exception, submitted to this determination: even the cardinal's brother, Bishop of Luna, was not excused. Petrarch, in his turn, presented himself to take the oath; the cardinal closed the book, and said, 'As to you, Petrarch, your word is sufficient.'

2. When George Washington, the president of the United States of America, was about six years of age, some one made him a present of a hatchet. Highly pleased with his weapon, he went about chopping every thing that came in his way; and going into the garden, he unhappily tried its edge on an English cherry tree, stripping it of its bark, and leaving little hope of its recovery. The next morning, when his father saw the tree, which was a great favourite, he inquired who had done the mischief, declaring he would not have taken five guineas for it; but no one could inform him of the offender. At length, however, came George, with the hatchet in his hand, into the place where the father was, who immediately suspected him to be the culprit. 'George,' said the father, 'do you know who killed that beautiful little cherry-tree yonder in the garden?' The child hesitated for a moment, and then said, '*I cannot tell a lie, father,*—you know that I cannot *tell a lie*— I did cut it with the hatchet.' 'Run to my arms. Glad am I, George, that you have killed my tree—you have paid me for it a thousand-fold. Such an act of heroism in my son is of more worth than a thousand cherry-trees, though blossoming with silver, and their fruits of gold.'

3. The Emperor Charles V having given his promise and safe conduct to Luther, to prevail on him to come to Worms, was afterwards urged to violate it by arresting Luther, on this ground, that 'he was a man of that character to whom he was not obliged to keep word.' To which he replied, 'When good faith may be banished from all the earth, it ought to be found with an emperor.'

4. Robert Fleming was a careful observer of that apostolic injunction, 'Speak evil of no man.' He once said to an intimate friend in London: 'I bless God, in fifteen years' time, I have not given any man's credit a thrust behind his back; when I have had grounds to speak well of any man, I have done so with faithfulness; but when I have lacked a subject that way, I have kept silence.'

5. Not many years ago, a man waited on a magistrate near Hitchin, in the county of Hertford, and informed him, that he had been stopped by a young gentleman in Hitchin, who had knocked him down and searched his pockets; but not finding anything, he suffered him to depart. The magistrate, astonished at this piece of intelligence, despatched a messenger to the young gentleman, ordering him to appear immediately, and answer to the charge exhibited against him. The youth obeyed the summons, accompanied by his guardian and an intimate friend. Upon their arrival at the seat of justice, the accused and the accuser were confronted. The magistrate hinted to the man that he was afraid he had made the charge with no other view than that of extorting money, and bade him take care how he proceeded; exhorting him most earnestly, to beware of the dreadful train of consequences attending perjury. The man insisted upon taking oath to what he had advanced; the oath was accordingly administered, and the business fully investigated, when the innocence of the young gentleman was established by the most incontrovertible evidence. The infamous wretch, finding his intentions thus frustrated, returned home much chagrined; and meeting soon afterwards with one of his neighbours, he declared he had not sworn to any thing but the truth, calling God to witness the same in the most

solemn manner, and wished, if it was not as he had said, his jaws might be locked, and that his flesh might rot upon his bones. It is recorded that his jaws were instantly arrested, and the use of the faculty he had so awfully perverted was denied him for ever! After lingering nearly a fortnight, he expired in the greatest agonies, his flesh literally rotting upon his bones.

Q. 78. *What is forbidden in the ninth commandment?*

A. The ninth commandment forbiddeth whatsoever is prejudicial to truth, or injurious to our own or our neighbour's good name.

1. 'It was but the other night,' says a godly gentleman, 'that I wandered across the bleak and barren mountains, at the foot of which stands the little cottage where I was born; and, O delightful thought, born again! Yes, it was at the humble spot that I first tasted the bitter cup of true repentance, and drank of the spring of peace, purity, and joy; the remembrance of which often fills my eyes with tears, and my heart with rapture. Seeing a cottage at a distance, I walked up to it, entered, and told the inmates the cause of my being there. I was most kindly received. Seven children were seated around the homely board; yet, sadness seemed to pervade the whole circle. When I asked the cause, the mother informed me that one of the children had been telling a falsehood; upon this a little girl was instantly covered with blushes, and a tear started from her eye. "Robert," said the father, "bring the Bible, and show your sister who it is she has offended." The little boy, younger than herself, read the ninth commandment, and the first eleven verses of the fifth chapter of the Acts. This being done, every member of the family brought a proof from Scripture of the sin and danger of lying. The father, then, with much affection, showed them that this was as offensive to God now, as it was when he struck Ananias and Sapphira dead; and that it was of the Lord's mercies we were not consumed. He then sung the 51st psalm, read a portion of the Word of God, frequently making pious and solemn observations as he went along, and afterwards prayed with his children most devoutly. On rising from prayer the offending girl wept bitterly. She approached her father with pensive looks, begged him to forgive the offence, and withdrew, that she might pray alone to God for His forgiveness. I was of course highly gratified. I returned home under the deep impression of the awfulness of the sin of lying, and could not help wishing that all parents would correct their children in a similar way, whenever they offended in a similar manner.'

2. 'Many years ago,' says a writer, 'I was witness to a very interesting scene at the house of a friend at Walworth, on a Sunday evening. A sermon had been preached in the morning, of which previous notice had been given, particularly addressed to poor children; and the master of the family had taken his own children to hear the discourse, having promised to distribute rewards amongst them, according to the proficiency with which they should

repeat the text, and state the heads and points of the sermon. As I entered the parlour, I was struck with the silent employment of the children, who were engaged in preparing themselves for their task; and after tea, they were called up in order. At this distance of time I remember only two circumstances connected with the result. One is, that the memories of the female children, in general, seemed better, and the facility of imparting their ideas greater, than those of the male branches of the family. The other relates to the youngest of the children, a little boy, who, though not expected to say any thing, requested to be heard. The text was too long for him to remember, but he delighted us all by the simple account which he gave of the sermon in the following words: "I heard the gentleman (the minister) say, *it was no disgrace to be poor, but it was a disgrace to tell lies.*" '

3. One day there happened a tremendous storm of lightning and thunder, as Archbishop Leighton was going from Glasgow to Dunblane. He was observed, when at a distance, by two men of bad character. They had not courage to rob him; but wishing to fall on some method of extorting money from him, one said, 'I will lie down by the wayside as if I were dead, and you shall inform the archbishop that I was killed by the lightning, and beg money of him to bury me.' When the archbishop arrived at the spot, the wicked wretch told him the fabricated story. He sympathized with the survivor, gave him money, and proceeded on his journey. But when the man returned to his companion he found him really lifeless. Immediately he began to exclaim, 'Oh, sir, he is dead! Oh, sir, he is dead!' On this, the archbishop, discovering the fraud, left the man with this important reflection, 'It is a dangerous thing to trifle with the judgments of God.'

4. Not long ago, a young girl, having stolen a silver spoon from her mother, who was blind, was accused by her of the theft, and repeatedly denied it. On being pressed with the charge, and conceiving what she had further to say might silence any more inquiry, she exclaimed, 'May God strike me dead if I have the spoon!' Judgment was visited on her instantly! She fell dead. On stripping the clothes from the body, there was found to the astonishment of all, the very article of which she had so positively declared her ignorance.

5. Inscription on the Market-Place of Devizes: 'The mayor and corporation of Devizes avail themselves of the stability of this building to transmit to future times the record of an awful event, which occurred in the market-place, in the year 1753—hoping that such record may serve as a salutary warning against the danger of impiously invoking Divine vengeance, or calling on the holy name of God, to conceal the devices of falsehood and fraud. On Tuesday, January, 1753, Ruth Pierce of Potterne in this county, agreed with three other women to buy a sack of wheat in the market, each paying her due proportion toward the same. One of the women, in collecting the money, discovered a deficiency, and demanded of Ruth Pierce the sum that was wanting to make good the amount. Ruth protested that she had paid her share, and said, she wished she might drop down dead if she had not. She rashly repeated the awful wish—when, to the consternation and terror of the surrounding multitude, she instantly fell down and expired, having the money concealed in her hand.'

6. Once, while the celebrated Robert Hall was spending an evening at the house of a friend, a lady who was there on a visit, retired, that her little girl of four years old, might go to bed. She returned in about half an hour, and said to a lady near her, 'She is gone to sleep. I put on my night-cap, and lay down by her, and she soon dropped off.' Hall, who overheard this, said, 'Excuse me, madam, do you wish your child to grow up a liar?' 'O dear no, sir; I should be shocked at such a thing.' 'Then bear with me while I say, you must never act a lie before her; children are very quick observers, and soon learn that that which assumes to be what it is not, is a lie, whether acted or spoken.' This was uttered with a kindness which precluded offence, yet with a seriousness that could not be forgotten.

7. The following may serve as a warning to young persons, against deception of every kind. A young man in a seaport town about seventy miles from London, was an excellent swimmer, and very fond of bathing. He frequently used to amuse himself, and deceive the boatmen, by swimming to a certain distance from the shore, and then pretend to be drowning; and when they had taken some trouble to come to his assistance, he would swim away, and laugh at them. One day, as he was bathing, he unfortunately entangled himself in the weeds, so that he could not extricate himself by any means. A boat was coming down the river, but he cried in vain to the men for assistance as they had so often been deceived by him. However, they watched him a short time, and began to suspect that he really wanted their assistance. They immediately went to him, but his spirit had taken its flight.

8. When any one was speaking ill of another, in the presence of Peter the Great, he at first listened to him attentively, and then interrupted him. 'Is there not,' said he, 'a fair side also to the character of the person of whom you are speaking? Come, tell me what good qualities you have noticed about him!'

Q. 79. *Which is the tenth commandment?*

A. The tenth commandment is, Thou shalt not covet thy neighbour's house, thou shalt not covet thy neighbour's wife, nor his man-servant, nor his maid-servant, nor his ox, nor his ass, nor any thing that is thy neighbour's.

Q. 80. *What is required in the tenth commandment?*

A. The tenth commandment requireth full contentment with our own condition, with a right and charitable frame of spirit toward our neighbour, and all that is his.

1. 'No doubt,' said John Brown of Haddington, 'I have met with trials as well as others; yet so kind has God been to me, that I think, if God were to give me as many years as I have already lived in the world, I would not

desire one single circumstance in my lot changed, except that I wish I had less sin. It might be written on my coffin, Here lies one of the cares of Providence, who early wanted both father and mother, and yet never missed them.'

2. An Italian bishop struggled through great difficulties without repining, and met with much opposition without ever betraying the least impatience. An intimate friend of his, who highly admired those virtues, which he thought it impossible to imitate, one day asked the bishop if he could communicate his secret of being always easy? 'Yes,' replied the old man, 'I can teach you my secret with great facility: It consists in nothing more than making a right use of my eyes.' His friend begged him to explain himself. 'Most willingly,' replied the bishop; 'in whatever state I am, I first of all look up to heaven, and remember that my principal business here, is to get there; I then look down on the earth, and call to mind how small a space I shall occupy in it when I am to be interred; I then look abroad on the world, and observe what multitudes there are who are, in all respects, more unhappy than myself. Thus I learn where true happiness is placed, where all our cares must end, and how very little reason I have to repine or complain.'

3. The danger of wealth and elevation may, with propriety, be used as a motive to contentment in a humble state. It is said of Pope Pius V that when dying he cried out despairingly, 'When I was in a low condition, I had some hopes of salvation; when I was advanced to be a cardinal, I greatly doubted it; but since I came to the popedom, I have no hope at all!'

4. If discontented persons would but look with a more impartial eye on the world, they would see themselves surrounded with sufferers; and find that they are only drinking out of that mixed cup which Providence has prepared for all. 'I will restore thy daughter again to life,' said an eastern sage, to a prince who grieved immoderately for the loss of a beloved child, 'provided thou art able to engrave on her tomb the names of three persons who have never mourned.' The prince made inquiry after such persons, but found the inquiry vain, and was silent.

5. The Greenlanders, David Crantz the missionary-historian tells us, are naturally the most selfish people in the world, and unwilling ever to give to any one, unless they hope for a return; and quite careless even for the welfare of their own friends and countrymen. When, however, the little flock of Greenlanders who had been converted to the faith of Christ were told by the missionaries of the distress to which the Christian Indians of North America were brought by a fire, which had destroyed their settlements, their hearts, now melted by the love of Christ, were full of love to His members, and their brethren in Him. With many tears, they heartily offered to do all in their power to relieve their sufferings. They had no money to give: 'but,' cried one, 'I have a fine reindeer skin—take it.' Another said, 'Here, I will give a new pair of reindeer boots.' Another offered a stock of train oil, 'that they may,' said he, 'have something to burn in their lamps, and a seal, that they may have somewhat to eat.' These gifts were of little value when turned into money; but the missionaries would not refuse the mite of the poor Greenlanders, who offered it with true joy: and they sent the value of their gifts to North America.

6. Two neighbouring farmers had a dispute about their right to some property, which they could not settle, and therefore an action was brought to determine it. On the day of the trial, one of the farmers, having dressed himself in his best clothes, called upon the other to accompany him to the judge, when he found his neighbour at work in his ground; on which he said, 'Is it possible that you can have forgotten that our cause is to be decided to-day?' 'No,' said the other, 'I have not forgotten it, but I cannot well spare the time to go; I knew you would be there, and I am sure you are an honest man, and will say nothing but the truth. You will state the case fairly, and justice will be done.' And so it turned out, for the farmer who attended, stated his neighbour's claims so clearly that he lost the case, and returned home to inform him that he had gained the property.

7. A very gratifying instance of generosity and kindly feeling was lately witnessed among the boys of a Sabbath school. One of their number having been absent for several Sabbaths, the boys were informed that the cause was his having no shoes, his parents being too poor to buy him any. The next Sabbath, they freely contributed a sufficient sum to enable their schoolfellow to appear among them, at their next meeting in school, with new shoes.

8. During the prevalence of the small-pox in Greenland, which proved very fatal, the Moravian missionaries showed the greatest kindness and attention to the poor inhabitants; they accommodated as many as their house would contain, surrendering to the afflicted even their own sleeping chambers; and thus though unable to make themselves distinctly understood by words, they preached by their conduct, and not without effect. One man who always derided them when in health, expressed his obligation to the minister shortly before he died: 'Thou hast done for us what our own people would not do; for thou hast fed us when we had nothing to eat— thou hast buried our dead, who would else have been consumed by the dogs, foxes, and ravens—thou hast also instructed us in the knowledge of God— and hast told us of a better life.'

Q. 81. *What is forbidden in the tenth commandment?*

A. The tenth commandment forbiddeth all discontentment with our own estate, envying or grieving at the good of our neighbour, and all inordinate motions and affections to any thing that is his.

1. 'When I was a lad,' says one, 'an old gentleman took some trouble to teach me some little knowledge of the world. With this view, I remember, he once asked me, when a man was rich enough? I replied, when he had a thousand pounds. He said, No.—Two thousand? No.—Ten thousand? No. —Twenty thousand? No.—An hundred thousand? which I thought would settle the business; but he still continuing to say no, I gave it up, and confessed I could not tell, but begged he would inform me. He gravely said,

When he has a little more than he has, and that is never! If he acquires one thousand, he wishes to have two thousand; then five, then ten, then twenty, then fifty; from that his riches would amount to a hundred thousand, and so on, till he had grasped the whole world; after which he would look about him, like Alexander, for other worlds to possess.'

2. A young person once mentioned to Benjamin Franklin his surprise that the possession of great riches should ever be attended with undue solicitude; and instanced a merchant, who, although in possession of unbounded wealth, was as busy as the most assiduous clerk in his counting-house, and much more anxious. The doctor, in reply, took an apple from the fruit basket, and presented it to a child in the room, who could scarcely grasp it in his hand. He then gave it a second, which filled the other hand; and choosing a third, remarkable for its size and beauty, he presented that also. The child, after many ineffectual attempts to hold the three apples, dropped the last on the carpet, and burst into tears: 'See, there,' said he, 'is a little man with more riches than he can enjoy.'

3. Dr. William Dodd, author and clergyman, in early life was an associate of Bishop Horne, Jones of Nayland, and, it is believed, of Wm. Romaine, and other religious persons of that age: and it was hoped that he would have continued in fellowship with them and their connections. But he yielded to the seductions of the world, became giddy with popular applause, sought and obtained admission within the circles of high life, gained preferment and royal favour, and eventually was a stranger among the companions of his better days. He was conscious of this desertion, and, on one occasion, meeting with a lady who belonged to the party he had abandoned, he asked her, what his former associates thought of him; she only answered, 'Demas hath forsaken us, having loved this present world'—a reply which, at the moment, deeply affected its object. Dr Dodd, however, pursued his career; and finally endeavouring, and with success, to defraud his former pupil, Lord Chesterfield, by forging his name to a financial document, he was convicted and executed.

4. Mutius, a citizen of Rome, was noted to be of so envious and malevolent a disposition, that Publius, one day observing him to be very sad, said 'Either some great evil has happened to Mutius, or some great good to another.'

5. A countryman presented Louis XI of France with a turnip of unusual size. The king, delighted with the simplicity of the man, commanded him to be presented with a thousand crowns; and the turnip (wrapped up in silk) to be reserved among his treasures. A covetous courtier observing this, in hopes of a greater sum, bought a very handsome horse, and made a present of him to the king, who cheerfully accepted the gift, and gave orders that the turnip should be presented to him, telling him it cost a thousand crowns.

6. A lady and gentleman, when taking a morning ride in their carriage, passed some reapers in a field near the road, immediately after they had finished their dinner. They were amusing themselves in the most cheerful and jovial manner. The lady asked her husband, whether he thought the reapers or they were the happier. 'There can be no difficulty,' said he, 'in

answering that question—undoubtedly *they* are by far the happier.' 'Do you suppose they think so?' 'No, I am certain they do not; for very probably some of them are now saying of us "O how happy these people must be, who have nothing else to do but to sit in their carriage, to look about them, and when they are tired, to go home to a good dinner: but here we must toil from morning to night for a poor pittance." '

7. A gentleman was once extolling at an extravagant rate the virtue of honesty; what a dignity it imparted to our nature; how it recommended us to the Supreme Being. He confirmed all by a celebrated line from Alexander Pope,

'An honest man's the noblest work of God.'

'Sir,' replied one, 'however excellent the virtue of honesty may be, I fear there are few men in the world that really possess it.' 'You surprise me,' said the stranger. 'Ignorant as I am of your character, sir, I fancy it would be no difficult matter to prove even you a dishonest man.' 'I defy you.' 'Will you give me leave then to ask you a question or two, and promise not to be offended?' 'Ask your questions and welcome.' 'Have you ever met with an opportunity of getting gain by unfair means?' The gentleman paused. 'I don't ask whether you made use of, but whether you have met with such opportunity. I for my part have, and I believe everybody else has.' 'Very probably I may.' 'How did you feel your mind affected on such an occasion? Had you no secret desire, not the *least* inclination to seize the advantage which offered? Tell me without any evasion, and consistently with the character you admire.' 'I must acknowledge, I have not always been absolutely free from every irregular *inclination*; but—' 'Hold, sir, none of your salvos, you have confessed enough. If you had the desire, though you never pursued it further, this shows you were dishonest in *heart*. This is what the Scriptures call concupiscence. It defiles the soul. It is a breach of that law which requires truth in the *inward parts;* and unless you are pardoned by the blood of Christ, it will be a just ground of your condemnation, when God shall judge the secrets of men.'

Q. 82. *Is any man able perfectly to keep the commandments of God?*

A. No mere man, since the fall, is able in this life perfectly to keep the commandments of God, but both daily break them in thought, word, and deed.

1. Dr John Gill was once preaching on human inability. A gentleman present was much offended, and took him to task for degrading human nature. 'Pray, sir,' said the doctor, 'what do you think that man can contribute to his conversion?' He enumerated a variety of particulars. 'And have you done all this?' said the doctor. 'Why, no, I cannot say I have yet; but I hope I shall begin soon.' 'If you have these things in your power, and have not done them, you deserve to be doubly damned, and are but ill qualified to be an advocate for free-will, which has done you so little good.'

2. Anne de Montmorency, a marshal of France, having been mortally

wounded at an engagement, was exhorted by those who stood around him, to die like a good Christian, and with the same courage which he had shown in his lifetime. To this he replied in the following manner: 'Gentlemen and fellow-soldiers! I thank you all very kindly for your anxious care and concern about me: but the man who has been enabled to endeavour to *live well*, for almost four score years past, can never need to seek now, how to *die well* for a quarter of an hour. But observe, my having been enabled to endeavour to live well, is not the ground of my dependence; no, my sole dependence is on Jesus Christ. It is by the grace of God, through Him, that I now am what I am.'

3. Some years ago, two pious weavers were conversing together, and complaining of the trouble which they found from vain and evil *thoughts* in the solemn duties of religion. Another person of the same business overheard them, and rushing forth, said, 'I always thought you two vile hypocrites; but now I know it from your own confession. For my part, I never had such vain and wicked thoughts in my life.' One of the men took a piece of money out of his pocket, and put it into his hand, adding, 'This shall be yours, if, after you come from the church the next time, you can say you had not one vain thought there.' In a few days he came, saying, 'Here take back your money, for I had not been five minutes in the church before I began to think how many looms could be set up in it.'

4. It is related of one of the ancients, that a man without learning came to him to be taught a psalm. He turned to the 39th, but when he had heard the first verse of it, 'I said, I will take heed to my ways, that I sin not with my tongue,' the man would hear no more, saying, this was enough, if he could practise it; and when the instructor blamed him, that he had not seen him for six months, he replied that he had not done the verse; and forty years after, he confessed he had been all that time studying it, but had not learned to fulfil it. 'If any man offend not in word, the same is a perfect man, and able also to bridle the whole body' (James 3. 2).

5. A young man of rank and fortune, just returned from making the grand tour on the Continent of Europe, had tinged himself with most of the vices and follies of the places through which he travelled. Among other *accomplishments* of this nature, he had gained a little knowledge of the *creative art*, which he frequently graced with an endless volubility of tongue. One day in particular, he was dealing out accounts of the number of presents which he had received while abroad, especially a rich bridle from the Emperor of Russia, the ornaments of which were of gold. 'It was so exquisitely fine,' said his lordship, 'that it can never be used in the mouth of a filthy horse. What shall I do with it, Colonel?' continued he to an old veteran in the army. '*Put it on your tongue, my lord*,' answered the soldier. His lordship was silenced.

6. A woman, professing to be under deep conviction, went to a minister, crying aloud that she was a sinner; but when he came to examine her in what point, though he went over and explained all the ten commandments, she would not own that she had broken one of them.

Q. 83. *Are all transgressions of the law equally heinous?*

A. Some sins in themselves, and by reasons of several ag-gravations, are more heinous in the sight of God than others.

1. On the 4th August, 1796, between eleven and twelve o'clock in the forenoon, a violent storm of thunder and lightning arose in the district of Montpellier, Southern France. In a field about a mile from the town, a body of nine hundred soldiers lay encamped. At a small distance from the camp, five of the soldiers were assisting a husbandman in gathering in the produce of the earth, for hire. When the storm came on, the whole party took refuge under a tree, where the five soldiers began to blaspheme God for interrupt-ing them in their labour; and one of them, in the madness of his presump-tion, took up his firelock, which he happened to have by him, and pointing it towards the skies, said he would fire a bullet at Him who sent the storm! Seized with horror at this blasphemous declaration, the husbandman made all the haste he could to quit their company; but scarcely had he got the dis-tance of ten paces from the tree, when a flash of lightning struck four of the soldiers dead, and wounded the fifth in such a manner, that his life was despaired of.

2. When that truly devoted missionary, Henry Martyn, was at Shiraz in Persia, translating the New Testament into the language of that country, he seems to have been delighted with the following incident, which he notices in his journal, June 28, 1811: 'The poor boy,' says he, 'while writing how one of the servants of the high priest struck the Lord on the face, stopped and said, Sir, *did not his hand dry up?*'

3. Edmund Bonner, Bishop of London, was one of the most bloody instru-ments of persecution during the cruel reign of Mary Tudor of England. Being confined in the Tower of London upon the accession of Queen Eliza-beth, which was the highest punishment inflicted on him, he went to visit some of the criminals kept in that prison, and wishing to ingratiate them, called them his *friends and companions.* One of them bade him begone, for they were none of his friends; adding, 'I killed but one man on a provoca-tion, and do truly repent of it; but you have killed many holy persons of all sorts, without any provocation from them, and are hardened in your im-penitence.' This fact is told by Bishop Jewel, in a letter to Peter Martyr.

4. 'I was lately called,' says one, 'to visit a sick person. On entering the room, I found him very weak in body, and troubled in mind. Seeing the Bible lying upon a table, near the chair upon which he sat, I said, "You have a blessed book here." "Yes," he replied; "but the sight of it is like a dagger to my heart." "Cannot you read it?" "O yes, yes! I have read it again and again; but I have not properly regarded it, nor minded what I read in it; it condemns my conduct—it troubles my mind, and now—O what must become of my soul!" I could not attempt, nor did I wish, to justify such neglect; I therefore spoke in a plain manner against such a course, and at the same time pointed out Jesus as the only possible means of escape, and way by which pardon and peace could be obtained. The advice

seemed to increase his sorrow and anguish. I closed the visit with prayer, and left the room, deeply impressed with the words of the wise man, "The spirit of a man will sustain his infirmity, but a wounded spirit who can bear?" Not many days after, I committed the mortal part to the earth, from whence it was taken, and the soul has been summoned to the bar of that God who gave it.'

5. An Indian chief, having been at one time a little intoxicated, his friend said to him, 'There is one thing very strange, and what I cannot account for —it is why the Indians get so much more drunk than the white people!' 'Do you think that to be strange?' said the old chief, 'it is not strange at all. The Indians think it no harm to get drunk whenever they can; but you white men say it is a sin, and get drunk nevertheless!'

Q. 84. *What doth every sin deserve?*

A. Every sin deserveth God's wrath and curse, both in this life, and that which is to come.

1. 'Walking in the country (says William Jay of Bath), I went into a barn, where I found a thrasher at his work. I addressed him in the words of Solomon, "My friend, in all labour there is profit." But what was my surprise, when, leaning upon his flail, he answered, and with much energy, "No, sir; that is the truth, but there is one exception from it: I have long laboured in the service of sin, but I got no profit by my labour." "Then," answered I, "you know something of the apostle's meaning, when he asked, *What fruit had ye in those things whereof ye are now ashamed?*" "Thank God," he replied, "I do; and I also know, that now, being freed from sin, and having become a servant unto righteousness, I have my fruit unto holiness, and the end everlasting life." '

2. A German prince travelling through France, visited the arsenal at Toulon, where the galleys were kept. The commandant, as a compliment to his rank, said he was welcome to set any one galley-slave at liberty, whom he should choose to select. The prince, willing to make the best use of his privilege, spoke to many of them in succession inquiring why they were condemned to the galleys. Injustice, oppression, false accusation, were the only causes they could assign; they were all innocent and ill-treated. At last he came to one, who, when he had asked the question, answered to this effect: 'My lord, I have no reason to complain. I have been a very desperate, wicked wretch; I have often deserved to be broken alive upon the wheel. I account it a great mercy that I am here.' The prince fixed his eyes upon him, gave him a gentle blow upon the head, and said, 'You wicked wretch, it is a pity you should be placed among so many honest men. By your own confession, you are bad enough to corrupt them all; but you shall not stay with them another day.' Then, turning to the officer, he said, 'This is the man, sir, whom I wish to be released.'

3. A venerable minister once preached a sermon on the subject of eternal punishment. On the next day, it was agreed among some thoughtless young

men, that one of them should go to him, and endeavour to draw him into a dispute, with the design of making a jest of him and of his doctrine. The wag accordingly went, was introduced into the minister's study, and commenced the conversation, by saying, 'I believe there is a small dispute between you and me, sir, and I thought I would call this morning and try to settle it.' 'Ah,' said the clergyman, 'what is it?' 'Why', replied the wag, 'you say that the wicked will go into everlasting punishment, and I do not think that they will.' 'Oh, if that is all,' answered the minister, 'there is no dispute between you and *me*. If you turn to Matt. 25. 46, you will find that the dispute is between you and the *Lord Jesus Christ*, and I advise you to go immediately and settle it with Him.'

4. Some time ago, a gentleman on Long Island, North America, was making too free with the Bible, and brought forward his strong argument against it, declaring in the face of all present, 'I am seventy years of age, and have never seen such a place as hell, after all that has been said about it.' His little grandson, of about seven years of age, who was all the while listening to the conversation, asked him, 'Grand-dad, have you ever been dead yet?'

Q. 85. *What doth God require of us, that we may escape His wrath and curse due to us for sin?*

A. To escape the wrath and curse of God due to us for sin, God requireth of us faith in Jesus Christ, repentance unto life, with the diligent use of all the outward means whereby Christ communicateth to us the benefits of redemption.

1. 'A pious young physician,' says one, 'whose father I knew, and of whose excellent character I had often heard, called on me one day, and after friendly salutations and expressions of Christian affection, said, "Do you know, sir, how much I am indebted to you for giving me a tract many years ago?" I told him I had no knowledge of ever presenting him with one; but recollecting that his father formerly kept a turnpike gate, and that often when I stopped to pay my toll, I used to give tracts to the children who were playing about the door, it occurred to me as possible, that on some of these occasions he had been among them. "When I was a boy," said he, "you gave me a tract, as you were riding by my father's house, and the first words that caught my eye were,

'Stop, poor sinner, stop and think.'

I was much affected with the whole hymn, beginning with these words, and committed it to memory. Five years ago, while a member of a university, in a time of universal attention to religion, I was present at a meeting for prayer and other devotional exercises, when they commenced singing the hymn,

'Stop, poor sinner, stop and think.'

My early impressions were all instantly revived; I saw that I was ruined by

I

sin; that an eternity of woe was before me; and I found no peace till I looked to the Saviour crucified for me; and, as I hope, by true repentance and faith in His blood, gave myself to Him, to be His for ever." ' The youth is now an active, godly praying physician.

2. John Brown of Haddington, towards the close of life, when his constitution was sinking under his multiplied and ceaseless labours, preached on the Monday after the dispensation of the Lord's Supper at Tranent near Edinburgh, a serious and animated sermon from these words: 'The grace of our Lord Jesus Christ be with you all. Amen.' After the service was concluded by prayer and praise, and he was just about to dismiss the congregation it occurred to him, that he had made no direct address to those who were destitute of the grace of the Lord Jesus; and, though worn out by his former exertions, he, at considerable length, and with most intense earnestness, represented the horrors of their situation, and urged them to have recourse, ere the season of forbearance was past, to the rich and sovereign grace of the long-despised Saviour. This unlooked-for exhortation apparently made a deep impression, and was long remembered by the more serious part of the hearers.

3. A certain man on the Malabar coast of India, having inquired of various devotees and priests how he might make atonement for his sins, was directed to drive iron spikes, sufficiently blunted, through his sandals; and on these spikes, he was enjoined to place his naked feet, and to walk about four hundred and eighty miles. If, through loss of blood, or weakness of body he was obliged to halt, he might wait for healing and strength. He undertook the journey, and while he halted under a large shady tree, where the gospel was sometimes preached, one of the missionaries came and preached in his hearing from these words: 'The blood of Jesus Christ, God's Son, cleanseth from all sin.' (1 John 1. 7). While he was preaching, the man rose up, threw off his torturing sandals, and cried out aloud—'This is what I want:' and he became a lively witness, that the blood of Jesus Christ does indeed cleanse from all sin.

4. In a Sabbath-school in Southwark, London, two instances of great diligence in committing the Word of God to memory, once occurred. In the twelvemonth from October 1826 to October 1827, William M—— repeated to his teacher all the chapters from the 11th of Luke, to the end of the 2nd Epistle to Timothy, besides various chapters from other parts of the Bible, making a total of above six thousand verses of Scripture. Another boy, in the same class, named James J——, committed to memory, and repeated to his teacher, from the New Testament, from the 14th chapter of Luke to the end of the Revelation; and, from the Old Testament, the whole of Proverbs, Ecclesiastes, Solomon's Song, and Isaiah, besides a few other chapters, making, in the whole, a total of above eight thousand verses repeated to his teacher in one year, which forms an average of one hundred and fifty verses every week. These two boys learned these portions of Scripture, in addition to the weekly lessons which were set them in common with the other boys in the class; and they learned them of their own accord. The teachers of the school wishing to encourage such uncommon application to the Scriptures, gave to each of them, as a token of their approbation,

a small gilt-edged Bible, with which the boys were much pleased and gratified.

5. A clergyman in the county of Tyrone (Ulster), had for some weeks observed a little ragged boy come every Sabbath, and place himself in the centre of the aisle, directly opposite the pulpit, where he seemed astonishingly attentive to the service, and, as it were, *eating* his words. He was desirous of knowing who the child was; and for this purpose hastened out after sermon, several times, but never could see him, as he vanished the moment service was over, and no one knew whence he came, or any thing about him. At length the boy was missed from his usual situation in the church for some weeks. At this time a man called on the minister, and told him a person very ill was desirous of seeing him; but added, 'I am really ashamed to ask you to go so far, but it is a child of mine, and he refused to have any one but you. He is altogether an extraordinary boy, and talks a great deal about things that I do not understand.' The clergyman promised to go, and kept his promise. The rain poured down in torrents, and he had six miles of rugged mountain to pass. On arriving where he was directed, he saw a most wretched cabin indeed; and the man he had seen in the morning was waiting at the door. He was shown in, and found the inside of the hovel as miserable as the outside. In a corner, on a little straw, he beheld a person stretched out, whom he recognised as the little boy who had so regularly attended his church. As he approached the wretched bed, the child raised himself up, and stretching forth his arms said, 'His own right hand hath gotten Him the victory,' and immediately expired!

6. Thomas Halyburton, when a young man, was asked by an aged minister, if he had ever sought a blessing from the Lord upon his learning. Halyburton confessed that he had not. The reverend man, looking him sternly in the face, replied, 'Unsanctified learning has done much harm to the church.' Halyburton was more conscientious afterwards in acknowledging God while pursuing his studies.

7. An incident is related in the life of Dr Robert Balmer, showing how early he had learned to think and reason on religious questions. When about ten years of age, an old man, a neighbour, came frequently at leisure hours to converse with his parents. This person was harrassed with doubts and fears about his interest in the Saviour. One day Robert listened while his mother argued with the man, and endeavoured to persuade him to dismiss his fears, and to commit himself trustingly to Christ. It was in vain. He still reiterated, 'Christ will have nothing to do with me.' Robert perceiving, it would seem, that the man was speaking under the influence of morbid feeling, and wilfully putting away consolation, at last put in his word. 'Then what is the use of your aye talk talking about Him to my mother? If He'll have nothing to do with you, can't you let Him alone?' 'Let Him alone, hinney!' the man replied, 'I would not let Him alone for a thousand worlds.' 'O then,' said the boy, 'I'm thinking you'll do well enough.'

Q. 86. *What is faith in Jesus Christ?*

A. Faith in Jesus Christ is a saving grace, whereby we receive and rest upon Him alone for salvation, as He is offered to us in the gospel.

1. 'Children,' says Richard Cecil, 'are capable of very early impressions. I imprinted on my daughter the idea of faith at a very early age. She was playing one day with a few beads, which seemed wonderfully to delight her. Her whole soul was absorbed in her beads. I said, "My dear, you have some pretty beads there?" "Yes, father." "And you seem vastly pleased with them? Well, now, throw them behind the fire." The tears started into her eyes; she looked earnestly at me, as if she ought to have a reason for so cruel a sacrifice. "Well, my dear, do as you please; but you know, I never told you to do any thing which I did not think would be for your good." She looked at me a few minutes longer, and then summoning up all her fortitude, her breast heaving with the effort, she dashed them into the fire. "Well," said I, "there let them lie; you shall hear more about them another time; but say no more of them now." Some days after, I bought her a box-ful of larger beads and toys of the same kind. When I returned home, I opened the treasure, and set it before her: she burst into tears of excessive joy. "These, my child," said I, "are yours, because you believed me when I told you to throw those paltry beads behind the fire; your obedience has brought you this treasure. But now, my dear, remember as long as you live, what FAITH is. I did all this to teach you the meaning of faith. You threw your beads away when I bade you, because you had faith in me, that I never advised you but for your good. Put the same confidence in God; believe every thing that He says in His Word. Whether you understand it or not, have faith in Him that He means your good." '

2. Walter Marshall, author of *The Gospel Mystery of Sanctification*, having been for several years under distress of mind, consulted Thomas Goodwin, an eminent divine, giving him an account of the state of his soul, and particularizing his sins, which lay heavy on his conscience. In reply, Goodwin told him he had forgotten to mention the greatest sin of all, the sin of unbelief, in not believing on the Lord Jesus Christ for the remission of his sins, and for the sanctifying of his nature. On this he set himself to the studying and preaching of Christ, and attained to eminent holiness, great peace of conscience, and joy in the Holy Ghost. Marshall's dying words were these: 'The wages of sin is death, but the gift of God is eternal life through Jesus Christ our Lord.'

3. A student at a theological academy was brought, in the course of providence, into the company of a young lady, who was just recovering from a dangerous illness. Speaking of her illness among other things, she said, 'At one time I sent for my parents, and beloved brothers and sisters, and took, as I thought, my last farewell of them. The physicians had given me up, and my friends expected to see me no more.' 'We seldom meet with a person,' said the student, 'who has been so near to death as you have been.

Tell me what were your feelings when you were on the verge of eternity?' 'I was happy,' she replied. 'And will you please to tell me what were your prospects?' 'I hoped to go to heaven, of course.' 'Had you no doubts, no fears, no suspicions?' 'None.' 'Perhaps almost all hope to go to heaven,' said the young man, 'but I fear there are very few who have a good founda- tion for their hope. On what was your hope founded?' 'Founded!' she replied, 'why, I had never injured any person, and I had endeavoured to do all the good in my power—was not this sufficient?' 'It is a delightful reflection,' said the student, 'that you have never injured any person, and it is still more delightful to think that you have done all the good in your power; but this is a poor foundation for a sinner to rest upon—was *this* the foundation of your hope?' She seemed quite astonished at the question, and eagerly inquired, 'Is not this sufficient?' The student did not give a direct answer, but observed, 'I am very thankful that you did not die.' 'What! do you think I should not have gone to heaven?' 'I am sure you could not in the way you mentioned. Do you not perceive that, according to your plan, you were going to heaven *without Christ?*—a thing which no sinner has done since Adam fell, and which no sinner will be able to do while the world stands. Be very thankful that you did not go out of life resting on this delu- sive foundation; for had you done so, the moment that you entered eternity it would have given way, and you would have fallen through it into the bottomless pit. Jesus says, "I am the Way, the Truth, and the Life; no man cometh to the Father but by Me." ' God carried home this word to her soul; light broke in upon her mind. From that day a decided change took place in the young lady's views; and a corresponding holiness, and love, and zeal, and usefulness adorned her life.

4. Dr. John Mitchell Mason, of New York, was requested to visit a dying lady who, together with her husband, openly avowed infidel principles, though they attended his ministry. On approaching her bedside, he asked if she felt herself a sinner, and her need of a Saviour. She frankly told him she did not, and that she believed the doctrine of a Mediator to be all a farce. 'Then,' said the doctor, 'I have no consolation for you, not one word of comfort. There is not a single passage in the Bible that warrants me to speak peace to one who rejects the Mediator provided; you must take the consequences of your infidelity.' He was on the point of leaving the room, when one said, 'Well, if you cannot speak consolation to her, you can pray for her.' To this he assented, and kneeling down by the bedside, prayed for her as a guilty sinner just sinking into hell; and then arising from his knees, he left the house. To his great surprise, a day or two after, he received a mes- sage from the lady herself, earnestly desiring that he would come down and see her, and that without delay. He immediately obeyed the summons. But what was his amazement, when, on entering the room, she held out her hand to him, and said with a benignant smile, 'It is all true—all that you said on the Sabbath is true. I have seen myself to be the wretched sinner you described me to be in prayer. I have seen Christ to be that all-sufficient Saviour you said He was; and God has mercifully snatched me from that abyss of infidelity in which I was sunk, and placed me on that Rock of Ages. There I am secure: there I shall remain—*I* know whom I have be-

lieved.' The minister's prayer, through the divine blessing, fastened on her mind; she was convinced of her guilty state, and enabled to rest wholly on the Saviour; and after solemnly charging her husband to educate their daughter in the fear of God, she died in peace.

5. A Franciscan friar, preaching during 1546 in Imola, Italy, told the people it behoved them to purchase heaven by the merit of their good works. A boy who was present exclaimed, 'That's blasphemy, for the Bible tells us that Christ purchased heaven by His sufferings and death, and bestows it on us freely by His merits.' A dispute of considerable length ensued between the youth and the preacher. Provoked at the pertinent replies of his juvenile opponent, and at the favourable reception which the audience gave them, 'Get you gone, you young rascal! (exclaimed the friar) you are but just come from the cradle, and will you take it upon you to judge sacred things, which the most learned cannot explain?' 'Did you ever read these words—"Out of the mouth of babes and sucklings God perfects praise?" ' rejoined the youth; upon which the preacher quitted the pulpit in wrathful confusion, breathing out threatenings against the poor boy, who was instantly thrown into prison.

6. David Dickson, once Professor of Divinity in Edinburgh, being asked, when on his deathbed, how he found himself, answered, 'I have taken my good deeds and bad deeds, and thrown them together in a heap, and fled from them both to Christ, and in Him I have peace.'

Q. 87. *What is repentance unto life?*

A. Repentance unto life is a saving grace, whereby a sinner, out of a true sense of his sin, and apprehension of the mercy of God in Christ, doth, with grief and hatred of his sin, turn from it unto God, with full purpose of, and endeavour after, new obedience.

1. A lady being visited with a violent disorder, was under the necessity of applying for medical assistance. Her doctor being a gentleman of great latitude in his religious sentiments, endeavoured in the course of his attendance to persuade his patient to adopt his creed, as well as to take his medicines. He frequently insisted, with a considerable degree of dogmatism that repentance and reformation were all that either God or man could require of us, and that consequently there was no necessity for an atonement by the sufferings of the Son of God. As the lady did not share the doctor's sentiments she contented herself with following his medical prescriptions, without embracing his creed. On her recovery, she forwarded a note to the doctor, desiring the favour of his company to tea when it suited his convenience, and requesting him to make out his bill. In a short time he made his visit, and the tea-table being removed, she addressed him as follows: 'My long illness has occasioned you a number of journeys; and I suppose, doctor, you have procured my medicines at considerable expense.' The doc-

tor acknowledged that 'good drugs were not to be obtained but at a very high price.' Upon which she replied, 'I am extremely sorry that I have put you to much labour and expense, and also promise that, on any future indisposition, I will never trouble you again. So you see I both repent and reform.' The doctor, immediately shrugging his shoulders, exclaimed, 'That will not do for me.' '*The words of the wise are as goads.*' (Eccles. 12. 11).

2. 'I have heard,' says Daniel Wilcox in one of his sermons 'of a certain person whose name I could mention, who was tempted to conclude his day over, and himself lost; that, therefore, it was his best course to put an end to his life, which, if continued, would serve but to increase his sin, and consequently his misery, from which there was no escape; and seeing he must be in hell, the sooner he was there, the sooner he would know the worst, which was preferable to his being worn away with the tormenting expectation of what was to come. Under the influence of such suggestions as these, he went to a river, with a design to throw himself in; but as he was about to do it, he seemed to hear a voice saying to him. *Who can tell?* As deep an impression was made upon him, as if these words had been audibly delivered. By this, therefore, he was brought to a stand; his thoughts were arrested, and thus began to work on the passage mentioned—*Who can tell?* (Jonah 3. 9) viz., what God can do when He will proclaim His grace glorious? *Who can tell*—how far God may suffer the tempter to prevail, and yet after all disappoint his malice? *Who can tell*—how long the Spirit may strive, and yet return with renewing efficacious grace? *Who can tell*—but such a one as I may find mercy? or what will be the issue of humble prayer to heaven for it? *Who can tell*—what purposes God will serve in my recovery? By such thoughts as these, it pleased God graciously to come in, and enable him, through all his doubts and fears, to throw himself, by faith, on Jesus Christ, as able to save to the uttermost all that come to God by Him, humbly desiring and expecting mercy for His sake, to his own soul. In this he was not disappointed, but afterwards became an eminent Christian and minister; and, from his own experience of the riches of grace, was greatly used to the conversion and comfort of others.'

3. In the second century, Celsus, a noted adversary of Christianity, distorting our Lord's expression (Matt. 9. 13), complained that Jesus Christ came into the world to create the most horrible and dreadful society, 'for He calls *sinners*, and not the *righteous*; so that the body He came to assemble is a body of profligates, separated from good people, among whom they before were mixed. He has rejected all the good and collected all the bad.' 'True,' says Origen, in reply, 'our Jesus came to call sinners; but to repentance. He assembles the wicked; but to convert them into new men, or rather to change them into angels. We come to Him covetous, He makes us liberal; lascivious, He makes us chaste; violent, He makes us meek; impious, He makes us religious.' 'If any man be in Christ Jesus, he is a new creature: old things are passed away, behold all things are become new' (2 Cor. 5. 17).

4. A woman who had once and again been guilty of a sin which incurred the censure of the church, and brought upon her public rebuke, presented herself before the parish session that she might be taken under discipline,

expecting, as a thing of course, that she would have to stand in the church and that then she would be restored to church privileges. But appearing to the ministers and elders to be a person who had no just sense of the evil of her sin, and exhibiting no signs of repentance, she was told that she could not be admitted to the privilege of the discipline and censure, which could be properly applied only to the penitent, and could be of no use to the hardened and insensible, such as she appeared to be. She went away greatly disappointed, because she was not to be rebuked, as she expected. She was in effect, though not in form, excommunicated. But the matter did not rest here. The sinner could find no peace in her conscience. The action taken by the church haunted her by night and by day; she began to reflect on her own character and conduct; she thought she must be a wicked creature indeed, seeing she was not reckoned worthy so much as to give public satisfaction for her sin. She was, in short, brought to consideration and deep repentance, on evidence of which, she was restored to church communion, and she maintained a good character all the rest of her life. When she applied to the session, she was very ignorant, and could not read; but, when awakened to a sense of her guilt, she immediately learned to read, so as to be able to read her Bible, and make it appear that she had profited by the merciful discipline of the church.

5. The faithful and laborious clergyman of a very large and populous parish had been accustomed, for a long series of years, to preserve notes of his visits to the afflicted, with remarks on the issue of their affliction, whether life or death, and of the subsequent conduct of those who recovered. He stated that, during forty years, he had visited no fewer than two thousand persons apparently dying, and who manifested such signs of penitence as would have led him to indulge a good hope of their safety if they had died at that time; they were restored to health, when he expected that they should bring forth fruits meet for repentance; but, alas! of the two thousand, not more than *two persons* manifested an abiding and saving change; the rest, when the terrors of eternity ceased to be in immediate prospect, forgot their religious impressions and their solemn vows, and returned with new avidity to their former worldly-mindedness and sinful pursuits, as the dog returns to his vomit again, and as the sow that was washed to her wallowing in the mire.

Q. 88. *What are the outward means whereby Christ communicateth to us the benefits of redemption?*

A. The outward and ordinary means whereby Christ communicateth to us the benefits of redemption, are His ordinances, especially the word, sacraments, and prayer; all which are made effectual to the elect for salvation.

1. John Berridge is said in one year to have been visited by a thousand

different persons under serious impressions; and it has been computed, that under his own and the joint ministry of Mr Hicks, about four thousand were awakened to a concern for their souls, in the space of twelve months. Incredible as this may appear, it is authenticated through a channel so respectable, that it would be illiberal to disbelieve it.

2. At a meeting of the Aberdeen Auxiliary Bible Society, the following pleasing anecdote was related by an eye-witness of the scene. 'Last year,' said he, 'a vessel from Stockholm was driven upon our coast in a tremendous gale, and became a total wreck. Her condition was such, that no human aid could possibly preserve the crew. In a short while after the vessel struck, she went to pieces. The persons on shore beheld with grief the awful state of those on board, but could render them no aid. They all perished except one lad; and he was driven by the waves upon a piece of the wreck, entwined among the ropes attached to the mast. Half-naked and half-drowned, he reached the shore. As soon as they rescued him, they saw a small parcel tied firmly round his waist with a handkerchief. Some thought it was his money; others, the ship's papers; and other said it was his watch. The handkerchief was unloosed, and to their surprise it was his BIBLE,—a Bible given to the lad's father by the British and Foreign Bible Society. Upon the blank leaf was a prayer written, that the Lord might make the present gift the means of saving his son's soul. Upon the other blank leaf, was an account how the Bible came into the father's hands, with expressions of gratitude to the Society from which he received it. To this was added a request to his son, that he would make it the man of his counsel; and that he could not allow him to depart from home without giving him the best pledge of his love—a Bible; although that gift deprived the other parts of the family of the Book. The Bible bore evident marks of having been often read with tears.'

3. John Skinner of Gloucestershire, was a strolling fiddler, going from fair to fair, and supplying music to any that would hire him. Having determined to incommode George Whitefield, who was going to preach, he obtained a standing on a ladder raised to a window near the pulpit; he remained a quiet, if not an attentive hearer, till the text was named, when he intended to begin his opposing and annoying exercise on the violin. It pleased God, while he was putting the instrument in tune, to convey the word spoken with irresistible power to the soul. His attention being diverted from its original design, and his purpose broken, that God's purpose according to election might stand, he heard the sermon out, after which he became altogether a changed character.

4. John Bailey of Lancashire, an eminent divine of the seventeenth century, was so honoured of God as to be made the instrument of the conversion of his own father, while he was yet a child. His mother was a remarkably godly woman, but his father was a very wicked character. The good instructions and frequent prayers of the former, were so blessed to the soul of little John, that he was converted to God while very young; and having a remarkable gift in prayer, his mother caused him to pray in the family. His father overhearing him engaged in this exercise, was so struck with remorse and shame at finding his child, then not above eleven or twelve years of age, performing a duty in his house which he had neglected himself,

that it brought on a deep conviction of his wretched state, and proved under God the means of his salvation.

5. 'The first seal of your missionary,' says the Report of the Baptist Home Missionary Society for 1828, 'was a poor woman, the wife of a day-labourer. Previously to this time, they had lived very happily together, but now the husband became a bitter persecutor; and because his wife would not relinquish the service of God, he frequently turned her out of doors in the night, and during the winter season. The wife, being a prudent woman, did not expose his cruelty to her neighbours, but, on the contrary, to avoid their observation, she went into the adjacent fields, and betook herself to prayer; and often, in a subordinate sense, it might be said of her,

> "Cold winter, and the midnight air,
> Witness'd the fervour of her prayer:
> The desert her temptation knew,
> Her conflict, and her victory too."

Greatly distressed, but not in despair, her only encouragement was, that with God all things are possible. She therefore resolved to set apart one hour every day, to pray for the conversion of her persecuting husband. This she was enabled to do, without missing one day for a whole year. Seeing no change in her husband, she formed a second resolution to persevere six months longer, which she did to the last day, when she retired at about twelve o'clock as usual, and, as she thought, for the last time. Fearing that her wishes in this instance might be contrary to the will of God, she resolved to call no more upon Him; her desire not being granted, her expectation appeared to be cut off. The same day, her husband returned from his labour in a state of deep dejection, and, instead of sitting down as usual to his dinner, he proceeded directly to his chamber. His wife followed and listened, and to her grateful astonishment, "he who used to mock, returned to pray." He came down stairs, but refused to eat, and returned again to his labour until the evening. When he came home, his wife affectionately asked him, "What is the matter?" "Matter enough," said he; "I am a lost sinner. About twelve o'clock this morning," continued he, "I was at my work, and a passage of Scripture was so impressed upon my mind, that I cannot get rid of it, and I am lost." His wife encouraged him to pray, but he replied, "O wife, it is of no use; there is no forgiveness for me!" Smitten with remorse at the recollection of his past conduct, he said to his wife, "Will you forgive me!" "O yes." "Will you pray for me?" "O yes, that I will." "Will you pray for me now?" "That I will with all my heart." They instantly fell on their knees, and wept, and made supplications. His tears of penitence mingled with her tears of gratitude and joy. Soon afterwards this godly couple agreed to have their house registered as a place of worship: and the scene of solitary intercession became a house of prayer; and he who was once a persecutor became a deacon in the church.'

6. A young man in America named Stoddart caused his mother much concern, for he lacked all interest in spiritual things. One night the pastor of the chapel which the mother attended saw him outside the building watch-

ing the people enter. In a joking and somewhat insolent tone he asked what they were at. 'Young man,' said the pastor, 'this is what we are at: your mother has asked us to meet tonight to pray for you.' Young Stoddart walked away saying, 'Then if these people are praying about me, it is high time I prayed for myself.' Before the meeting was over, in he crept, and with great joy the believers heard him say that he thanked them for praying for him and desired also to pray for himself. The Lord made him a preacher, one sermon that he preached being the prelude to a great revival.

7. The pious George Herbert built a new church at Leighton Bromswold in Huntingdonshire, and by his order the reading desk and pulpit were a little distance from each other, and both of an equal height; for he often said, 'They should neither have a precedency nor priority of the other; but that prayer and preaching, being equally useful, might agree like brethren, and have an equal honour and estimation.'

8. A minister of Exeter, named Kilpin, marked every pew in his chapel, on the divisions of the paper which covered his parlour study, with the names, in short-hand, of their occupants, lest one should be forgotten. Here he daily presented his petitions to God for the spiritual prosperity of each according to their various situations and wants, as far as he knew their characters, temptations, and trials.

Q. 89. *How is the word made effectual to salvation?*

A. The Spirit of God maketh the reading, but especially the preaching of the word, an effectual means of convincing and converting sinners, and of building them up in holiness and comfort, through faith, unto salvation.

1. A certain libertine of a most abandoned character happened one day to stroll into a church, where he heard the 5th chapter of Genesis read, importing that such and such persons lived for so long, and yet the conclusion in all cases was, 'they died.' Enos lived 905 years, and he died—Seth 912, and he died—Methuselah 969, and he died. The frequent repetition of the words *he died*, notwithstanding the great length of years they had lived, struck him so deeply with the thought of death and eternity, that, through divine grace, he became a most exemplary Christian.

2. Dr Edmund Staunton was called 'the searching preacher'. Once when preaching at Warborough, in Oxfordshire, a man was so much affected with his first prayer, that he ran home and desired his wife to get ready and come to church, for there was one in the pulpit who prayed like an angel. The woman hastened away and heard the sermon, which, under the divine blessing, was the means of her conversion; and she afterwards proved an eminent Christian.

3. An aged minister addressing a young minister at his ordination, said, 'I cannot conclude without reminding you, my young brother, of some things that may be of use to you in the course of your ministry. 1. Preach

Christ crucified, and dwell chiefly on the blessings resulting from His righteousness, atonement, and intercession. 2. Avoid all needless controversies in the pulpit; except it be when your subject necessarily requires it; or when the truths of God are likely to suffer by your silence. 3. When you ascend the pulpit, leave your learning behind you: endeavour to preach more to the hearts of your people than to their heads. 4. Do not affect too much oratory. Seek rather to profit, than to be admired.'

4. 'I was conversing,' says Charles G. Finney, in his 'Lectures on Revivals of Religion,' 'with one of the first advocates in America. He said, the difficulty which preachers find in making themselves understood is, that they do not repeat enough. Says he, "In addressing a jury, I always expect that whatever I wish to impress upon their minds, I shall have to repeat at least twice, and often I repeat it three or four times, and even more. Otherwise, I do not carry their minds along with me, so that they can feel the force of what comes afterwards." If a jury, under oath, called to decide on the common affairs of this world, cannot apprehend an argument, unless there is so much repetition, how is it to be expected that men will understand the preaching of the gospel without it?'

5. A young man, gay, thoughtless, and dissipated, with a companion like himself, was passing along the street, intending to go to one of the theatres. A little boy ran by his side, and attempted to put a letter into his hand: he repulsed the boy, but he persevered: and when his companion attempted to take it, the boy refused him, saying to the other, 'It is for you, sir.' He opened the paper, and read its contents. They were simply these words, 'Sir, remember the day of judgment is at hand.' It pleased God that these words should meet his attention; he was struck with them; he felt disinclined to go to the theatre, and said he would return home. His companion rallied him, but he took leave of him, and bent his course homewards. On his way he observed a chapel open, and though he was not accustomed to attend such places, he went in. A venerable minister was about to preach, and just then reading his text. He had chosen as his text: 'This is the finger of God.' The sermon was blessed to him, and he became a new man.

6. Archbishop Leighton, before he attained his high dignity in the church, being asked why he did not preach on the times, as the rest of his brethren did, replied, 'That if they all preached *on time*, might not one poor brother be allowed to preach *on eternity!*'

7. A minister, one Sabbath morning, opened his Bible to mark the passage he had been studying throughout the week, and from which he intended to deliver a discourse that day; but to his great surprise, he could not find the passage: for neither words nor text could he recollect. He endeavoured to recall the subject to memory, and made it a matter of prayer; but all to no effect. While thinking how he should be confounded before the congregation another passage darted into his mind with peculiar energy. He accordingly preached from it, and during the discourse he observed a person, apparently in a clerical habit, enter the place. After having heard a little he seemed bathed in tears, and never raised his head through the whole of the sermon. The minister never had more liberty in preaching. In the evening, this person called on him, and after expressing his obliga-

tions for the sermon he had heard, he added, 'Two or three years ago, I heard you, in such a place, preach upon a subject, and ever since I have been under the spirit of conviction and bondage. This day I took my horse and rode to hear you, and blessed be God, He has now given me to see Him as my reconciled God and Father in Jesus Christ, and has also given me to enjoy that liberty wherewith He makes His people free.' 'After some interesting conversation, we both,' says the minister, 'began to see the good hand of God in this matter, and His good providence in determining me in such a remarkable manner, to preach upon a subject I had never before proposed, and which He had accompanied with such a powerful efficacy. To me it was one of my best days, and one which, both by him and me, will be remembered through a joyful eternity.'

8. Hugh Clark, a pious minister of Northamptonshire, in Queen Elizabeth's reign, having in his sermon announced the just judgment of God against certain particular sins to which the people were much addicted, the next morning a young man came to his house wishing to see him. Mr Clark, having invited him into his chamber, and knowing his vicious character, sharply reproved him, and warned him of his awful danger. God wrought so effectually upon his heart by this pointed and faithful dealing that the man, falling on his knees, and crying for pardon, pulled out a dagger by which he had determined to murder him. 'I came hither,' said the man, 'with a full resolution to stab you, but God has prevented me. This was occasioned by your terrifying sermon yesterday. But, if you please to forgive me, I shall, by the grace of God, never attempt any such thing again.' Clark freely pardoned the offence, and, after giving him suitable advice, dismissed him.

Q. 90. *How is the word to be read and heard, that it may become effectual to salvation?*

A. That the word may become effectual to salvation, we must attend thereunto with diligence, preparation, and prayer; receive it with faith and love, lay it up in our hearts, and practise it in our lives.

1. When Archbishop Cranmer's edition of the Bible was printed in 1538, and fixed to a desk in all parochial churches, the ardour with which men flocked to read it was incredible. They who could procured it; and they who could not, crowded to read it, or to hear it read in churches, where it was common to see little assemblies of workmen meeting together for that purpose after the labour of the day. Many even learned to read in their old age, that they might have the pleasure of instructing themselves from the Scriptures. John Foxe mentions two apprentices who joined each his little stock, and bought a Bible, which at every interval of leisure they read; but being afraid of their master, who was a zealous papist, they kept it under the straw of their bed.

2. When the arrival of the cart, which carried the first sacred load of the

Scriptures to Wales in 1816, sent by the British and Foreign Bible Society, was announced, the Welsh peasants went out in crowds to meet it. Welcoming it as the Israelites did the ark of old they drew it into the town, and eagerly bore off every copy as rapidly as they could be dispersed. The young people were to be seen spending the whole night in reading it. Labourers carried it with them to the field, that they might enjoy it during the intervals of their labour, and lose no opportunity of becoming acquainted with its sacred truths. Let those consider this, who despise or neglect the Bible; who have it, but seldom open it, or when they do, slumber over it, as a record in which they have little or no interest, and soon lay it aside in weariness or disgust.

3. As a minister named Nicoll of Exeter was once preaching, he saw several of the aldermen asleep, and thereupon sat down. Upon his silence, and the noise that presently arose in the church, they awoke, and stood up with the rest, upon which *he* arose, and said, 'The sermon is not yet done, but now you are awake, I hope you will hearken more diligently,' and then went on.

4. 'I was once preaching a charity sermon,' says Richard Cecil, 'when the congregation was very large, and chiefly of the lower order. I found it impossible by my usual method of preaching to gain their attention. It was in the afternoon, and my hearers seemed to meet nothing in my preaching which was capable of rousing them out of the stupefaction of a full dinner. Some lounged, and some turned their backs on me. "I must have attention," I said to myself; "I will be heard." The case was desperate; and, in despair, I sought a desperate remedy. I exclaimed aloud, "Last Monday morning a man was hanged at Tyburn." Instantly the face of things was changed and all was silence and expectation! I caught their ear, and retained it through the sermon.'

5. The first day that Dr Robert Balmer went with his mother to attend public worship at Jedburgh, having formerly gone with his father, during his life-time, to Morebattle, was one on which the sacrament of the Lord's Supper was dispensed. The action sermon, as it is called, was preached from a tent erected in a green adjoining the church. Robert sat before his mother on the grass. She, having never seen his demeanour in the public assembly before, was surprised and somewhat grieved by his apparent restlessness, but took no notice. However, when the services were concluded, and the little band which came from Eckford-moss were returning, and talking by the way of what they had heard, and endeavouring to recall the particulars of the sermons delivered, he was found able to supply much of what the older people had forgotten. He had several times thus assisted them to the recollection both of the heads of the discourses and of remarks made in illustration, when an elder who was among them, looking to his mother, said, 'Margaret, do you know wha's laddie that is?' She might, no doubt, have felt something of maternal pride as she replied, 'The boy is mine.'

6. The pastor of a congregation in America, after many years labour among his people, was supposed by some of them to have declined much in his vigour and usefulness; in consequence of which two gentlemen of the

congregation waited upon him, and exhibited their complaints. The minister received them with much affection, and assured them that he was equally sensible of his languor and little success, and that the cause had given him very great uneasiness. The gentlemen wished he would mention what he thought was the cause. Without hesitation, the minister replied, 'The loss of my prayer-book.' 'Your prayer-book?' said one of the gentlemen with surprise; 'I never knew that you used one.' 'Yes,' replied the minister, 'I have enjoyed the benefit of one for many years till lately, and I attribute my want of success to the loss of it. The prayers of my people were my prayer-book; and it has occasioned great grief to me that they have laid it aside. Now, if you will return and procure to me the use of my prayer-book again, I doubt not I shall preach much better, and that you will hear more profitably.' The gentlemen, conscious of their neglect, thanked the minister for the reproof, and wished him a good morning.

7. A merchant at Boston in America, according to his wonted liberality, sent a present of chocolate and sugar to a minister of the gospel, with a note desiring his acceptance of it, as a comment on Gal. 6. 6, 'Let him that is taught in the word, communicate to him that teacheth, in all good things.' The minister, who was then confined by sickness, returned his compliments to the merchant, thanked him for his excellent *family expositor*, and wished him to give him a practical exposition of Matt. 25. 36, 'I was sick, and ye visited me.'

8. A poor woman in the country went to hear a sermon, wherein, among other evil practices, the use of dishonest weights and measures was exposed. With this discourse she was much affected. The next day, when the minister, according to his custom, went among his hearers and called upon the woman, he took occasion to ask her what she remembered of his sermon. The poor woman complained much of her bad memory, and said she had forgotten almost all he had delivered. 'But one thing,' said she, 'I remembered—I remembered to burn my bushel.' A doer of the word cannot be a forgetful hearer.

9. 'There was one thing,' said an individual, who was then following his godly parents in the path to heaven, 'which, in my wildest days, I never could get over, and that was the holy and devoted conduct of my father and mother. I watched them constantly and intently, in the hope of finding something which would supply me with a reason for thinking meanly of religion; but I watched in vain. Their whole conduct so exemplified their creed, and so adorned the gospel, as to leave me without excuse.'

10. Two learned physicians, and a plain honest countryman, happening to meet at an inn, sat down to dinner together. A dispute presently arose between the two doctors, on the nature of aliment, which proceeded to such a height, and was carried on with so much fury, that it spoiled their meal, and they parted extremely indisposed. The countryman, in the meantime, who understood not the cause, though he heard the quarrel, fell heartily to his meat, gave thanks to God, digested it well, returned in the strength of it to his honest labour, and at evening received his wages. 'Is there not sometimes,' adds Bishop Horne, 'as much difference between the polemical and the practical Christian?'

Q. 91. *How do the sacraments become effectual means of salvation?*

A. The sacraments become effectual means of salvation, not from any virtue in them, or in him that doth administer them; but only by the blessing of Christ, and the working of His Spirit in them that by faith receive them.

1. A lady who was present at the observance of the Lord's Supper, where Ebenezer Erskine was assisting, was much impressed by his discourse. Having been informed who he was, she went next Sabbath to his own place of worship to hear him. But she felt none of those strong impressions she experienced on the former occasion. Wondering at this, she called on Erskine, and stating the case, asked what might be the reason of such a difference in her feelings; he replied, 'Madam, the reason is this—last Sabbath you went to hear Jesus Christ; but to-day, you have come to hear Ebenezer Erskine.'

2. During the residence of Sir Ralph Abercrombie at Tullibody, the ancient seat of his family, in Clackmannanshire, his humility and Christian deportment pointed him out as a proper person to fill the office of an elder in the parish church. Being ordained according to the rites of the Church of Scotland, when the solemnity was ended, he addressed the minister to the following purpose: 'Sir, I have often been entrusted by my sovereign with honourable and important commands in my profession as a soldier, and his Majesty has been pleased to reward my services with distinguished marks of his royal approbation; but to be the humble instrument, in the office of an elder, of putting the tokens of my Saviour's dying love into the hands of one of the meanest of *His* followers, I conceive to be the highest honour that I can receive on this side heaven.'

3. Colonel James Gardiner mentions in a letter the pleasure with which he had attended a preparation sermon on the Saturday before the dispensation of the Lord's Supper. 'I took a walk,' says he, 'on the mountains over against Ireland; and I persuade myself, that were I capable of giving you a description of what passed there, you would agree that I had much better reason to remember my God from the hills of Port-Patrick, than David from the land of Jordan, and of the Hermonites, from the hill Mizar. In short, I wrestled some hours with the Angel of the covenant, and made supplications to Him with floods of tears and cries, until I had almost expired; but He strengthened me so, that, like Jacob, I had power with God, and prevailed. You will be more able to judge of this, by what you have felt yourself upon the like occasions. After such a preparatory work, I need not tell you how blessed the solemn ordinance of the Lord's Supper proved to me: I hope it was so to many.'

Q. 92. *What is a sacrament?*

A. A sacrament is a holy ordinance instituted by Christ; wherein, by sensible signs, Christ and the benefits of the new covenant, are represented, sealed, and applied to believers.

1. In the year 1805, when an installation of the knights of the garter was approaching, and his Majesty, George III was conversing with some persons of high rank on the subject, a distinguished nobleman said to the king, 'Sir, are not the new knights about to be installed, obliged to take the sacrament before the ceremony?' His Majesty, changing countenance, and assuming a severe look, replied, 'No; that religious institution is not to be mixed with our profane ceremonies. Even at the time of my coronation, I was very unwilling to take the sacrament; but when they told me it was indispensable and I must take it, before I approached the communion-table, I took off the bauble from my head. The sacrament, my lord, is not to be profaned by our Gothic institutions.'

2. The famous Scottish preacher Robert Bruce was once ministering at a Communion Service at Larbert, Stirlingshire. On rising to address the communicants he continued gazing at them in silence. At length, with much concern, he broke out: 'There is some person at this table guilty of an unrepented sin, for my Master has shut my mouth and I can say nothing till he remove. In the Lord's Name I charge him to withdraw from this holy table'. Having thus spoken he sat down and waited. Amid a breathless silence a man rose up from the table and left the building. Upon this Bruce resumed the service and proceeded with much power to minister the Word.

3. 'On Sabbath last,' says a good man, 'we were enabled to keep our New Testament passover; it was a good day, a day of salvation. At the sacred banquet my hard heart melted, and the tears flowed plentifully from my eyes; but they were tears of joy; my heart was full. On Monday, a minister preached from these words: "And one shall say, I am the Lord's." (Is. 44. 5). O what a sermon to me! My heart made the happy claim and cheerful surrender again and again. My soul said, I am the Lord's; and with my heart I subscribed it, and I hope and believe will never unsay it.

"Sweet was the hour I freedom felt,
    To call my Jesus mine,
To see His smiling face, and melt
    In pleasures all divine."

Truly I am Thy servant—I am Thy servant, the son of Thine handmaid; Thou hast loosed my bonds. Why me, O Lord? Why me? What am I, or what is my father's house, that Thou hast brought me hitherto?'

4. Joseph Williams of Kidderminster, in his diary, relates his happy experience on a communion Sabbath (August 26, 1744). 'The whole administration of the Lord's Supper to-day, was,' says he, 'through adorable grace, a sweet opportunity, a most delightful gospel feast. How did my heart burn within me! How tenderly did it throb! What streams of tears, even tears of joy, joy unspeakable and full of glory, flowed from my gushing eyes, while the minister was in his introductory discourse! "As often as ye eat this bread, and drink this cup, ye do show forth the Lord's death till He come."

K

With what humble boldness did I appeal to the omniscient God, to the Father, the Son, and the Holy Ghost, that each of the Divine Persons knew the sincerity and integrity of my heart, midst all the imperfections and frailties with which I am encompassed! With what holy freedom and confidence could I desire of God to search and try me, my own heart not condemning me! How did my heart glow with thankfulness and admiration, at the amazing condescension and love of God in Christ Jesus, to a creature so mean, so vile, and sinful! Had the tide of sacred joy swelled a few degrees higher, I could hardly have restrained myself from crying out in the congregation, "O He is come! He is come!" '

Q. 93. *Which are the sacraments of the New Testament?*

A. The sacraments of the New Testament are, Baptism and the Lord's Supper.

1 Matthew Henry, the author of the excellent commentary on the Bible, baptized one of his children himself. His friends thought this not so proper but he judged it as fit as it is for a minister to communicate in the Lord's Supper, which he himself administers.

2. 'In a recent journey,' says a minister, 'I said to a fellow-passenger, an apparently intelligent young woman, "Are you a Christian?" "Yes, sir," was the prompt reply. "How long have you been one?" was my next inquiry. "Ever since I was christened, sir!" And this was all she knew about the matter.'

3. The following anecdote is extracted from the Memoirs of Casanova an Italian adventurer of the eighteenth century: 'While at St Petersburg, I was present at a scene which much surprised me—I mean, the blessing of the waters of the river on the day of Epiphany, at a time when the ice on the Neva was five feet thick. They christened children by dipping them in a hole which they had cut in the ice. It happened on this occasion, that the bishop who performed the ceremony of baptizing, let a child fall out of his hands into the water; and it instantly disappeared. The bishop, without at all endeavouring to recover the child, turned coolly round, and desired the attendants to hand him another child. This was instantly done. What surprised me most, however, was the joy of the parents at their child's being drowned. I learned afterwards that the people here believe that a child drowned under such circumstances, is sure of going instantly into paradise.'

4. 'We can truly say,' observes a Moravian missionary, 'that among the very considerable number of Esquimaux who live with us, we know of few who are not seriously desirous to profit by what they hear, and to experience and enjoy for themselves that which they see their countrymen possess. Our communicants give us pleasure; for it is the wish of their very hearts to live unto the Lord, and their conduct affords proofs of the sincerity of their profession; thus, for example, Esquimaux sisters, who have no boat of their

own, venture across bays some miles in breadth, sitting behind their husbands, on their narrow kayaks, in order to be present at the holy sacrament, though at the peril of their lives.' What a lesson is this for those who live near, and make any trifling thing an excuse!

5. Melancthon relates a story of a tragedy that was to be acted, of the death and passion of Christ. But he that personated the Redeemer on the cross, was wounded to death by one that should have thrust his sword into a bladder of blood; and he, by his fall, killed one that acted a woman's part, lamenting under the cross. The brother of him who was first killed, slew the person who stabbed him, for which he was apprehended and executed. So speedily was their daring impiety punished.

Q. 94. *What is baptism?*

A. Baptism is a sacrament, wherein the washing with water, in the name of the Father, and of the Son, and of the Holy Ghost, doth signify and seal our ingrafting into Christ, and partaking of the benefits of the covenant of grace, and our engagement to be the Lord's.

1. Philip Henry drew up the following short form of the baptismal covenant, for the use of his children: 'I take God the Father to be my chief good and highest end. I take God the Son to be my Prince and Saviour. I take God the Holy Ghost to be my Sanctifier, Teacher, Guide, and Comforter. I take the Word of God to be my rule in all my actions, and the people of God to be my people in all conditions. I do likewise devote and dedicate unto the Lord, my whole self, all I am, all I have, and all I can do. And this do I deliberately, sincerely, freely, and for ever.' This he taught his children; and they each of them solemnly repeated it every Lord's-day in the evening, after they were catechised, he putting his *amen* to it, and sometimes adding, 'So say, and so do, and you are made for ever.'

2. Matthew Henry has left the following testimony in his *Treatise on Baptism*: 'I cannot but take occasion to express my gratitude to God for my infant baptism; not only as it was an early admission into the visible body of Christ, but as it furnished my pious parents with a good argument (and, I trust, through grace, a prevailing argument) for an early dedication of my own self to God in my childhood. *If God has wrought any good work upon my soul, I desire with humble thankfulness, to acknowledge the moral influence of my infant baptism upon it.*'

3. Philip Henry declined the private administration of the Lord's Supper to sick persons, as judging it not consonant to the rule and intention of the ordinance. He very rarely, if ever, baptized in private, but would have children brought to the solemn assembly on the Lord's-day, that the parents' engagement might have the more witnesses to it, and the child the more prayers put up for it, and that the congregation might be edified. He very much persuaded his friends to put off feasting till another occasion, observ-

ing, that Abraham made a great feast the same day that Isaac was weaned, not the same day that he was circumcised.

4. A Greenlander for many years had communication with the Moravian missionaries, but could never resolve to forsake his land, where he was held in great respect. On one occasion, however, being at the capelin fishery, he got a sight of his daughter, who had removed from him, and was baptized, and showed his resentment at it. But she modestly told him the reasons that induced her to it and set forth the happiness of believers, concluding with these words: 'So happy may *you* also be; but if you will not, I cannot stay and perish with you.' This softened his heart, and he began to weep, went with her to the missionary, and declared his intention now was, not to take away his daughter from the baptized, but rather go with her. He expressed his resolution to remain with the missionaries, and his wish that the rest of his children might be baptized. 'As for myself,' said he, 'I dare not think of baptism, as I am very bad, and old too, and incapable of learning much more; but yet I will live and die with you, for it is very reviving to me to hear of our Saviour.'

Q. 95. *To whom is baptism to be administered?*

A. Baptism is not to be administered to any that are out of the visible church, till they profess their faith in Christ, and obedience to Him; but the infants of such as are members of the visible church are to be baptized.

1. As an instance of the misapplication and abuse of the sacred ordinance of baptism, the author of the *Protestant* publishes, in that excellent work, a description sent him by a correspondent, of the ceremony of the baptism of a *bell*, which took place at Naples. A noble lord was god-father to the bell, and a lady of quality was god-mother. Most of the prayers said on the occasion, ended with the following words: 'That Thou wouldst be pleased to rinse, purify, sanctify, and consecrate these bells with Thy heavenly benediction.' The following were the words of consecration: 'Let the sign be consecrated and sanctified, in the name of the Father, and of the Son, and of the Holy Ghost.' The bishop then turning to the people, said, 'The bell's name is Mary.' He had previously demanded of the god-father and god-mother, what name they would have put upon the bell, and the lady gave it this name.

2. A careless parent one evening entered Murray M'Cheyne's house, and asked him to come with him to baptize a dying child. He knew that neither this man nor his wife ever entered the door of a church; but he rose and went with him to the miserable dwelling. There an infant lay, apparently dying, and many of the female neighbours, equally depraved with the parents, stood round. He came forward to where the child was, and spoke to the parents of their ungodly state, and fearful guilt before God, and concluded by showing them that, in such circumstances, he would consider it sinful

in him to administer baptism to their infant. They said, 'You might at least do it for the sake of the poor child.' He told them that it was not baptism that saved a soul, and that out of true concern for themselves, he must not do as they wished. The friends around the bed then joined the parents in upbraiding him as having no pity on the poor infant's soul! He stood among them still, and showed them that it was they who had been thus cruel to their child; and then lifted up his voice in solemn warning, and left the house amidst their ignorant reproaches.

3. A parish minister, preaching in the presence of Philip Henry and his family, and many of his friends being present, was earnestly cautioning people not to go to nonconformist meeting-places, and used this as an argument against it, 'that they were baptized into the Church of England.' Philip Henry's catholic charity could not well digest this monopolizing of the great ordinance of baptism, and thought it time to bear his testimony against such narrow principles, of which he ever expressed his dislike in all parties and persuasions. Accordingly he took the next opportunity that offered itself, publicly to baptize a child, and desired the congregation to bear witness, 'that he did not baptize that child into the Church of England, nor into the Church of Scotland, nor into the church of the dissenters, nor into the church at Broad-Oak, where he was a minister, but into the visible catholic church of Jesus Christ.'

4. 'An assembly of sixty-six pastors,' says Joseph Milner, 'men who had stood the trial of a grievous persecution, and sound in the faith, was called by Cyprian, in the year 253 of the Christian era, to decide, not whether infants should be baptized at all, but whether it should be done immediately, or on the eighth day. If infant baptism had been an innovation, it must have been now of considerable standing. The disputes about Easter show that such an innovation must have formed a remarkable era in the church. It is impossible to account for the silence of all antiquity, but on the footing that it had once been allowed, and that infant baptism was the practice of the first churches.'

Q. 96. *What is the Lord's Supper?*

A. The Lord's Supper is a sacrament, wherein by giving and receiving bread and wine, according to Christ's appointment, His death is showed forth; and the worthy receivers are, not after a corporal and carnal manner, but by faith, made partakers of His body and blood, with all His benefits, to their spiritual nourishment, and growth in grace.

1. John Beck, one of the Moravian missionaries, on one occasion, with much fervour and energy described the agonies and death of Jesus; and exhorted the Greenlanders to think seriously how much it had cost the Saviour to redeem man, and entreated them not to withhold from Him their hearts,

which He had so dearly earned; for He had been wounded, shed His blood, and died to purchase them. He read, at the same time, from the New Testament, the history of our Saviour's agony in the garden, and insisted upon that anguish of soul that made Him sweat great drops of blood. Kaiarnack, their first convert, being much impressed by the discourse, stepped forward and said, in an earnest and affecting tone, 'How was that? tell me that once more, for I would fain be saved too.' 'These words,' said Beck, in relating them, 'the like of which I had never heard from a Greenlander before, thrilled through my inmost soul, and kindled such an ardour, that I gave a general account of our Saviour's life and death, and the whole counsel of God for our salvation, while the tears ran down my cheeks.'

2. 'A more devout communicant at the table of the Lord,' says Dr Philip Doddridge, in his *Life of Colonel James Gardiner*, 'has perhaps seldom been any where known. Often have I had the pleasure to see that manly countenance softened into all the marks of humiliation and contrition on this occasion; and to discern, in spite of all his efforts to conceal them, streams of tears flowing down from his eyes, while he has been directing them to those memorials of his Redeemer's love. And some who have conversed intimately with him, after he came from that ordinance, have observed a visible abstraction from surrounding objects, by which there seemed reason to imagine that his soul was wrapt in holy contemplation. And I particularly remember, that when we had once spent a great part of the following Monday in riding together, he made an apology to me for being so absent as he seemed, by telling me that his heart was flown upwards before he was aware, to Him whom having not seen he loved: and that he was rejoicing in Him with such unspeakable joy, that he could not hold it down to creature converse.'

3. William Warburton and Josiah Tucker were contemporary bishop and dean of the same (Gloucester) cathedral. Both were eminent but very different in the line of their studies. For many years they were not even on speaking terms. It was on a Good Friday, not long before Warburton's death, they were at the holy table together. Before he gave the cup to the dean, he stooped down, and said in tremulous emotion—'Dear Tucker, let this cup be the cup of reconciliation between us.' It had the intended effect; they were friends again to their mutual satisfaction.

4. Afoofoo, an interesting Malay youth, who resided for some months in Greenock, till he met with a premature death by drowning, was once present at the dispensation of the Lord's Supper. A clerical friend, who met him coming out, asked, 'What have you seen in church to-day?' He answered, 'I see people take bread and wine.' 'And what does that mean?' 'The body and blood of Jesus Christ.' 'Is it really the body and blood of Jesus Christ?' 'O no,' said he, 'not all same—it keep in mind His body and blood. He die for sinners.'

5. 'Supposing,' says Archbishop Tillotson, 'the doctrine of transubstantiation had been delivered in Scripture in the very same words that it is decreed in the Council of Trent, by what clearer evidence could any man prove to me that such words were in the Bible, than I can prove to him that bread and wine after consecration are bread and wine still? He could

but appeal to my eyes to prove such words to be in the Bible; and with the same reason and justice might I appeal to several of his senses, to prove to him that the bread and wine, after consecration, are bread and wine still.'

6. One Sabbath morning, during the reign of James II of England, as a captain with a party of soldiers went out to hunt down the Protestants, as they termed it, they met a young woman, a servant-maid, running along the road early in the morning, without either shoes or stockings. The captain of the band asked her where she was going so early in the morning, and what was the urgency of the business that made her run so fast. She told him that she had learned that her elder brother was dead, and she was going to receive her share of the riches he had bequeathed to her, as well as to her other brothers and sisters; and she was afraid she should be too late. The commander was so well pleased with her answer, that he gave her half-a-crown to buy a pair of shoes, and also wished her success; but if he had known the real business she was going on, which was to a sacrament, he would most probably have prevented her from going that day to the place where she hoped to receive 'durable riches.'

7. One of the converted Greenlanders, who had taken a seal, rather than be absent from the missionary settlement when the Lord's Supper was to be administered, rowed the whole night in his kayak with the animal in tow, and when his exertion was mentioned—'How could I,' said he, 'stay where I was? My soul hungers and thirsts after the Lord and His communion.'

Q. 97. *What is required to the worthy receiving of the Lord's Supper?*

A. It is required of them that would worthily partake of the Lord's Supper, that they examine themselves of their knowledge to discern the Lord's body, of their faith to feed upon Him, of their repentance, love, and new obedience; lest, coming unworthily, they eat and drink judgment to themselves.

1. The three questions which Philip Henry advised people to put to themselves in self-examination before the sacrament were, What am I? What have I done? and What do I want?

2. Joseph Woodward was a nonconformist minister in England settled at Dursley in Gloucestershire. He found it needful to set about the reform of many disorders of discipline and manners that existed among the people to whom he ministered. In particular, he declared his resolve to admit none to the Lord's table save those who, besides the usual marks of conversion, had a competent knowledge of divine things. A certain man obstinately said that he would not submit to examination and that if the minister would not give him the sacrament he would take it! In pursuance of this impious resolution, this man attended the church on sacrament day, but had scarcely set foot in the building before he fell dead, the Lord thus making clear to

all the church members that the solemn admonitions addressed to the Church of the Corinthians by the apostle in the first Christian century were ageless in their solemn application.

3. During the ministry of Andrew Gray at Glasgow, William Guthrie of Fenwick on one occasion assisted him at the dispensation of the Lord's Supper. Some of Cromwell's officers, then in Glasgow, acting on the principle of promiscuous admission to the Lord's table, were coming irregularly without having acquainted the minister, or giving evidence that they were prepared for the observance of that holy ordinance. Guthrie addressed them when leaving their pews to come to the table, with such gravity, resolution, and zeal, that they were quite confounded, and sat down again, without causing any further disturbance.

4. In a speech in the House of Lords in 1719, Lord Lansdowne said, 'The receiving of the Lord's Supper was never intended to be as a qualification for an office, but as an open declaration of one's being and remaining a sincere member of the Church of Christ. Whoever presumes to receive it with any other view, profanes it, and may be said to seek his promotion in this world, by eating and drinking his own damnation in the next.'

5. In the capacity of envoy from the Augustinians of Germany, Luther was invited to several assemblies of distinguished ecclesiastics. One day in particular, he happened to be at table along with several prelates; the latter showed themselves to him without reserve in their accustomed buffoonery of manners and impiety of conversation, and did not hesitate to play off a thousand jests in his presence, thinking him, no doubt, a man of their own stamp. Amongst other things, they told the monk with laughter and boasting, how, when reading mass at the altar, instead of the sacramental words that were to 'convert' the bread and wine into the Saviour's flesh and blood, they pronounced these derisive words over them, 'Bread thou art, and bread thou shalt remain; wine thou art, and wine thou shalt remain.' 'Then,' they continued, 'we elevate it, and all the people adore.' The jocularity of Rome was shocking to him. 'I was,' he says, 'a young and pious monk; words like these gave me acute pain. If they speak thus in Rome at table, freely and openly, I thought to myself, what would be the consequence if their actions corresponded to their words, and if pope, cardinal, courtiers, and all, said mass in this fashion. Me, too, who have heard them read so many times with such devotion, how they would have deceived me!'

6. At an ordination of elders, Robert Murray M'Cheyne of Dundee made the following statement. 'When I first entered upon the work of the ministry among you, I was exceedingly ignorant of the vast importance of church discipline. I thought that my great and almost only work was to pray and preach. I saw your souls to be so precious, and the time so short, that I devoted all my time and care and strength, to labour in word and doctrine. When cases of discipline were brought before me and the elders, I regarded them with something like abhorrence. It was a duty I shrank from; and I may truly say it nearly drove me from the work of the ministry among you altogether. But it pleased God, who teaches His servants in another way than man teaches, to bless some of the cases of discipline to the manifest and undeniable conversion of the souls of those under our care;

and from that hour a new light broke in upon my mind, and I saw that if preaching be an ordinance of Christ, so is church discipline. I now feel very deeply persuaded that both are of God—that two keys are committed to us by Christ, the one the key of doctrine, by means of which we unlock the treasures of the Bible, the other the key of discipline, by which we open or shut the way to the sealing ordinances of the faith. Both are Christ's gift, and neither is to be resigned without sin.'

Q. 98. *What is prayer?*

A. Prayer is an offering up of our desires unto God, for things agreeable to His will, in the name of Christ, with confession of our sins, and thankful acknowledgment of His mercies.

1. Amyntor, at a memorable period of his life, was under great distress of conscience, and harrassed by violent temptations. He made his case known to an experienced friend, who said, '*Amyntor, you do not pray.*' Surprised at this, he replied, 'I pray, if such a thing be possible, too much. I can hardly tell how many times in the day I bow my knee to God, almost to the omission of my other duties, and the neglect of my necessary studies.' 'You mistake my meaning, dear Amyntor; I do not refer you to the ceremony of the knee, but to the devotion of the *heart*, which neglects not any business, but intermingles prayer with *all:* which in every place looks unto the Lord; and on every occasion lifts up an indigent longing soul, for the supply of His grace. This,' he added with peculiar force, '*this* is prayer, which all the devils in hell cannot withstand.'

2. A poor old man, when a child of three years of age, had been taught by his mother to repeat a prayer every night, which he did till he was seventy-three years old; and not a little proud was he to say, that he had not omitted saying his prayers every night for seventy years! At this advanced age it pleased God to afflict him severely; he was led by the Holy Spirit to see that he was a poor sinner who had been living in a form of godliness, but had never felt its power. He was enabled to spend the last few years of his life in humble dependence on the grace of Christ; and when he referred to himself, he would often add, 'I am the old man who said his prayers for seventy years, and yet all that time never prayed at all.'

3. A poor man once went to a pious minister, and said, 'Mr Carter, what will become of me? I work hard, and fare hard, and yet I cannot thrive.' Mr Carter answered, 'Still you want one thing; I will tell you what you must do. Work hard, and fare hard, and *pray* hard; and I will warrant you shall thrive.'

4. Dr Johnson once reproved the Rev. Dr Maxwell for saying grace in his presence, without mentioning the name of the LORD JESUS CHRIST; and hoped he would be more mindful in future of the apostolical injunction.

5. A gentleman of very considerable fortune, but a stranger both to personal and family religion, one evening took a solitary walk through part

of his grounds. He happened to come near a mean hut, where a poor man lived with a numerous family, who earned their bread by daily labour. He heard a continued and rather loud voice. Not knowing what it was, curiosity prompted him to listen. The man, who was piously disposed, happened to be at prayer with his family. So soon as he could distinguish the words, he heard him giving thanks, with great affection, to God for the goodness of His providence, in giving them food to eat and raiment to put on, and in supplying them with what was necessary and comfortable in the present life. He was immediately struck with astonishment and confusion, and said to himself, 'Does this poor man, who has nothing but the meanest fare, and that purchased by severe labour, give thanks to God for His goodness to himself and family; and I, who enjoy ease and honour, and every thing that is pleasant and desirable, have hardly ever bent my knee or made any acknowledgment to my Maker and Preserver?' It pleased God to make this providential occurrence the means of bringing him to a real and lasting sense of religion.

6. Over a century ago, on a winter night, when the snow was falling heavily, a poor woman, with five children, reached a village in Essex, just as a farmer's lad was shutting up a barn. She begged him to ask his master's leave for them to pass the night in the barn. The lad did so; and the master who was a kind, feeling man, ordered him to take a bundle of straw, and make them a comfortable bed. The poor woman felt grateful, and asked the lad if he would like to hear a song. He hoped that it would be something amusing, and replied 'Yes;' upon which she and her children sung one of Watts's hymns. The lad felt interested—she asked him if he had ever prayed to God, and thanked Him for the mercies he had enjoyed; and said that she was going to pray with her children, and he might stay if he pleased. The lad stayed while she offered up her thanks for the mercies she enjoyed; and begged for a blessing upon him. He then went away, but could not rest, and after passing a sleepless night, he resolved on going again to the barn to talk with the woman. She was gone—he saw her no more, but from that day he became a changed character.

7. It is good when rooms in our homes are definitely associated with prayer, but the people of God are sometimes obliged to seek a place of prayer out of doors, as did the Lord Jesus Christ Himself. A godly young man in the army, not finding a convenient place in the barracks where he was quartered, went one night, when dark, into an adjoining field for the purpose of prayer. Two men belonging to the same regiment, in whose hearts enmity had long subsisted against each other, were resolved to end it, as they said, by battle, being prevented from going during the day by the fear of punishment. They were providentially led to the very field where the young man was engaged in his secret spiritual exercise. Surprised to hear a voice in the field at that hour of night, and much more so when they drew nearer to it and heard a young man at prayer, they stopped and gave attention. Through the divine blessing the prayer had such an effect on both men that their enmity ended. They took each other by the hand, and cordially confessed that there existed no longer, in their hearts, hatred to each other. It is not recorded whether the young man at prayer learned of

the use which the Lord had made of the exercise in which he had been so happily engaged.

8. The Roman Emperor, Antoninus, one of the persecutors of the Christians, was once surrounded by his enemies, and it seemed likely that he and his army would perish from lack of water. He commanded the Christians in his army to pray for rain. Immediate relief came to him, his army was preserved and his enemies defeated. He then wrote to the Roman senate in favour of the Christians and said, 'They are a people who are content with God whom they always carry about with them in their bosoms, and though we may think them wicked, they have God in their conscience for their bulwark.' 'When a man's ways please the the Lord, He maketh even his enemies to be at peace with him' (Prov. 16. 7).

9. At the Metropolitan Tabernacle, London, a woman once came to C. H. Spurgeon at the end of a service. 'She was accompanied,' says Spurgeon, 'by two of her neighbours and entered my vestry in deep distress. Her husband had fled the country; and, in her sorrow, she had gone to the house of God, and something I said in the sermon made her think that I was personally familiar with her case. Of course, I had really known nothing about her; I had made use of a general illustration which just fitted her particular case. She told me her story, and a very sad one it was. I said, "There is nothing that we can do but kneel down, and cry to the Lord for the immediate conversion of your husband." We knelt down, and I prayed that the Lord would touch the heart of the deserter, convert his soul and bring him back to his home. When we rose from our knees, I said to the poor woman, "Do not fret about the matter. I feel sure your husband will come home; and that he will yet become connected with our church."

'She went away, and I forgot all about her. Some months afterwards, she reappeared, with her neighbours, and a man, whom she introduced to me as her husband. He had indeed come back, and he had returned a converted man. On making enquiry, and comparing notes, we found that, the very day on which we had prayed for his conversion, he, being at that time on board a ship far away on the sea, stumbled most unexpectedly upon a stray copy of one of my sermons. He read it; the truth went to his heart; he repented, and sought the Lord; and, as soon as possible, he came back to his wife and to his daily calling. He was admitted as a member at the Tabernacle, and his wife who up to that time had not joined the church, was also received into fellowship with us.

'That woman does not doubt the power of prayer. All the infidels in the world could not shake her conviction that there is a God that heareth and answereth the supplications of His people.'

Q. 99. *What rule hath God given for our direction in prayer?*

A. The whole word of God is of use to direct us in prayer; but the special rule of direction is that form of prayer which Christ taught His disciples, commonly called *The Lord's Prayer.*

1. A good man was told one day by a girl of prayer, 'When I was a child my mother taught me to pray, but now the Lord makes me.' Being asked how she knew the Lord's teaching from that of her mother, her reply was: 'The Lord makes me both to rejoice and weep; He makes my heart glad, and gives me new words.'

2. When Thomas Watson was in the pulpit on a lecture-day, before the infamous Bartholomew Act of 1662 took place, among other hearers, 'there came in,' says Dr Calamy, 'that reverend and learned prelate, Bishop Richardson, who was so well pleased with his sermon, but especially with his prayer after it, that he followed him home, to give him thanks, and earnestly desired a copy of his prayer. "Alas!" said Mr Watson, "that is what I cannot give; for I do not use to pen my prayers: it was no studied thing, but uttered as God enabled me, from the abundance of my heart and affection." Upon which the good bishop went away wondering that any man could pray in that manner *extempore*.'

3. A Hottentot of immoral character, being under deep conviction of sin, was anxious to know how to pray. He went to his master, a Dutchman, to consult with him; but his master gave him no encouragement. A sense of his own wickedness increased, and he had no one near to direct him. Occasionally, however, he was allowed to join with the family at the time of prayer. The portion of Scripture which was one day read by the master, was the parable of the Pharisee and Publican. While the prayer of the Pharisee was read, the poor Hottentot thought within himself, 'This is a *good* man: here is nothing for me;' but when his master came to the prayer of the Publican, 'God be merciful to me a sinner.'—'This suits me,' he cried: 'now I know how to pray!' With this prayer he immediately retired, and prayed night and day for two days, and then found peace. Full of joy and gratitude, he went into the fields, and as he had no one to whom he could speak, he exclaimed, 'Ye hills, ye rocks, ye trees, ye rivers, hear what God has done for my soul!—He has been merciful to me a sinner.'

4. A Sabbath school boy in London, who had been well taught, received a visit from a country cousin, about the same age, and it was agreed they should sleep together. When they went to their room, the Sabbath school boy knelt down by the bedside, and said his prayers; but the country cousin stripped off his clothes, and jumped into bed. When the other arose from his knees, he asked his cousin how he could think of going to bed without saying a prayer. He replied that he did not know any; however this did not satisfy the Sabbath scholar; he made his cousin get out of bed, and repeat the evening prayer after him.

5. A minister was once endeavouring to prevail with a young believer, to begin to pray in his family. The person said he had a great desire to engage in this work, but he feared he had not sufficient gifts to pray publicly. The minister said he would write him a prayer if he would promise to use it. He said he certainly would. The prayer was composed, and the man devoutly used it for some time, both morning and evening; but on one occasion as he was reading his prayer, the candle went out; however, the good man proceeded with great comfort and enlargement; and he found no need of a written prayer ever after.

6. 'Once,' said William Romaine, 'I uttered the Lord's prayer without a wandering thought, and it was the worst prayer I ever offered. I was on this account as proud as the devil.'

7. James Hervey, giving an account of his method of catechising children, says, 'As to instructing children, my method is to ask them easy questions, and to teach them easy and short answers. The Lord's prayer was the subject of our last explanation. In some such manner I proceeded: Why is this prayer called the Lord's prayer? Because our Lord taught it.—Why is Christ called *our* Lord? Because He has bought us with His blood.—Why does He teach us to call God Father? That we may go to Him as children to a father.—How do children go to God as a Father? With faith, not doubting but He will give them what they want.—Why our Father in *heaven*? That we may pray to Him with reverence.—What is meant by God's name? God Himself, and all His perfections.—What by *hallowed*? That He may be honoured and glorified.—How is God to be honoured? In our hearts, with our tongues, and by our lives'.

Q. 100. *What doth the preface of the Lord's prayer teach us?*

A. The preface of the Lord's prayer (which is, *Our Father which art in heaven*), teacheth us to draw near to God with all holy reverence and confidence, as children to a father, able and ready to help us; and that we should pray with and for others.

1. A child about four years of age would often remark to her mother, with great horror, how Mr G. (a person in the family) swore, and wished to reprove him, but for some time durst not. One day she said to her mother, 'Does Mr G. say, *Our Father*?' (a term she used to express in her prayers). The mother replied, she could not tell; she then said, 'I will watch, and if he does, I will tell him of swearing so.' She did watch, and heard him say his prayers privately in bed. Soon after this she heard him swear bitterly; upon which she said to him, 'Did you not say *Our Father* this morning?—How dare you swear? Do you think He will be your Father if you swear?' He answered not a word, but seemed amazed; and well he might. He did not live long after this, but was never heard to swear again. 'Out of the mouth of babes and sucklings God has ordained strength.'

2. Theodorus, speaking of Luther, says, 'Once I overheard him in prayer; but oh! with what life and spirit did he pray! It was with so much reverence as if he were speaking to God; yet with so much confidence as if he had been speaking to a friend.' Perceiving the interest of religion to be low, he be took himself to prayer. Rising off his knees, he came out of his closet triumphantly saying to his friends, 'We have overcome, we have overcome.' At which time it was observed, there came out a proclamation from Charles V that none should be further molested for their profession of the gospel.

3. 'My grandfather,' says Job Orton, 'once solicited a very excellent but modest minister to pray in his family, when there were several others present; he desired to be excused, alleging that he had not thought of it, and, there were so many other ministers present. My grandfather replied, "Sir, you are to speak to your Master, and not to them; and my Bible tells me He is not so critical and censorious as men are." '

4. A missionary to the heathen writes thus: 'Some impressions of the importance and necessity of true religion, were made upon my mind at a very early period. The first particular one that I recollect, was, I think, when I was about five years of age. There happened one day a very violent storm of thunder and lightning in our neighbourhood; on which occasion a few Christian friends, who lived near us, terrified by its violence, came into my father's house. When under his roof, in a moment there came a most vivid flash, followed by a dreadful peal of thunder, which much alarmed the whole company, except my father, who, turning toward my mother and our friends, with the greatest composure repeated these lines of Dr Watts—

> "The God that rules on high,
>   And thunders when He please:
> That rides upon the stormy sky,
>   And manages the seas:
> This awful God is ours:
>   Our Father and our love,
> He will send down His heavenly powers
>   To carry us above."

These words, accompanied with such circumstances, sunk deep into my heart. I thought how safe and happy are those who have the great God for their father and friend; but being conscious that I had sinned against Him, I was afraid that He was not my father, and that, instead of loving me, He was angry with me; and this for some time after, continued to distress and grieve my mind.' He then proceeds to say, that these early impressions were succeeded by others, occasioned by parental admonitions, the death of a sister, the conversation of godly friends, and the reading of useful books, which terminated in his conversion.

5. A wealthy planter in Virginia, who had a great number of slaves, found one of them reading the Bible, and reproved him for the neglect of his work, saying there was time enough on Sundays for reading the Bible, and that, on other days, he ought to be in the tobacco-house. The slave repeating the offence, he ordered him to be whipped. Going near the place of punishment, soon after its infliction, curiosity led him to listen to a voice engaged in prayer, and he heard the poor black implore the Almighty to forgive the injustice of his master, to touch his heart with a sense of his sin, and to make him a good Christian. Struck with remorse, he made an immediate change in his life, which had been careless and dissipated, burnt his profane books and cards, liberated all his slaves, and began to study how to render his wealth and talents useful to others.

6. There was a man in England, whose son was thought to be dying.

He went to a curate, requesting prayer to be made for him. The curate desired the disconsolate father to return home, and pray himself for the recovery of his son. He had never prayed before, but now he was very earnest. On rising from his knees, he inquired after his son, who had greatly recovered while he was praying. The father was astonished that God should hear the very first prayer that ever he had offered to Him. The providence was made a blessing to this man; for he became a praying Christian.

7. John Ryland of Northampton, being on a journey, was overtaken by a violent storm, and compelled to take shelter in the first inn he came to. The people of the house treated him with great kindness and hospitality. They would fain have shown him into a parlour, but being very wet and cold, he begged permission rather to take a seat by the fireside with the family. The good old man was friendly, cheerful, and well stored with entertaining anecdotes—and the family did their utmost to make him comfortable; they all supped together, and both the residents and the guest seemed mutually pleased with each other. At length, when the house was cleared, and the hour of rest approached, the stranger appeared uneasy, looking up every time a door opened, as if expecting the appearance of something essential to his comfort. His host informed him that his chamber was prepared whenever he chose to retire. 'But,' said he, 'you have not had your family together.' 'Had my family together? for what purpose? I don't know what you mean,' said the landlord. 'To read the Scriptures, and to pray with them,' replied the guest: 'surely you do not retire to rest in the omission of so necessary a duty?' The landlord confessed that he had never thought of doing such a thing. 'Then, sir,' said Ryland, 'I must beg you to order my horse immediately.' The landlord and family entreated him not to expose himself to the inclemency of the weather at that late hour of the night, observing that the storm was as violent as when he first came in. 'It may be so,' replied Ryland, 'but I had rather brave the storm than venture to sleep in a house where there is no prayer. Who can tell me what may befall us before morning. No, sir, I dare not stay.' Ryland, however, proposed to conduct family worship, to which all readily consented. The family being assembled, he called for a Bible, but no such book could be produced. However he was enabled to supply the deficiency, as he always carried a small Bible or Testament in his pocket. He read a portion of Scripture, and prayed with much fervour and solemnity, acknowledging the goodness of God, that none had been struck dead by the storm, and imploring protection through the night. He earnestly prayed that the attention of all might be awakened to the things belonging to their everlasting peace, and that the family might never again meet in the morning, or separate at night, without prayer. A deep impression was made on the family, and much interesting conversation ensued, when worship was over. Ryland conducted family worship next morning, and obtained from the landlord a promise that, however feebly performed, it should not in future be omitted. This was indeed the beginning of days to the family; most, if not all of them, became sincere followers of the Lord Jesus, and were instrumental in diffusing a knowledge of the gospel in a neighbourhood which had before been remarkably dark and destitute.

8. M'Cheyne of Dundee wrote thus to a youth: 'Pray that the Holy

Spirit would not only make you a believing and a holy lad, but make you wise in your studies also. A ray of divine light in the soul sometimes clears up a mathematical problem wonderfully. The smile of God calms the spirit, the left hand of Jesus holds up the fainting head, and His Holy Spirit quickens the affection, so that even natural studies go on a million times more easily and comfortably.'

Q. 101. *What do we pray for in the first petition?*

A. In the first petition (which is *Hallowed be Thy name*), we pray that God would enable us and others to glorify Him in all that whereby He maketh Himself known; and that He would dispose all things to His own glory.

1. Robert Boyle, one of the greatest scientists of the seventeenth century, had such a veneration of God, and such a sense of His presence, that he never mentioned the name of God without a pause, and a visible stop in his discourse.

2. In the life of William Wyndham, (Lord Grenville) prefixed to his Speeches in Parliament, it is remarked, that nothing so highly offended him as any careless or irreverent use of the name of the Creator. 'I remember,' says his biographer, 'that, on reading a letter addressed to him, in which the words, "My God," had been made use of on a light occasion, he hastily snatched a pen, and before he could finish reading the letter, blotted out the misplaced exclamation.'

3. When Thomas Scott was speaking to John Newton about a call to God's service which seemed to conflict with a man's personal interests, Newton told him the story of a nobleman who was selected as ambassador by his queen, but excused himself on the grounds of his family, and urgent concerns at home; but was answered, 'You must go; only do you mind my concerns heartily, and I will take care of yours.' 'Thus,' says Newton, 'God, as it were, says to you.'

4. One day when James Durham and Andrew Gray were to preach in the same town, as they were walking together, Durham, observing multitudes thronging into the church where Gray was to preach, and but one here and there dropping into the one he was to preach in, said to Gray, 'Brother, I perceive you are like to have a thronged church to-day.' To which Gray answered, 'Truly, brother, they are fools to leave you and come to me.' To which Durham nobly replied, 'Not so, dear brother, for a minister can receive no such honour and success in the ministry, except it be given him from Heaven. I rejoice that Christ is preached, and that His honour and esteem do increase, though my esteem in people's hearts should decrease, and be diminished; for I am content to be anything, so that Christ may be all in all.'

5. Terentius, captain to the Emperor Adrian, presented a petition to that monarch, praying that the Christians might have a temple by themselves,

to worship God apart from the Arians. The emperor tore up his petition, and threw it away, desiring him to ask something for himself, and it should be granted; but he modestly gathered up the pieces of his petition again, and told him, 'If he could not be heard in God's cause, he would never ask anything for himself.'

6. Edward Gibbon, who, in his celebrated *History of the Decline and Fall of the Roman Empire*, has left an imperishable memorial of his enmity to the gospel, resided many years in Switzerland, where with the profits of his works, he purchased a considerable estate. This property descended to a gentleman, who out of his rents, expended a large sum annually in the promulgation of that very gospel which his predecessor insidiously tried to undermine, not having the courage openly to assail it.

Q. 102. *What do we pray for in the second petition?*

A. In the second petition (which is, *Thy kingdom come*), we pray, that Satan's kingdom may be destroyed; and that the kingdom of grace may be advanced, ourselves and others brought into it, and kept in it; and that the kingdom of glory may be hastened.

1. A little girl sent about ten shillings to a gentleman for the purchase of some missionary tracts; and in her letter she said: 'She who takes this freedom to ask so much of a stranger, began this letter with a trembling hand. She is indeed young in years, and in knowledge too, and is not able to talk much with a gentleman on religion; but her mother has taught her, almost eleven years, to say, *Thy kingdom come;* and she believes she cannot be saying it sincerely, if she does nothing to help it on among the heathen. This thought emboldens her to write to a stranger, almost as though he were a friend.'

2. 'There are at Haworth,' says Newton, in his *Life of William Grimshaw*, 'two feasts annually. It had been customary with the innkeepers, and some other inhabitants, to make a subscription for horse-races at the latter feast. These were of the lowest kind, attended by the lowest of the people. They exhibited a scene of the grossest and most vulgar riot, profligacy, and confusion. Grimshaw had frequently attempted, but in vain, to put a stop to this mischievous custom. His remonstrances against it were little regarded. Unable to prevail with men, he addressed himself to God; and for some time before the races began, he made it a subject of fervent prayer, that the Lord would be pleased to stop these evil proceedings in His own way. When the race time came, the people assembled as usual, but they were soon dispersed. Before the race could begin, dark clouds covered the sky, which poured forth such excessive rains, that the people could not remain upon the ground; it continued to rain incessantly during the three days appointed for the races. This event, though it took place nearly forty years since, is still

L

remembered and spoken of at Haworth, with the same certainty as if it had happened but a few months past. It is a sort of proverbial saying among them, that old Grimshaw put a stop to the races by his prayers. And it proved an effectual stop. There have been no races in the neighbourhood of Haworth from that time to the present day.'

3. Melancthon, going once upon some great service for the Church of Christ, and having many doubts and fears about the success of his business, was greatly relieved by a company of poor women and children, whom he found praying together for the prosperity of the Church.

4. 'I one day dined on board the *Duff* (missionary ship),' wrote a minister of the gospel, 'and much pleased I was with the thought, that amidst all the hundreds of vessels I saw in the river, trading to different parts of the globe, carrying the perishing things of this world from one nation to another, there was one trading for heaven, engaged in conveying the everlasting gospel to benighted heathens perishing for lack of knowledge. Perhaps it is the first vessel that in any age of the world was ever solely so employed. I thought the nation highly honoured by the event, as well as the persons principally concerned.'

5. A godly man and woman had an only son, named Thomas, who to the great grief of his parents, began to turn out wild. A worthy minister named Rees, went to lodge at the house, and the father and mother with many tears, informed him of the ungodliness of their son. The following morning, before family prayer, the minister took hold of the young man's hand, and spoke very seriously and affectionately to him respecting his salvation. In family worship he prayed for him with great enlargement, and amongst others, used the following expression: 'O Lord, say *to this Thomas*, "be not faithless, but believing."' The words, to use the young man's own expression, entered his heart like a sword, and a permanent change was effected: he soon became a church member, and was an ornament to his Christian profession till death.

6. 'I know,' says William Fenner, 'an old man that used constantly to go to the labourers in the fields, and talk to them about religion as they were reaping and working. He would go to men's shops where he was acquainted, and stir them up to the care of their souls; and, by this means, brought about forty men and women to seek for heaven, who before had no more care that way, than if they had been a company of beasts. Wouldest thou not be glad to do good? Thou wilt never be able to do it except thou be zealous. Paul had women and sundry private Christians who laboured with him in the gospel. This—this—beloved, would cause religion to thrive here amongst us!'

7. Dr James Spener, some days before his death, gave orders that nothing of black should be on his coffin—'For,' said he, 'I have been a sorrowful man these many years, lamenting the deplorable state of Christ's church militant upon earth; but now being upon the point of retiring into the church triumphant in heaven, I will not have the least mark of sorrow left upon me; but my body shall be wrapped up all over in white, for a testimony that I die in expectation of a better and more glorious state of Christ's church to come, even upon earth.'

Q. 103. *What do we pray for in the third petition?*

A. In the third petition (which is, *Thy will be done on earth as it is in heaven*), we pray that God by His grace would make us able and willing to know, obey, and submit to His will in all things as the angels do in heaven.

1. There was a good woman, who, when she was ill, being asked whether she was willing to live or die, answered, 'Whichever God pleaseth.' 'But,' said one standing by, 'if God should refer it to you, which would you choose?' 'Truly,' said she, 'if God should refer it to me, I would even refer it to Him again.'

2. A Christian widow in London saw, with great alarm, her only child taken dangerously ill. As the illness increased, she became almost distracted, from a dread of losing the child. At length it became so extremely ill, and so convulsed, that she kneeled down by the bed deeply affected, and in prayer said, 'Now, Lord, Thy will be done.' From that hour the child began to recover, till health was perfectly restored.

3. 'The most remarkable and astonishing instance of resignation I ever remember to have met with,' says Toplady, 'is to be found in Fenelon, Archbishop of Cambray. When his illustrious pupil (the Duke of Burgundy, if I mistake not) lay dead in his coffin, and the nobles of the court, in all the pomp of silent sadness stood weeping around, the archbishop came into the apartment, and having fixed his eyes for some time on the corpse, broke out at length in terms to this effect: "There lies my beloved prince, for whom my affection was equal to that of the tenderest parent. Nor was my affection lost—he loved me in return with the ardour of a son. There he lies; and all my worldly happiness lies dead with him. But if the turning of a straw would call him back to life, I would not for ten thousand worlds be the turner of that straw, in opposition to the will of God." '

4. A godly man, who had lost his only son, retired to his room, to pour out his heart to God in prayer. On coming out, he declared, that, for such refreshing and abundant consolation as he had enjoyed in communion with his God, he would be willing to lose an only son every day.

5. 'What occasions that melancholy look?' said a gentleman to one of his young favourites one morning. He turned away his face, to hide a tear that was ready to start from his eyes. His brother answered for him—'Mother is very angry with him,' said he, 'because he would not say his prayers last night; and he cried all day, because a sparrow died, of which he was very fond.' The little mourner turned hastily round, and looking at me, exclaimed, 'I could not say *Thy will be done*, because of my poor bird.' The gentleman took him by the hand, and pointing to his school-fellows, 'Mark the observation,' said he, 'from the youngest present, only six years old; for it explains the nature of prayer, of which perhaps some of you are ignorant. Many persons repeat words, who never prayed in their lives. My dear boy, I am very glad to find you were afraid to say to God what you could

not truly say from your heart; but you may beg of Him to give you submission to His will.'

6. Thomas Potter, whom Dr Doddridge mentions in his *Life of Colonel
Gardiner*, was a plain and simple man. Though very deficient in natural
things, yet he enjoyed the gift of a most retentive memory, both of Scripture
phrases and Scripture places; and had an aptness of applying suitable texts,
in a wonderful, though awkward, manner. Two young persons, who intended to be married in a short time, applied to him, acquainting him with
their circumstances, and requesting a text; he immediately pointed them to
Psalm 46. 10, 'Be still and know that I am God,' as altogether suitable to
their case. The parties were quite at a loss how to apply this to their situation,
and supposing that he must be mistaken, asked for another; but Thomas
insisted on it—he had no other for them. They then retired; but Providence
soon explained that Scripture, for within a few days, by a sudden illness, one
of them died, and the survivor was left to learn the needful lesson of submission to His will, who does as it pleases Him, in heaven and in earth.

7. A Sabbath school teacher, instructing his class on the third petition
of the Lord's prayer, said to them—'You have told me, my dear children,
what is to be done—*the will of God*; and *where* it is to be done—*on earth;
how* it is to be done—*as it is done in heaven.* How do you think the angels and
happy spirits do the will of God in heaven, as they are to be our pattern?'
The first child replied, 'They do it *immediately.*' The second, 'They do it
diligently.' The third, 'They do it *always.*' The fourth, 'They do it *with all
their hearts.*' The fifth, 'They do it *all together.*' Here a pause ensued, and no
other child appeared to have any answer; but after some time a little
girl rose and said, 'Why, sir, they do it *without asking any questions.*'

8. Thomas Charles of Bala, in Wales, intended to go to Liverpool, but
his wife was not willing, knowing the danger in which he had before been.
The night prior to the day on which he was to set off, one of the children
fell from the bed upon the floor, and it was at first much feared that one of
its arms was broken; which happily did not turn out to be the case. But the
event had a happy effect on her mind. 'God,' says she, 'can bring a judgment on us while at home, as well as when we are from home; therefore,'
she added, 'I will trust you in His hand, to do what He pleases with you,
while you are doing His work either on sea or land.'

Q. 104. *What do we pray for in the fourth petition?*

A. In the fourth petition (which is, *Give us this day our daily
bread*), we pray, that of God's free gift we may receive a competent portion of the good things of this life, and enjoy His
blessing with them.

1. Professor Francke, who founded an orphanage, relates that at one
time all his provision was spent; 'but in addressing myself,' says he, 'to the
Lord, I found myself deeply affected with the fourth petition of the Lord's

prayer, "Give us this day our daily bread," and my thoughts were fixed in a more especial manner upon the words, *this day*, because on the very same day we had great occasion for it. While I was yet praying, a friend of mine came before my door in a coach, and brought the sum of 400 crowns.'

2. A godly woman used to say she should never want, because her God would supply her every need. In a time of persecution, she was taken before an unjust judge for attending a conventicle, as they styled her offence. The judge, on seeing her, rejoiced over her, and tauntingly said—'I have often wished to have you in my power, and now I shall send you to prison, and then how will you be fed?' She replied, 'If it be my heavenly Father's pleasure, I shall be fed from your table.' And that was literally the case; for the judge's wife being present at her examination, and being greatly struck with the good woman's firmness, took care to send her victuals from her table, so that she was comfortably supplied all the while she was in confinement: and the other found her reward, for the Lord was pleased to work on her soul, to her real conversion.

3. Cornelius Winter observes, that in a time when he was destitute and knew not where to look for a supply, he received a letter, of which the following is a copy, and which he kept, as he said, to record the kind providence of the Lord: 'Dear and Rev. Sir, I enclose you twenty pounds, as I suppose your purse may be low. I commend you to the grace and love of Jesus; may He long shine upon you and bless you. My dear friend, yours affectionately, J. THORNTON.'

4. Henry Erskine, minister of the gospel at Durham, but ejected from the Church of England in 1662, and the father of Ebenezer and Ralph Erskine, was at one time in very destitute circumstances. Once when he and his family had supped at night, there remained neither bread, meal, flesh, nor money in the house. In the morning, the young children cried for their breakfast, and their father endeavoured to divert them, and did what he could at the same time to encourage himself and his wife to depend upon that Providence which feeds the young ravens when they cry for food. While he was thus engaged a country-man knocked hard at the door, and called on some one to help him off with his load. Being asked whence he came, and what he would have, he told them that he came from Lady Raeburn, with some provisions for Mr Erskine. They told him he must be mistaken, and that it was very likely to be for another Mr Erskine in the same town. He replied, No, he knew what he said; he was sent to Mr Henry Erskine, and cried, 'Come, help me off with my load, or else I will throw it down at the door.' They then took the sack from him, and on opening it, found it well filled with provisions.

5. In the years 1821 and 1822, the Hottentots could scarcely procure a morsel of bread, and their garden vegetables almost entirely failed; they were driven for their chief support to the wild fruits of the fields and woods. Those among them who had felt the power of the grace of God, displayed its influence in a very striking manner. A missionary said, 'It is distressing to see what hunger they sometimes endure, but also edifying to find them so firm in their faith and confidence in God. I asked some who had formerly enjoyed plenty and comfort, whether they had not rather return, as they

found living so hard.' One said, 'No, indeed, in that place I had food for my body, but not for my soul; the gospel that I hear in this place, is more to me than victuals and drink.' 'It is true,' said another, 'I often go to bed with an empty stomach, but I pray to the Saviour to make me satisfied, and feel no inclination to complain. It will not be always so, and though my garden fruits are all burnt up, I will plant again and again, till it shall please God to make it grow.' Their hope in the providence of God was not disappointed.

6. A poor servant, who had a wife and children to support, was once reduced to such distress, that, with the concurrence of his wife, he went to his master's flock, and brought home a lamb, which was killed, and a part of it dressed, and set on the table. The next thing to be done before their hunger could be relieved, *was to ask a blessing on the food*. The poor man's heart was filled with anguish. How could he ask a blessing from God on the fruit of unrighteousness? Tears gushed from his eyes. He rose, went directly to his master, told him what he had done, and implored his forgiveness. His master knew him to be not only a sober and industrious, but an honest and well-disposed man, and that nothing but the greatest straits could have tempted him to be guilty of what he had done. After a suitable admonition, he assured him of his hearty forgiveness, told him he was welcome to what he had got, and that he should not be disappointed in any future application which he might find it necessary to make to him, for the supply of his wants. The servant returned home with joy; and with his family he ate with gladness, that food which was now his own and praised the Lord.

7. A minister of the gospel went to dine at the house of one of his hearers, whom he was in the habit of visiting. Dinner being on the table, the master of the house requested the preacher to ask a blessing. It was no sooner said, than one of the children, a boy about seven years old, asked the following appropriate and memorable question. 'Father, what is the reason we *always* have a blessing asked when the minister dines with us, and *never* at any other time?'

Q. 105. *What do we pray for in the fifth petition?*

A. In the fifth petition (which is, *And forgive us our debts, as we forgive our debtors*), we pray, That God, for Christ's sake, would freely pardon all our sins; which we are the rather encouraged to ask, because by His grace we are enabled from the heart to forgive others.

1. Who can forgive sins but God only? (Mark 2. 7). When Tetzel, the seller of papal indulgences, was at Leipsic, and had collected a great deal of money from all ranks of people, a nobleman who had suspected the imposition, put the question to him, 'Can you grant absolution for a sin which a man intends to commit in the future?' 'Yes' replied the commissioner; 'but on condition that the proper sum of money be actually paid down.' The nobleman instantly produced the sum demanded; and in return re-

ceived a diploma, sealed and signed by Tetzel, absolving him from the un-explained crime, which he secretly intended to commit. Not long after, when Tetzel was about to leave Leipsic, the nobleman made inquiry re-specting the road he would probably travel, waited for him in ambush at a convenient place, attacked and robbed him; then beat him soundly with a stick, and sent him back again to Leipsic with his chest empty, and at parting said, 'This is the fault I intended to commit, and for which I have your absolution.'

2. The Marquis of Argyle, who suffered in the reign of King Charles II, was employed in the morning of the day of his execution in settling his worldly affairs. To those about him he spoke right joyfully: 'I am now ordering my affairs, and God is sealing my charter to a better inheritance, and just now saying to me, Son, be of good cheer, thy sins are forgiven thee.' Having with great cheerfulness dined with his friends, he retired for a little while. Upon his opening the door, a minister of the gospel said to him, 'What cheer, my lord?' He replied, 'Good cheer, sir; the Lord hath again confirmed, and said to me from heaven, Thy sins be forgiven thee.'

3. A gentleman once went to Sir John Eardley Wilmot (at one time Lord Chief Justice of the Court of Common Pleas), under the impression of great wrath and indignation at a real injury he had received from a per-son high in the political world, and which he was meditating how to resent in the most effectual manner. After relating the particulars, he asked Sir Eardley, if he did not think it would be *manly* to resent it? 'Yes,' said he, 'it will be *manly* to resent it, but it will be *Godlike* to forgive it.' The gentle-man declared that this had such an instantaneous effect upon him, that he came away quite a different man, and in a very different temper from that in which he went.

4. In a school at Youghall, in Ireland, during the master's accidental absence, one boy having been provoked, struck another. On hearing the complaint, the master determined to punish the culprit, when the aggrieved entreated pardon for the offender. On being asked why he would interpose to prevent a just example, he said: 'I was reading in the New Testament lately, that Jesus Christ said we should forgive our enemies, and I wish to forgive him, and I beg he may not be punished for my sake.' This Christian plea was too powerful to be resisted. The offender was pardoned, and the parent of the boy was highly pleased at the circumstance.

5. A little African Negro, only ten years of age, went to hear the preach-ing of one of the missionaries, and became through his instrumentality a convert to the Christian religion. His master (an inveterate enemy to mis-sions) hearing of it, commanded him never to go again, and declared he would have him whipped to death if he did. The little boy, in consequence of this mandate, was very miserable. He could scarcely refrain from going, yet knew his death was inevitable if he did. In this critical situation, he sought direction and assistance at the throne of grace, and after having done this, he felt convinced that it was still his duty to attend, but to be careful that he should never interfere with his master's business, and, for the rest, to leave himself in the hands of God. He therefore went, and on his return was summoned to his master's presence. After much violent and

abusive language, he received five-and-twenty lashes, and then, in a sarcastic tone of blasphemous ridicule, his master exclaimed, 'What can Jesus Christ do for you now?' 'He enables me to bear it patiently,' said the child. 'Give him five-and-twenty lashes more,' said the inhuman wretch. He was obeyed. 'And what can Jesus Christ do for you now?' asked the unfeeling monster. 'He helps me to look forward to a future reward,' replied the little sufferer. 'Give him five-and-twenty lashes more,' vociferated the cruel tyrant in a transport of rage. They complied; and while he listened with savage delight to the extorted groans of his dying victim, he again demanded, 'What can Jesus Christ do for you now?' The youthful martyr, with the last effort of expiring nature, meekly answered, 'He enables me to pray for you, massa;' and instantly breathed his last.

6. John Owen, a godly and devoted servant of the Lord, having, on a particular occasion, endeavoured in vain to accommodate a matter in dispute between two friends, for both of whom he felt much respect, evinced the amiableness of his disposition, by retiring and writing, impromptu, the following lines, which he transmitted to the disputants:

'How rare that toil a prosperous issue finds,
Which seeks to reconcile divided friends!
A thousand scruples rise at passion's touch,
This yields too little, and that asks too much.

Each wishes each with other eyes to see,
And many efforts can't make two agree:
What mediation then the Saviour showed,
Who singly reconciled us all to God!'

7. John Wesley, in the course of a voyage to America, hearing an unusual noise in the cabin of General Oglethorpe, the Governor of Georgia, with whom he sailed, stepped in to inquire the cause of it. The General thus addressed him; 'Mr Wesley you must excuse me, I have met with a provocation too great for a man to bear. You know the only wine I drink is Cyprus wine; I therefore provided myself with several dozens of it, and this villain Grimaldi (his foreign servant, who was present, and almost dead with fear), has drunk up the whole of it, but I will be revenged on him. I have ordered him to be tied hand and foot, and to be carried to the man-of-war which sails with us. The rascal should have taken care how he used me so, for I never forgive.' 'Then I hope, sir,' said Mr W., looking calmly at him, 'you never sin?' The General was quite confounded at the reproof; and, putting his hand into his pocket, took out a bunch of keys, which he threw at Grimaldi—'There, villain,' said he, 'take my keys, behave better for the future.'

Q. 106. *What do we pray for in the sixth petition?*

A. In the sixth petition (which is, *And lead us not into temptation, but deliver us from evil*), we pray that God would either keep us from being tempted to sin, or support and deliver us when we are tempted.

1. A plain countryman, who was effectually called by divine grace under a sermon from Zech. 3. 2, was some time afterwards accosted by a one-time companion of his drunken fits, and strongly solicited to accompany him to the alehouse. But the good man strongly resisted all his arguments, saying, 'I am a brand plucked out of the fire.' His old companion not understanding this, he explained it thus: 'Look ye,' said he, 'there is a great difference between a brand and a green stick; if a spark flies upon a brand that has been partly burned, it will soon catch fire again; but it is not so with a green stick. I tell you, I am that brand plucked out of the fire, and I dare not venture into the way of temptation, for fear of being set on fire.'

2. 'I once went to a friend,' says Richard Cecil, 'for the express purpose of calling him out into the world; I said to him, "It is your duty to accept the loan of ten thousand pounds, and to push yourself forward into an ampler sphere." But he was a rare character, and his case was rare. His employers had said, "We are ashamed you should remain so long a servant in our house, with the whole weight of affairs upon you. We wish you to enter as a principal with us, and will advance you ten thousand pounds. It is the custom of the city—it is your due—we are dissatisfied to see you in your present sphere." I assured him that it appeared to me to be his duty to accede to the proposal. But I did not prevail. He said, "Sir, I have often heard from you that it is no easy thing to get to heaven. I have often heard from you that it is no easy thing to master the world. I have everything I wish. More would encumber me—increase my difficulties—and endanger me." '

3. Dr Pendleton and Lawrence Saunders, meeting together in the beginning of Queen Mary's reign, talked of the persecution which would likely arise; with regard to which Saunders showed much weakness and fear. Pendleton, on the other hand, boasted of his resolution, that he would endure the severest treatment, rather than forsake Jesus Christ, and the truth which he had professed. Yet not long after, the feeble, faint-hearted Saunders, through the goodness of God, sealed the truth with his blood, while proud Pendleton played the apostate, and turned papist.

4. The following anecdote may perhaps illustrate the promise, 'As thy days so shall thy strength be.'—Under the reign of paganism, a Christian, notwithstanding her pregnancy, was condemned to die for her profession. The day before her execution, she fell into labour, and crying out in her pangs, the jailor insulted her, saying, 'If you make a noise to-day, how will you endure a violent death to-morrow?' To this she replied, 'To-day I suffer what is ordinary, and have only ordinary assistance; to-morrow I am to suffer what is more than ordinary, and shall hope for more than ordinary assistance.' O, woman! great was thy faith.

5. One night, John Newton found a notice put up at the church of St Mary Woolnoth upon which he commented a great deal when he came to preach. The notice was to this effect: 'A young man, having come to the possession of a very considerable fortune, desires the prayers of the congre-

gation, that he may be preserved from the snares to which it exposes him.'
'Now, if the man,' said Newton, 'had lost a fortune, the world would not
have wondered to have seen him put up a notice; but this man has been
better taught.'

6. Legh Richmond was once conversing with a brother clergyman, on
the case of a poor man who had acted inconsistently with his religious
profession. After some angry and severe remarks on the conduct of such
persons, the gentleman with whom he was discussing the case, concluded
by saying, 'I have no notion of such pretences; I will have nothing to do
with him.' 'Nay, brother,' replied Richmond, 'Let us be humble and moderate. Remember who has said, "Making a difference." With opportunity on
the one hand, and Satan on the other, and the grace of God at neither,
where should you and I be!'

7. A lady who moved in high society introduced herself to Samuel Kilpin, a gospel minister, with the apology that she thought it her duty to inform him, that some years before, she was passing along the street as a
stranger, on the Sabbath, when seeing many persons enter a passage, she
followed them, and found herself within his chapel. Every object was new;
but she listened, and was interested in the sermon. Immediately after, she
left England, and, with some young friends, became the inmate of a convent
in France, to finish her education. While there, every argument was employed to convert them to the Roman Catholic religion. Her English associates were overcome by these persuasions. 'Your discourse, sir,' said she,
'which I could never get from my mind, has been my preservation, from
that period to the present, though I have been beset with every snare from
family connections.' Mr Kilpin recommended suitable books to her attention, and devoutly committed her to the God of heaven, while she knelt with
him bathed in tears.

Q. 107. *What doth the conclusion of the Lord's prayer teach us?*

A. The conclusion of the Lord's prayer (which is, *For Thine
is the kingdom, and the power, and the glory, for ever, Amen*), teacheth
us, to take our encouragement in prayer from God only, and
in our prayers to praise Him, ascribing kingdom, power, and
glory to Him. And in testimony of our desire, and assurance
to be heard, we say, Amen.

1. Alexander the Great had a famous but indigent philosopher in his
court. This adept in science was once particularly straitened in his circumstances. To whom alone, should he apply, but to his patron, the conqueror
of the world? His request was no sooner made than granted. Alexander
gave him a commission to receive of his treasurer whatever he wanted. He
immediately demanded, in his sovereign's name, ten thousand pounds. The
treasurer, surprised at so large a demand, refused to comply; but waited

upon the king, and represented to him the affair, adding withal, how un-reasonable he thought the petition, and how exorbitant the sum. Alexander heard him with patience; but as soon as he had ended his remonstrances, replied, 'Let the money be instantly paid. I am delighted with this philoso-pher's way of thinking; he has done me a singular honour; by the largeness of his request, he shows the high idea he has conceived, both of my superior wealth and my royal munificence.' Thus let us honour what the inspired penman styles *the marvellous loving kindness of* JEHOVAH. 'He that spared not His Son, but delivered Him up for us all, how shall He not with Him also freely give us all things!' (Rom. 8. 32).

2. 'A valuable person whom I once knew,' says James Hervey, 'was roused from a habit of indolence and supineness, to a serious concern for his eternal welfare. Convinced of his depraved nature and aggravated guilt, he had recourse to the Scriptures and to frequent prayer; he attended the ordinances of Christianity, and sought earnestly for an interest in Christ, but found no steadfast faith, and tasted very little comfort; at length he ap-plied to an eminent divine, and laid open the state of his heart. Short but weighty was the answer: "I perceive, sir, the cause of all your distress; you will not come to Christ as a sinner; this mistake lies between you and the joy of religion; this detains you in the gall of bitterness, and take heed, O take heed, lest it consign you to the bond of iniquity!" This admonition never departed from the gentleman's mind, and it became the means of re-moving the obstacles to his peace.'

3. John Janeway, when on his deathbed, was employed chiefly in praise. 'O,' said he to his friends, 'help me to praise God; I have now nothing else to do. I have done with prayer and all other ordinances. Before a few hours are over, I shall be in eternity, singing the song of Moses and the Lamb. I shall presently stand upon Mount Zion, with an innumerable company of angels and spirits of just men made perfect, and with Jesus the Mediator of the new covenant. I shall hear the voice of much people, and with them shall cry, Hallelujah, glory, salvation, honour and power unto the Lord our God. And again we shall say, Hallelujah!' In this triumphant manner he expired in the twenty-second year of his age.

4. A lady, who had just sat down to breakfast, had a strong impression upon her mind that she must instantly carry a loaf of bread to a poor man who lived about half a mile from her house, by the side of a common. Her husband wished her either to postpone taking the loaf of bread till after breakfast, or to send it by her servant; but she chose to take it herself in-stantly. As she approached the hut, she heard the sound of a human voice. Willing to hear what it was, she stept softly, unperceived, to the door. She now heard the poor man praying, and among other things he said— 'O Lord, help me; Lord, Thou wilt help me; Thy providence cannot fail; and although my wife, self, and children, have no bread to eat, and it is now a whole day since we had any, I know Thou wilt supply me, though Thou shouldest again rain down manna from heaven.' The lady could wait no longer; she opened the door. 'Yes,' she replied; 'God has sent you relief. Take this loaf, and be encouraged to cast your care upon Him who careth for you; and when you ever want a loaf of bread, come to my house.'

Some Related Banner of Truth Titles

The Shorter Catechism Explained from Scripture by Thomas Vincent. No London pastor made more effective use of *The Shorter Catechism* than Vincent, and when his 'explanation' was first published in 1674, John Owen, Thomas Watson along with 38 other signatories to the Preface, declared their belief that it would 'be greatly useful to all Christians in general.' Numerous reprints were to verify their judgment of this Puritan classic.

The Confession of Faith by A.A. Hodge. It is the purpose of the author of this book to analyze the chapters and sections of The Confession of Faith drawn up at Westminster in 1646 by over one hundred leading Puritan divines. Hodge, the eminent son and successor of Charles Hodge, was finely equipped for this work. He was considered one of the greatest teachers that America has ever produced. This volume reveals his strong convictions, his power of analysis, and his ability to make sharp and discriminating definitions.

A Body of Divinity, The Ten Commandments, The Lord's Prayer by Thomas Watson. These three volumes make up Watson's complete Body of Practical Divinity. C.H. Spurgeon declared, "One of the most precious of the peerless works of the Puritans, and those best acquainted with it prize it most."

Letters from the South Seas by Margaret Whitecross Paton. *John G. Paton: Missionary to the New Hebrides* is a missionary classic. In this companion volume, Margaret Whitecross Paton, John Paton's second wife, gives an enthralling account of missionary life in the New Hebrides from the 1860s to the 1890s. The steady advance of the gospel in the islands is vividly described, and the whole account is set against the background of the joys and sorrows of family life. Margaret Paton writes with rare grace, humor and pathos. This is an inspiring story, full of the triumphs of Christian faith and love, and a missionary classic in its own right - a book to prize.

The Banner of Truth, PO Box 621, Carlisle PA 17013

The Banner of Truth Trust, The Grey House, 3 Murrayfield Rd Edinburgh, EH12 6EL

Other SGCB Classic Reprints

In addition to *The Shorter Catechism Illustrated* that you now possess, Solid Ground Christian Books is delighted to announce that we have also published the following by Robert Hawker:

Hawker's Poor Man's Old Testament Commentary in six wonderful volumes. This set contains more than 4,200 pages of exposition and reflection by the man who loved Christ and delighted to make Him known to others. The volumes are as follows:

> Volume One: Genesis - Numbers
> Volume Two: Deuteronomy - 2 Samuel
> Volume Three: 1st Kings - Esther
> Volume Four: Job - Psalms
> Volume Five: Proverbs - Lamentations
> Volume Six: Ezekiel - Malachi

Hawker's Poor Man's New Testament Commentary in three wonderful volumes. This set contains more than 2,100 pages of exposition and reflection by the man who loved Christ and delighted to make Him known to others. The volumes are as follows:

> Volume One: Matthew - John
> Volume Two: Acts - Ephesians
> Volume Three: Philippians - Revelation

Hawker's Poor Man's Morning and Evening Portions which is a daily devotional work of more than 900 pages. Pastor Don Fortner has said:

> "Robert Hawker's **Poor Man's Daily Portions** is, in my opinion, the very best book of daily devotional readings I have yet read. My wife and I have used it for many years, always with great profit to our souls. Why is it such a blessing? It is full of Christ and full of grace. Every reading leaves the reader looking to, resting in, and rejoicing in our all-glorious Savior."

Solid Ground Christian Books
2090 Columbiana Rd, Suite 2000
Birmingham AL 35266
(205) 443-0311
sgcb@charter.net
http://solid-ground-books.com

LaVergne, TN USA
24 March 2010
177030LV00003B/48/A